Research in Criminology

Series Editors
Alfred Blumstein
David P. Farrington

Research in Criminology

Understanding and Controlling Crime: Toward A New Research Strategy
D.P. Farrington, L.E. Ohlin and J.Q. Wilson

The Social Ecology of Crime
J.M. Byrne and R.J. Sampson (Eds.)

The Reasoning Criminal: Rational Choice Perspectives on Offending
D.B. Cornish and R.V. Clarke (Eds.)

The Reasoning Criminal

Rational Choice Perspectives on Offending

Edited by
Derek B. Cornish
Ronald V. Clarke

With 12 Illustrations

Springer-Verlag
New York Berlin Heidelberg Tokyo

Derek B. Cornish
Department of Social Science and Administration, London School of Economics and Political Science, London WC2A 2AE, England

Ronald V. Clarke
Department of Criminal Justice, Temple University, Philadelphia, Pennsylvania 19122, U.S.A.

Series Editors
Alfred Blumstein
School of Urban and Public Affairs, Carnegie-Mellon University, Pittsburgh, Pennsylvania 15213, U.S.A.

David P. Farrington
Institute of Criminology, University of Cambridge, Cambridge, CB3 9DT, England

Library of Congress Cataloging in Publication Data
Main entry under title:
The reasoning criminal.
 (Research in criminology)
 Bibliography: p.
 Includes index.
 1. Criminal psychology—Congresses. 2. Crime and criminals—Congresses. 3. Decision-making—Congresses. 4. Choice (Psychology)—Congresses.
I. Cornish, Derek B. (Derek Blaikie), 1939-   .
II. Clarke, R. V. G. III. Series.
HV6080.R38 1986   364.3   86-1275

Typeset by Ampersand Publisher Services, Inc., Rutland, Vermont.
Printed and bound by R.R. Donnelley & Sons, Harrisonburg, Virginia.
Printed in the United States of America.

9 8 7 6 5 4 3 2 1

ISBN 0-387-96272-7 Springer-Verlag New York Berlin Heidelberg Tokyo
ISBN 3-540-96272-7 Springer-Verlag Berlin Heidelberg New York Tokyo

Preface

The assumption that rewards and punishments influence our choices between different courses of action underlies much economic, sociological, psychological, and legal thinking about human action. Hence, the notion of a reasoning criminal—one who employs the same sorts of cognitive strategies when contemplating offending as he and the rest of us use when making other decisions—might seem a scarcely novel contribution to the debate about crime control.

This conclusion would be mistaken. For such is the confusion which characterizes our thinking about offending that contradictory notions about crime and the nature of criminal man happily co-exist in the public and professional consciousness. At the same time as we recognize the mundane, opportunistic, and rational nature of much offending, our deeply held and abiding fears about crime depict it as irredeemably alien to ordinary behavior—driven by abnormal motivations, irrational, purposeless, unpredictable, potentially violent, and evil. It is no part of our purpose at this time either to question the existence of pathological elements in some criminal behaviors, or to deny the relevance of moral discourse: Emphasizing the unique quality of criminal behavior may serve important, though not clearly understood deterrent, socializing, and social control functions. But it is our belief that the recurring (and often politically disingenuous) tendency to "overpathologize" offending, or otherwise discount its rational components, fosters an atmosphere that hinders more constructive attempts both to analyze criminal behavior effectively and to devise better crime-control strategies.

How has this confusion in our thinking about crime come about? Primarily, we think, as the result of two trends, one in criminological, and the other in lay thinking. In the past, repeated attempts by criminologists to identify differences between criminal and noncriminal groups that could explain offending have reinforced assumptions that offenders are similar to each other and different from everybody else. Small-scale clinical or ethnographic studies of offending subgroups have merely added to the problem, since extrapolation from such narrow data bases has presented theories about specific offenses or offender groups as general explanations of crime. The net effect of these tendencies has been the persistent blurring of important distinctions among crimes and among criminals: Instead, criminals have more often been treated as a homogeneous group and crimes as functionally equivalent. The violent and sensationalized typifications of crime to be found in political debate, the news, and entertainment media—which provide much of the information upon which lay opinion is constructed—have further encouraged tendencies to exaggerate differences between offenders and others, and to minimize differences (among offenders, motives, and types of crime) within the criminal population.

By contrast, the present volume—which is the outcome of a multidisciplinary conference held at Christ's College, Cambridge, in July 1985—develops an alternative approach, termed the "rational choice perspective," to the explanation of criminal behavior. Instead of emphasizing the differences between criminals and noncriminals, it stresses some of the similarities. In particular, while it does not deny the existence of irrational and pathological components in some crimes, it suggests we examine more closely the rational and adaptive aspects of offending. A number of further implications would follow from this. If crimes are the result of broadly rational choices based on analyses of anticipated costs and benefits, it suggests that, instead of seeing crime as a unitary phenomenon, our analysis of criminal behavior must become much more crime-specific; and that, instead of concentrating attention solely on the criminal and on factors governing his involvement in particular crimes, adequate attention must be paid to the criminal event itself and the situational factors that influence its commission.

A wide choice of terms, all of which attempt to capture aspects of the notion of a reasoning criminal, exists: adaptive choice, strategic analysis, decision making, and bounded or limited rationality. Use of the term "rational choice perspective" was adopted more for the pragmatic reason that it has now achieved a certain currency than for any intrinsic superiority over others. But its component terms also sum up salient features of the approach; the term "rational" emphasizes the notion of strategic thinking—of processing information, of evaluating opportunities and alternatives; the term "choice" emphasizes the notion that criminals make decisions; and the term "perspective" stresses that the approach is not intended as a theory but as an organizing framework—a way of rearranging existing theory and data to throw new light on criminal behaviors. Lastly, it is hoped that the changes of emphasis outlined above will provide a policy-relevant perspective on criminal behavior.

The contributors to this volume have arrived at a broadly similar destination *via* many different paths, disciplines, and preoccupations. But it seems worthwhile mentioning our own route briefly since it illustrates the close connection that we see between the emergence of the rational choice approach and the continuing development of policy-relevant research. Our interest in this topic derived from evaluative research we had undertaken in the 1960s and 1970s for the Home Office on institutional treatments for delinquents. Like so many other investigators, we found little evidence of any long-term effects of treatment. However, somewhat inconsistently, we did find that the institutional regime exerted a powerful immediate effect on behavior, as shown by the great variation in rates of absconding and other misconduct among institutions receiving essentially similar populations. We reconciled these findings by positing that immediate environmental variables, including situational inducements and opportunities for crime, were much more important in determining delinquency than had usually been thought. This line of argument was to influence later Home Office research on crime prevention where it was decided to concentrate on the development of situational measures to reduce opportunities for crime, rather than on measures to ameliorate social and psychological disadvantage.

Situational prevention leaves open the question of criminal disposition. Regardless of how much an offender might want to commit crime, or commit a particular crime, situational crime prevention or deterrence would make it more difficult for him. Unless one envisaged the criminally inclined as uniformly relentless in their quest for targets and victims—the stuff of nightmares—situational methods (which were after all nothing new to the policeman, householder, and businessman) could be expected to deter the more opportunistic, lazy, or fearful offender, and (at the least) to increase the effort required from the more experienced. But it was clear from other research (on gambling behavior, for example) that to be maximally effective situational crime prevention and deterrence policies needed better information about how criminals themselves perceived penal sanctions, environmental opportunities, rewards, and costs. And, given the arguments by critics of the situational approach that it merely displaced offending, a better understanding of criminal decision making itself seemed called for if this possibility was to be investigated.

In offering the rational choice perspective as an addition to the conceptual armory of criminology, we wish to make no undue claims as to its likely benefits, and any tendency to see it as replacing other legitimate approaches to crime prevention and reduction should be resisted. At this stage in criminology, "triangulation" through a plurality of approaches should be encouraged. Again, while the rational choice perspective pays attention to the rational decision-making elements governing criminal involvement and criminal events, it recognizes that the degree of reasoning involved will vary from offender to offender and from crime to crime. Nor does it exclude the operation of pathological motives acting in concert with rational means to secure "irrational" ends.

Finally, it offers no easy solution to the question of criminal responsibility. It does provide, however, a way of pulling together many diverse strands of criminological theory and research. It also provides both a fresh agenda for empirical enquiry concerning offenders' perspectives and, we believe, the prospect of new light on the likely effects of various crime-control policies.

Many people and organizations have assisted us in the production of this volume. We would like to extend our thanks: to Michael Tonry, Norval Morris, Al Reiss, and Frank Zimring, for helpful comments on our review of the criminal decision-making literature, which suggested the need for a conference; to the Home Office Research and Planning Unit for funding the conference; to Christ's College, Cambridge, for providing such a pleasant venue; to all the participants from Britain and overseas who made the event an enjoyable and fruitful occasion—especially to Mary Tuck, Head of the Research and Planning Unit, and James Stewart, Director of the National Institute of Justice, Washington, D.C., for their particular interest in the area of offender perceptions; to the contributors to the volume, who made our editorial task so easy and who worked quickly and efficiently to tight conference and publication deadlines; to David Farrington, Series Editor to Springer-Verlag, for his encouragement to publish these proceedings; to the editorial staff at Springer-Verlag, for their help during preparation of the manuscript for publication; and to Chicago University Press for permission to reproduce Figures 1 through 4 in Chapter 1.

Finally, we would like to thank a number of institutions for their assistance. Derek Cornish thanks the United Nations Social Defense Research Institute in Rome, its past (Professor Tolani Asuni) and current (Professor Ugo Leone) directors and their staff for their welcome and support during the period in which the original literature review was being completed; and the Social Research Division of the London School of Economics for assistance with travel costs. Both of us are grateful to our respective departments and institutions, past and present, for the time and facilities that were made available during the course of this project.

D.B.C.
R.V.C.

Contents

Chapter 1   Introduction   1
Derek Cornish and Ronald Clarke

Rational Choice Approaches to Crime   1
Empirical Studies of Criminal Decision Making   5
Theoretical Issues   10
Conclusions   13

Part One   Empirical Studies of Criminal Decision
Making

Chapter 2   Shoplifters' Perceptions of Crime Opportunities:
A Process-Tracing Study   19
John Carroll and Frances Weaver

Editors' Note   19
Criminal Rationality   20
Appropriate Methods   24
A Study of Shoplifters' Thoughts   25
Generalizations   31

Chapter 3   Victim Selection Procedures Among Economic
Criminals: The Rational Choice Perspective   39
Dermot Walsh

Editors' Note   39
Introduction: Contrasting Attitudes to Rationality   40
Differing Conceptions of Rationality   40
Rationality and Risk   42
Present Research: Aims and Methods   42
Results   43
Conclusions   49

Chapter 4   Robbers as Decision-Makers   53
             Floyd Feeney

             Editors' Note   53
             The Decision to Rob   55
             Planning   59
             Decisions Concerning Means   61
             Decisions Concerning Weapons and Force   63
             Learning and Decisions to Continue   65
             Rationality   66
             Implications for Research   67
             Implications for Policy   68

Chapter 5   The Decision to Give Up Crime   72
             Maurice Cusson and Pierre Pinsonneault

             Editor's Note   72
             Shock   73
             Delayed Deterrence   75
             Assessment   77
             A Reevaluation of Goals   78
             The Decision   78
             Aging   79
             Backsliding   79
             Women and Jobs   79
             Conclusion   80

Chapter 6   A Decision-Making Approach to Opioid
             Addiction   83
             Trevor Bennett

             Editors' Note   83
             Searching for Causes: A Look Backward   85
             Understanding Drug-Taking Careers: A Look
             Forward   88
             The Cambridge Study of Opioid Users   93
             Summary and Discussion   97
             A Final Comment   98

Part Two   Theoretical Issues

Chapter 7   On the Compatibility of Rational Choice and
             Social Control Theories of Crime   105
             Travis Hirschi

             Editors' Note   105
             Social Disorganization   108

Social Control Theory 108
Integrated Theory in Sociology 109
Causation and Determinism 112
Crime and Criminality 113
Mindlessness and Intellectualism 115
Correlates of Crime 116
Conclusion 117

Chapter 8   Linking Criminal Choices, Routine Activities,
             Informal Control, and Criminal Outcomes 119
             Marcus Felson

             Editors' Note 119

Chapter 9   Models of Decision Making Under Uncertainty:
             The Criminal Choice 129
             Pamela Lattimore and Ann Witte

             Editors' Note 129
             The Expected Utility Model 131
             Criticisms of the Expected Utility Model 134
             The Prospect Theory Model 137
             Expected Utility and Prospect Theory Models of
             Criminal Choice 144
             Summary 148
             Appendix I 149
             Appendix II 150

Chapter 10   The Theory of Reasoned Action: A Decision
             Theory of Crime 156
             Mary Tuck and David Riley

             Editors' Note 156
             Deterrence Research 157
             Wider Criminological Theories 159
             A Theory Expounded 160
             TORA and Situational Theory...................... 162
             The Normative Measure 163
             The Moral Commitment Variable.................... 164
             Crime and Secrecy 165
             TORA and Judgmental Heuristics 165
             Levels of Specificity 166
             Conclusion: The Need for Empirical Work 167

Chapter 11   The Decision to Commit a Crime: An Information-
             Processing Analysis 170
             Eric Johnson and John Payne

             Editors' Note 170

Decision Making and Criminality 171
Constructing Representations....................... 173
Evaluating Alternatives 179
Conclusion 183

Chapter 12 Offense Specialization: Does It Exist? 186
Kimberly Kempf

Editors' Note 186
Previous Research................................ 187
Data... 189
Variables.. 190
Methods 191
Results.. 192
Summary of Results 197
Conclusion 198
Appendix 199

Chapter 13 Criminal Incapacitation Effects Considered in an
Adaptive Choice Framework 202
Philip J. Cook

Editors' Note 202
Research on Incapacitation 204
Adaptive Behavior 205
The Effects of a Selective Incapacitation Policy:
A Numerical Example............................ 208
Expanding the Conceptual Framework 213

Chapter 14 Practical Reasoning and Criminal Responsibility:
A Jurisprudential Approach 217
Alan Norrie

Editors' Note 217
Juridical Individualism and Practical Rationality 220
Situated Reasoning and the Rational Choice Model
of Crime 225
Conclusion 228

Author Index 231

Subject Index 237

Contributors

Trevor Bennett Institute of Criminology, University of Cambridge, Cambridge CB3 9DT, England.

John Carroll Sloan School of Management, Massachusetts Institute of Technology, Cambridge, Massachusetts 02139, U.S.A.

Ronald Clarke Department of Criminal Justice, Temple University, Philadelphia, Pennsylvania 19122, U.S.A.

Philip J. Cook Institute of Policy Sciences and Public Affairs, Duke University, Durham, North Carolina 27706, U.S.A.

Derek Cornish Department of Social Science and Administration, London School of Economics and Political Science, London WC2A 2AE, England.

Maurice Cusson École de Criminologie, Université de Montréal, Montréal, P.Q. H3C 3J7, Canada.

Floyd Feeney School of Law, University of California at Davis, Davis, California 95616, U.S.A.

Marcus Felson Social Science Research Institute, University of Southern California, Los Angeles, California 90089-1111, U.S.A.

Travis Hirschi Department of Sociology, University of Arizona, Tucson, Arizona 85721, U.S.A.

Eric Johnson Graduate School of Industrial Administration, Carnegie-Mellon University, Pittsburgh, Pennsylvania 15213, U.S.A.

Kimberly Kempf Center for Studies in Criminology and Criminal Law, University of Pennsylvania, Philadelphia, Pennsylvania 19104, U.S.A.

Pamela Lattimore Department of Economics, University of North Carolina, Chapel Hill, North Carolina 27514, U.S.A.

Alan Norrie   Department of Law, University of Dundee, Dundee DD1 4HN, Scotland.

John Payne   The Fuqua School of Business, Duke University, Durham, North Carolina 27706, U.S.A.

Pierre Pinsonneault   École de Criminologie, Université de Montréal, Montréal, P.Q. H3C 3J7, Canada.

David Riley   Home Office Research and Planning Unit, Queen Anne's Gate, London SW1H 9AT, England.

Mary Tuck   Home Office Research and Planning Unit, Queen Anne's Gate, London SW1H 9AT, England.

Dermot Walsh   Department of Sociology, University of Exeter, Exeter EX4 4RJ, Devon, England.

Frances Weaver   Loyola University, Chicago, Illinois 60611, U.S.A.

Ann Witte   Department of Economics, Wellesley College, Wellesley, Massachusetts 02181, U.S.A.

1
Introduction

Derek Cornish and Ronald Clarke

The chapters in this volume are the outcome of a conference sponsored by the Home Office at Christ's College, Cambridge, England, in July 1985. The conference was designed to provide a forum for exploring and elaborating a decision-making approach to the explanation of crime. This perspective, the organizers believed (Clarke and Cornish, 1985), was one increasingly being adopted by a number of social scientists in disciplines with an interest in criminal behavior. At the least, these various approaches—drawn from psychology, sociology, criminology, economics, and the law—seemed to assume that much offending was broadly rational in nature (Simon, 1978). Hence the "reasoning criminal" of this volume's title. In other respects, however, their concepts, aims, preoccupations, and terminologies were often quite different, and in consequence it was not always easy to appreciate how much common ground they shared. More tantalizingly, it was unclear to what extent the insights provided by the various disciplines could be integrated into a more comprehensive and satisfactory representation of criminal behavior. The organizers had already made one attempt to provide such a framework in the paper referred to above, and the conference provided a further opportunity to test out the possibilities for some such synthesis.

Rational Choice Approaches to Crime

The synthesis we had suggested—a rational choice perspective on criminal behavior—was intended to locate criminological findings within a framework particularly suitable for thinking about policy-relevant research. Its starting point was an assumption that offenders seek to benefit themselves by their criminal behavior; that this involves the making of decisions and of choices, however rudimentary on occasion these processes might be; and that these processes exhibit a measure of rationality, albeit constrained by limits of time and ability and the availability of relevant information. It was recognized that this conception of crime seemed to fit some forms of offending better than others. However, even in the case of offenses that seemed to be pathologically motivated or impulsively executed, it was felt that rational components were also often present and that the identification and description of these might have lessons for crime-control policy.

Second, a crime-specific focus was adopted, not only because different crimes may meet different needs, but also because the situational context of decision making and the information being handled will vary greatly among offenses. To ignore these differences might well be to reduce significantly one's ability to identify fruitful points for intervention (similar arguments have been applied to other forms of "deviant" behavior, such as gambling: cf. Cornish, 1978). A crime-specific focus is likely to involve rather finer distinctions than those commonly made in criminology. For example, it may not be sufficient to divide burglary simply into its residential and commercial forms. It may also be necessary to distinguish between burglaries committed in middle-class suburbs, in public housing, and in wealthy residential enclaves. Empirical studies suggest that the kinds of individuals involved in these different forms of residential burglary, their motivations, and their methods all vary considerably (cf. Clarke and Hope, 1984, for a review). Similar cases could be made for distinguishing between different forms of robbery, rape, shoplifting, and car theft, to take some obvious cases. (In lay thinking, of course, such distinctions are also often made, as between mugging and other forms of robbery, for example.) A corollary of this requirement is that the explanatory focus of the theory is on crimes, rather than on offenders. Such a focus, we believe, provides a counterweight to theoretical and policy preoccupations with the offender.

Third, it was argued that a decision-making approach to crime requires that a fundamental distinction be made between criminal involvement and criminal events. Criminal involvement refers to the processes through which individuals choose to become initially involved in particular forms of crime, to continue, and to desist. The decision processes in these different stages of involvement will be influenced in each case by a different set of factors and will need to be separately modeled. In the same way, the decision processes involved in the commission of a specific crime (i.e., the criminal event) will utilize their own special categories of information. Involvement decisions are characteristically multistage, extend over substantial periods of time, and will draw upon a large range of information, not all of which will be directly related to the crimes themselves. Event decisions, on the other hand, are frequently shorter processes, utilizing more circumscribed information largely relating to immediate circumstances and situations.

The above points can be illustrated by consideration of some flow diagrams that the editors previously developed (Clarke and Cornish, 1985) to model one specific form of crime, namely, burglary in a middle-class residential suburb. Figure 1.1, which represents the processes of

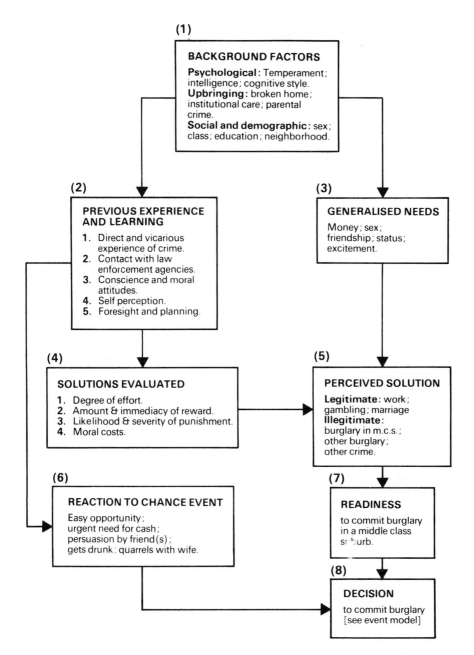

FIGURE 1.1. Initial involvement model (example: burglary in a middle-class suburb). (From *Crime and Justice*, vol. 6, M. Tonry and N. Morris (eds.), University of Chicago Press, 1985. By permission.)

initial involvement in this form of crime, has two decision points. The first (Box 7) is the individual's recognition of his or her "readiness" to commit the specific offense in order to satisfy certain needs for money, goods, or excitement. The preceding boxes indicate the wide range of factors that bring the individual to this condition. Box 1, in particular, encompasses the various historical (and contemporaneous) background factors with which traditional criminology has been preoccupied; these have been seen to determine the values, attitudes, and personality traits that dispose the individual to crime. In a rational choice context, however, these factors are reinterpreted as influencing the decisions and judgments that lead to involvement. The second decision (Box 8) actually to commit this form of burglary is the outcome of some chance event, such as an urgent need for cash, which demands action.

Figure 1.2, which is much simpler, depicts the further sequence of decision making that leads to the burglar selecting a particular house. The range of variables influencing this decision sequence is much narrower and reflects the influence of situational factors related to opportunity, effort, and proximal risks. In most cases this decision sequence takes place quite quickly. Figure 1.3 sketches the classes of

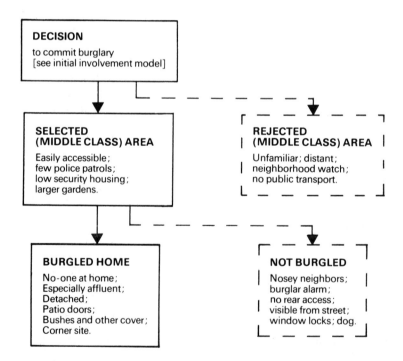

FIGURE 1.2. Event model (example: burglary in a middle-class suburb). (From *Crime and Justice*, vol. 6, M. Tonry and N. Morris (eds.), University of Chicago Press, 1985. By permission.)

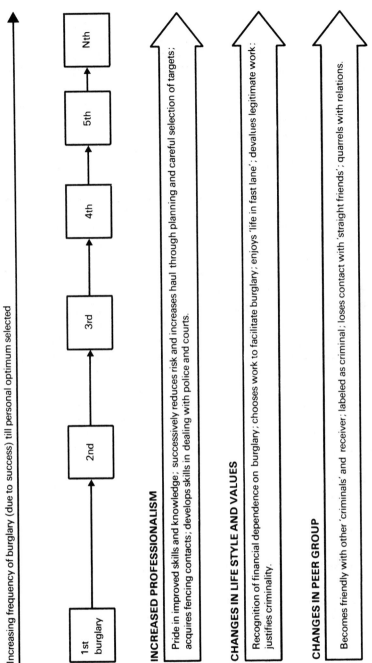

FIGURE 1.3. Continuing involvement model (example: burglary in a middle class suburb). (From *Crime and Justice*, vol. 6, M. Tonry and N. Morris (eds.), University of Chicago Press, 1985. By permission.)

variables, relating to changes in the individual's degree of professionalism, peer group, life-style, and values, that influence the constantly reevaluated decision to continue with this form of burglary.

Figure 1.4 illustrates, with hypothetical data, similar reevaluations that may lead to desistance. In this case, two classes of variables are seen to have a cumulative effect: life-events (such as marriage), and those more directly related to the criminal events themselves.

These, then, are the main features of the framework that was developed out of our review of recent work in a variety of disciplines that have an interest in crime. It differs from most existing formal theories of criminal behavior, however, in a number of respects. It is true that, like many other criminological theories, the rational choice perspective is intended to provide a framework for understanding all forms of crime. Unlike other approaches, however, which attempt to impose a conceptual unity upon divergent criminal behaviors (by subsuming them under more general concepts such as delinquency, deviance, rule breaking, short-run hedonism, criminality, etc.), our rational choice formulation sees these differences as crucial to the tasks of explanation and control. Unlike existing theories, which tend to concentrate on factors disposing individuals to criminal behavior (the initial involvement model), the rational choice approach, in addition, emphasizes subsequent decisions in the offender's career. Again, whereas most existing theories tend to accord little influence to situational variables, the rational choice approach explicitly recognizes their importance in relation to the criminal event and, furthermore, incorporates similar influences on decisions relating to involvement in crime. In consequence, this perspective also recognizes, as do economic and behaviorist theories, the importance of incentives—that is, of rewards and punishments—and hence the role of learning in the criminal career. Finally, the leitmotif encapsulated in the notion of a "reasoning" offender implies the essentially nonpathological and commonplace nature of much criminal activity.

Empirical Studies of Criminal Decision Making

Part 1 of this volume consists of a number of empirical studies of shoplifting (Carroll and Weaver), robbery (Cusson and Pinsonneault, Feeney, Walsh), commercial burglary (Walsh), and opioid use (Bennett). Considered merely as additions to the crime-specific literature, these studies contribute greatly to our knowledge about particular offenses. This may be illustrated by a few of the more unexpected findings: that many robberies are impulsive and unplanned (Feeney, Walsh), that some robbers avoid burglary for fear of encountering the householder (Feeney),

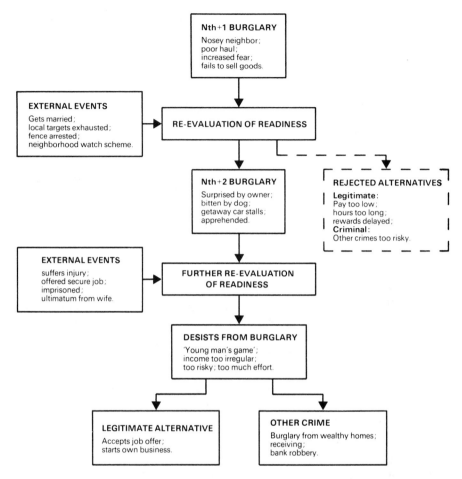

FIGURE 1.4. Desistance model (example: burglary in a middle class suburb). (From *Crime and Justice*, vol. 6, M. Tonry and N. Morris (eds.), University of Chicago Press, 1985. By permission.)

and that, prior to their first experience of drug use, many opioid users had already apparently decided that they wanted to become part of the "drug scene" (Bennett). Additionally, although not necessarily designed with the above formulation of the rational choice approach in mind, these studies also exemplify the kind of detailed empirical work needed to test, refine, and elaborate our models.

In our discussion of the rational choice perspective we identified three main components: the image of a reasoning offender, a crime-specific focus, and the development of separate decision models for the involvement processes and the criminal event. The empirical studies both give some support to the above analysis and permit further refinements. In regard to the nature of offender decision making, the present studies suggest that, although offenders act in a broadly rational fashion, normative economic models such as the expected utility (EU) paradigm fail to capture the cognitive activities involved. (This point is referred to again below.) Furthermore, there is evidence from Carroll and Weaver's study that information-processing strategies change with growing expertise. As far as the second element is concerned, the importance of a crime-specific approach has already been noted above in relation to the insights provided about particular crimes. The necessity of such a focus is reinforced by Walsh's comparisons between commercial burglars and robbers: Although similar proportions in each group claimed to plan their offenses, there was some evidence of differences in the form and content of the reasoning involved. Within categories of crime, too, it seems that further differentiation may have some value: Feeney, for example, found that commercial robberies were more often planned than those committed against individuals. Blazicek's recent (1985) study of target selection by commercial robbers tends to support this finding, and his results also indicate that a further breakdown of commercial robbery into more specific categories might be useful. More generally, information from his respondents suggests that, when selecting their commercial targets, such robbers apparently attach more importance to the overall scenario—numbers of people inside the establishment, its size and location—than to the personal characteristics of the human victims involved. Since studies like Lejeune's (1977) on mugging have shown victim characteristics to play a more central role in relation to target selection, it would be interesting to know more about the relative importance of scene and victim characteristics for other offenses.

The empirical studies support in general terms the separate modeling of event and involvement processes. (This issue, too, relates to the nature of criminal decision-making processes and will be discussed in more detail later.) However, they also suggest the need for some qualifications: For example, Cusson and Pinsonneault's analysis, with its emphasis on the possibility of "backsliding," suggests that desistance from a particular type of crime may not always be the smooth process of disengagement that our model might suggest. Their concepts of "shock" and of "delayed deterrence" leading to desistance further stress the discontinuities involved. (In passing it should be noted that the concept of desistance, and indeed of involvement, assumes repeated offenses. Although this assumption undoubtedly holds for many crimes, there is a limited class, including domestic murder, for which it will not.)

Lastly, the authors of these chapters (in particular, Carroll and Weaver, Walsh) raise some of the methodological problems commonly encountered when carrying out such empirical research. Many of these considerations will be especially relevant to studies of event decisions, but others will be found to apply equally to questions of involvement, continuance, and desistance. The problems can be divided into two broad categories: those of contacting and enlisting the cooperation of "real" criminals, and those of providing a research context and, where relevant, a decision task likely to elicit valid information about criminal decision making. Unfortunately, these two groups of requirements often tend to conflict. To guarantee the representativeness of one's sample, it might seem sensible to contact those convicted of such offenses, large clusters of whom are, in any case, conveniently located in prisons. Although these populations do not (as is often claimed) necessarily contain an overrepresentation of unsuccessful offenders—the criminal records of convicted burglars and robbers are likely to be only the tips of their personal offending icebergs—the data may well contain other systematic distortions: for example, the presence of large numbers of older, more serious, and more persistent offenders may exaggerate the role of experience and planning in decision making.

Although problems in gaining the cooperation of incarcerated offenders may be encountered (Walsh), the difficulties are considerably magnified where the decision is made to use those currently at liberty. The confidentiality of agency files, the covert nature of criminal activity, and the difficulty of penetrating criminal networks all make the task of identifying and contacting criminals (cf. Klockars, 1974; Carroll and Weaver) and ex-criminals (Cusson and Pinsonneault) a hard one; even when respondents are found, the problems remain of verifying their credentials and estimating their representativeness.

Such problems interact with those of trying to ensure that information about criminal decision making is elicited in ways that guarantee authenticity and verisimilitude. Bennett has elsewhere (Bennett and Wright, 1984) graphically cataloged the practical difficulties of undertaking process-tracing research with burglars. Moreover, the well-documented ethical and legal problems of carrying out participant observation studies with criminals (cf. Weppner, 1977)—to say nothing of the personal dangers sometimes involved—will usually place similar constraints on process tracing, limiting the method at best to the study of induced behavioral intentions rather than the commission of criminal acts. This will mean that, although questions of procedural rationality can be addressed by such studies, the effectiveness of the identified decision processes in achieving their outcomes cannot be directly explored. Even this research might be viewed as ethically dubious where serious personal crimes are being studied, especially those regarded as having pathological components, if those using the procedure were to be suspected of condoning, colluding in, or encouraging the consideration of such offenses.

However, in vitro techniques, such as process tracing using video recordings (cf. Bennett and Wright, 1984) or retrospective interviewing using still photographs to stimulate discussion and simulate important aspects of the decision problem, may fail to capture essential elements of the real-life task or decision-making processes, even if the method enables the salient information being used to be correctly identified. At worst there is the danger that a largely fictional gloss of rationality, born out of the demands of the researcher and the needs of the offender, could be imposed post hoc on previous offending or arise more adventitiously through faulty memory and ignorance of or inability to articulate the real mechanisms involved. On the other hand, some offenders—even if their offense has been adjudicated, and certainly before—may, out of professional habit or personal needs, remain anxious to conceal any exercise of foresight and planning (Walsh). Indeed, most of the methodological problems traditionally to be met with in ethnographic research, whether by interview or observation, apply in some measure to the studies reported here. These difficulties relate inter alia to the motivations of respondents in supplying information; to the reactive effects of unanticipated interactions between experimenter (or interviewer) and subject (or respondent); to the intrusiveness of any technical instrumentation and other props; to the wealth of material generated; and to problems of analysis (a problem for process-tracing research; cf. Payne et al., 1978).

The list, of course, is endless, but such are the inevitable intellectual challenges and frustrations of undertaking research into real-life criminal decision making. It is hoped that the present chapters, taken singly or as a group, give some indication of the corresponding rewards.

Theoretical Issues

Part 2 of this volume collects chapters addressing some general theoretical issues. One of these concerns the place of a rational choice perspective in theoretical criminology. This topic is discussed in chapters by Hirschi and by Felson, both of whom believe that rational choice approaches complement rather than supplant existing theory. Hirschi sees rational choice theory as being concerned mainly with explaining crimes (or "events"), in contrast to his "control theory," which is primarily a theory of criminality (or "involvement"). Felson attempts to provide a synthesis among routine activities, social control, and rational choice perspectives. In his view, rational choice theory deals mainly with the content of decisions; routine activity approaches, in contrast, are seen to deal with the ecological contexts that supply the range of options from which choices are made.

We, too, see no essential conflict among these various theoretical positions, which, as Hirschi points out, share basic assumptions about the nature of human beings. On the other hand, we believe that rational choice models deal not just with crimes but also with criminality, and not merely with the form and content of decision making itself but also with the historical and contemporaneous background to decisions. In other words, we see a rational choice perspective as providing a framework within which to incorporate and locate existing theories. This does not reflect an imperialistic ambition on our part to encroach upon the territory of other theories; indeed, it seems to us that a plurality of criminological theories is desirable. However, there is also a need for some integration of theory, and our perspective represents one such attempt. We also believe that theories are primarily of heuristic rather than intrinsic value, and the standard by which we should like to see the rational choice approach judged is the degree to which it enhances thinking about crime-control policies.

A second general issue, which is directly addressed in chapters by Lattimore and Witte (economists), by Tuck and Riley, and by Johnson and Payne (all psychologists), concerns the nature of the criminal decision-making process. This issue is also raised in some of the empirical chapters. Taken together, these chapters suggest that normative economic and decision theory models and related perspectives, such as the theory of reasoned action (TORA), may fail to capture the nature of the actual decision-making processes involved. In brief, such models often appear to require from decision makers more complex and sophisticated information-handling skills than they generally seem either willing or able to employ. Because the descriptive value of a model is vital to its usefulness in developing an understanding of criminal decision making detailed enough to provide pointers for policymaking, this conclusion is an important one. It should, however, be accompanied by some qualifications. In particular, it may be premature given the present concentration on event decisions and the limited range of crimes (mainly predatory) so far studied. The more protracted time scales of involvement decisions may allow greater scope for information processing along the lines that EU models seem to require; in a similar way, the latter may yet prove to provide appropriate descriptions of decision making (even in relation to event decisions) where offenses requiring a greater degree of deliberation and planning, such as some forms of corporate crime, are concerned.

However, the rapid information processing often demanded by the search and evaluation procedures involved in the assessment of criminal opportunities, and in the planning and commission of offenses, must favor explanations that emphasize the role of noncompensatory strategies (cf. Johnson and Payne). The end result of these strategies would be to lighten the load upon the human cognitive system. It seems likely, therefore, that the burden is reduced in other ways, too. Part of the expertise involved in criminal decision making may well consist in the ability to manage fears, moral scruples, and guilt by dealing with these issues at the time of first considering (or reconsidering) involvement, and thereafter treating them as temporarily settled (in Cook's [1980] terms, as "standing decisions"). There is some evidence from Bennett's study (and from his previous research on burglars' perceptions: cf. Bennett and Wright, 1984) and from Feeney's and from Carroll and Weaver's research that this may occur.

The third general issue examined in part 2 (in the chapter by Kempf) concerns the role of specialization in criminal behavior. Our crime-specific focus may appear to rely on the notion that offenders tend to specialize. This, of course, runs counter to most of the empirical evidence (Wolfgang et al., 1972), although 78% of Feeney's sample of robbers claimed to be specialists. In fact, such an assumption is not necessary to our models, the foci of which are on crimes rather than on offenders, and which therefore treat of offenders, whether generalists or specialists, only in relation to that particular form of crime. In a sense, therefore, the question of whether offenders are generalists or specialists is a tangential one and would only become salient were the models to be used to explain a particular offender's career, in which case the links between various crime-specific involvement models would need to be described. There is, in addition, the purely practical point that it may be inefficient to develop separate involvement (though *not* event) models for specific crimes that tend to be committed by largely the same kind of offenders. Nevertheless, given the difficulty of making the distinction between crime-based and offender-based models, there is no doubt that the value of the approach would be more readily appreciated the greater the degree of specialization that could be demonstrated. Seen in this light, Kempf's findings, using data from the second Philadelphia cohort, of a moderate degree of specialization are encouraging, and sufficient to keep the issue open.

The final group of issues raised by the chapters in part 2 of this volume concerns the implications for policy of a rational choice approach. The view, for example, that offenders will act rationally to adapt their behavior to changes in penal sanctions is put forward by Cook in his telling exploration of some of the possible unforeseen consequences of incapacitation. Elsewhere (Cornish and Clarke, forthcoming) we have argued, in relation to situational crime prevention, that an understanding of factors affecting target choice is the key to the management of the displacement problem. Displacement refers to the possibility that, in response to reduced opportunities to commit a particular crime, offenders will adapt by choosing other targets, offending at a different time or place, changing their methods, or committing other forms of crime (Reppetto, 1976). Rational choice perspectives provide a fruitful way of conceptualizing the displacement phenomenon and of assessing the degree to which it might undermine crime-control measures. More generally, a focus on offender decision making seems to offer a more useful framework within which to discuss deterrence than do most existing criminological theories, which seem geared toward rehabilitation and social prevention. The distinction between involvement and event models, for example, provides a convenient basis for locating decisions about, respectively, the distal and proximal risks of offending.

In the wider context of criminal justice policy, Norrie's paper raises important questions about the extent to which a rational choice approach, with its apparent emphasis upon individual choice and responsibility, supports a "just deserts" philosophy. The distinction he develops between "situated" rationality, under which people are seen as making genuine choices, albeit from a restricted range of possibilities dictated by their position in the socioeconomic structure, and the "abstracted" notion of rationality implicit in the criminal law, provides a strong support for our own reluctance to see the rational choice perspective as necessarily supporting juridical individualism. Thus, the mere ability to be a reasoning criminal cannot of itself provide a basis for ascribing criminal responsibility to actions, and the rational choice perspective is therefore neutral with respect to the free will–determinism debate.

Conclusions

The view that formed the starting point for this volume—that it can be useful to see offenders as reasoning decision makers—is borne out by its contents. The empirical studies of part 1 provide further evidence that, with regard to the offenses studied, criminals exercise some degree of planning and foresight and adapt their behavior to take account of proximal and distal contingencies. It also seems that the rational choice models we have provided serve to locate the findings of individual studies within a policy-relevant explanatory framework. The approach seems, for example, particularly useful for thinking about situational crime prevention and deterrence.

The studies in part 1 were carried out by workers from a variety of academic backgrounds. The value of a rational choice perspective as an impetus to interdisciplinary cooperation is also supported by the theoretical work in part 2 and bears out Simon's (1978) judgment about how much common ground is already shared. Whereas the empirical work serves to flesh out the rational choice framework, the second set of chapters identifies some of the theoretical issues that need to be tackled if this perspective is to be taken further. For example, it is important that a rapprochement be reached with other theoretical perspectives, that a fuller understanding of the cognitive processes involved in criminal decisions be achieved, and that the implications of a rational choice approach for crime control and the wider criminal justice policies be more fully debated.

The present volume goes some way toward dealing with these issues.

Nevertheless, much work remains to be done. In addition, a number of other issues require urgent attention. Perhaps the most pressing of these concerns the need to extend the reach of rational choice approaches to a wider variety of crimes. Considering the clear applicability of a rational choice perspective to corporate crimes, it is to be hoped that the approach will act as a further stimulus to research in this neglected area. It is particularly important, however, to ascertain the extent to which such an analysis can be applied to violent offenses. The few relevant studies that exist in this area (Lejeune's 1977 study of mugging, Athens's 1980 study of rape and homicide, and Dobash and Dobash's 1984 study of spouse abuse) suggest that many such offenses do indeed exhibit a substantial degree of rationality. Feeney's findings indicate that the use of weapons and of force, or threatened force in robbery, may be rationally calculated to gain swift control over an uncertain situation. It may be that our reluctance to construe aggressive or violent behavior as instrumental rather than expressive (or normal rather than pathological) sometimes has more to do with our own fears than with the facts of the matter. One must also be wary of definitions of rationality that rely too much on evidence of planning. From Walsh's and Feeney's data on personal robbery, it seems likely that "pattern planning" would be sufficient for offenses that rely largely for their success on surprise, intimidation, and a general ability to seize the initiative and think on one's feet.

Although a number of chapters in the present volume have been concerned with the nature of decision-making processes, in terms of both their form and their content, a question that has barely been addressed (except in the clinical research of Yochelson and Samenow, 1976) is whether characteristically criminal thinking patterns exist. To handle guilt and shame, for example, do criminals employ unique thinking patterns, or do they make much greater use of commonplace cognitive devices such as excuses, justifications, and defense mechanisms like repression or denial, or is it that their thinking processes are similar to those of nonoffenders but the informational content differs? On the evidence of Carroll and Weaver's chapter in this volume, and of Johnson and Payne's discussion of noncompensatory strategies, it certainly seems that, in relation to decisions about the criminal event, the more experienced offender behaves in much the same way as any expert decision maker.

All methods for studying cognitive processes are liable to error. The primary data collection technique employed by the empirical studies in this volume was the interview, a technique whose strengths and limitations are too well known to require further rehearsal here. A range of other methods to study criminal decision making exists (such as participant and nonparticipant observation, the life history approach, and process tracing), and criminal decision making can be studied using a range of tasks in a variety of settings from the natural to the contrived.

Each of these approaches has its own special application: Process tracing, for example, is more suited to the study of events than of involvement, whereas the life history method may be especially useful where the sequential decisions of the criminal career are to be explored. Neither should more indirect methods of studying criminal decision making be forgotten: Interviews with victims and with police experienced in handling particular types of crime, surveys of previously victimized targets (cf. Winchester and Jackson, 1982)—all these can provide useful evidence against which to validate data obtained directly from offenders. For the future, apart perhaps from more carefully defining the offenses under investigation, there is a need to move from the pilot study to more methodologically rigorous research. This will involve increased attention to the representativeness of the samples and the reactiveness of whatever method is employed. Given that the field is still new, however, the need to encourage continuing methodological innovation and triangulation of research techniques cannot be overemphasized. In particular, it is to be hoped that the historical reluctance of some deviancy sociologists (particularly in Britain) to explore the implications of their ethnographic research for crime-control policies will not prevent a fuller appreciation of the insights that this work can provide.

Lastly, it remains to draw attention to two somewhat disquieting questions concerning this new image of a reasoning criminal. One, mentioned in Hirschi's paper, refers to the possibility that criminologists may now be tending to see the offender as more thoughtful and intellectually sophisticated than he or she really is—an image with which, perhaps, the middle-class academic feels more at ease. A second and related question concerns the likely long-term consequences of thus "depathologizing" crime. If most criminal behavior is portrayed as rational, normal, and commonplace, what will be the effect upon everyday thinking and moralizing about crime?

References

Athens, Lonnie
   1980   Violent Criminal Acts and Actors: A Symbolic Interactionist Study. London: Routledge and Kegan Paul.
Bennett, Trevor and Richard Wright
   1984   Burglars on Burglary. Aldershot, Hants, England: Gower.
Blazicek, Donald L.
   1985   "Patterns of victim selection among robbers: a theoretical and descriptive analysis." Paper presented at the Fifth International Symposium on Victimology, Zagreb, Yugoslavia, August 18–23.
Clarke, Ronald V. and Derek B. Cornish
   1985   "Modeling offenders' decisions: a framework for research and policy." Pp. 147–85 in M. Tonry and N. Morris (eds.), Crime and Justice: An

Annual Review of Research, Volume 6. Chicago: University of Chicago Press.

Clarke, Ronald V. and Tim Hope
1983   Coping with Burglary: Research Perspectives on Policy. Boston: Kluwer-Nijhoff.

Cook, Philip J.
1980   "Research in criminal deterrence: laying the groundwork for the second decade." Pp. 211–68 in N. Morris and M. Tonry (eds.), Crime and Justice: An Annual Review of Research, Volume 2. Chicago: University of Chicago Press.

Cornish, Derek B.
1978   Gambling: A Review of the Literature and Its Implications for Policy and Research. Home Office Research Studies No. 42. London: HMSO.

Cornish, Derek B. and Ronald V. Clarke
        "Situational prevention, displacement of crime and rational choice theory." In Kevin Heal and Gloria Laycock (eds.), Situational Crime Prevention: From Theory Into Practice. London: HMSO (in press).

Dobash, R. Emerson and Russell P. Dobash
1984   "The nature and antecedents of violent events." British Journal of Criminology 24:269–88.

Klockars, C.
1974   The Professional Fence. London: Tavistock.

Lejeune, Robert
1977   "The management of a mugging." Urban Life 6(2):123–48.

Payne, J.W., M.L. Braunstein and J.S. Carroll
1978   "Exploring predecisional behavior: an alternative approach to decision research." Organizational Behavior and Human Performance 22:17–44.

Reppetto, Thomas A.
1976   "Crime prevention and the displacement phenomenon." Crime and Delinquency 22:166–77.

Simon, Herbert A.
1978   "Rationality as process and product of thought." American Economic Review 8(2):1–11.

Weppner, R.S. (ed.)
1977   Street Ethnography: Selected Studies of Crime and Deviance in a Natural Setting. Beverly Hills, CA: Sage.

Winchester, S.W.C. and H. Jackson
1982   Residential Burglary: The Limits of Prevention. Home Office Research Studies No. 74. London: HMSO.

Wolfgang, Marvin E., Robert M. Figlio and Thorsten Sellin
1972   Delinquency in a Birth Cohort. Chicago: University of Chicago Press.

Yochelson, S. and S.E. Samenow
1976   The Criminal Personality (2 volumes). New York: Aronson.

Part One   Empirical Studies of Criminal Decision Making

2
Shoplifters' Perceptions of Crime Opportunities: A Process-Tracing Study

JOHN CARROLL AND FRANCES WEAVER

Editors' Note

The nature of the rationality to be ascribed to criminals is a theme that preoccupies most of the contributors to this volume. This discussion of normative versus bounded rationality by John Carroll and Frances Weaver emphasizes the need to develop empirically based descriptive models to account for the operation of criminal expertise within the context of limited information-processing capacities and establishes a context for the rest of the studies in part 1 of this volume. However, the particular interest of their chapter lies in the empirical investigation they undertook to throw further light upon these theoretical issues. For this purpose they used a process-tracing technique designed to elicit verbal reports of people's thinking when actually engaged in assessing information and making decisions—to study, in the real-life settings of retail stores, the perceptions and judgments of experienced and novice shoplifters when considering crime opportunities. Their results provide further evidence for the viability of the general rational choice perspective outlined in the Introduction to this volume. Although only issues of procedural rationality could be addressed by the data, it was clearly the case that experienced shoplifters, especially those in whom a behavioral intention was induced, were much more expert than novices at analyzing shoplifting opportunities. This difference was as much in terms of the reasoning strategies adopted as in the content. The detailed information about expert shoplifters' perceptions gained from this type of study once again emphasizes the usefulness of crime-specific analyses of this nature and their potential relevance to policymaking. Similarly, the benefit of making analytic distinctions between involvement and even decisions was also borne out. On the whole, it was the novices who were preoccupied with the distal consequences of shoplifting and any associated moral considerations and fears—factors that might be expected to enter into the initial decision to shoplift. Once formed, the intention to shoplift seemed to focus subsequent reasoning on strategic issues concerning specific tactics and risks (cf. also Feeney, this volume).

Criminologists are taking a new look at the thought processes of potential criminals (Carroll, 1982; Cook, 1980; Clarke and Cornish, 1985). In an era of social science research that has emphasized the cognitive determinants of behavior (Bandura, 1977; Simon, 1957; Petty and Cacioppo, 1981), interest has converged on the interpretation of criminal behavior as the product of reasoned judgments about the costs and benefits of criminal and noncriminal acts. Such interpretations have potential policy implications regarding the deterrence or reduction of crime.

In the first section of this chapter we argue two points: (1) that our growing knowledge of human reasoning suggests that the rationality of crime perceptions will be limited, in contrast to the economic or normative rationality underlying our existing theories of deterrence, and (2) that the study of crime perceptions demands methods that allow the collection of appropriate observations, specifically, individual judgments of realistic crime opportunities. In the second section we present an empirical study of shoplifting, using experienced and novice shoplifters who described their thoughts during consideration of actual crime opportunities in retail stores.

Criminal Rationality

Normative Rationality

Economists view crime as a rational act resulting when individuals evaluate the expected utility of both criminal and noncriminal activities and then choose the alternative with the highest net payoff (e.g., Becker, 1968). If committing a crime has a higher utility than not committing the crime—that is, an acceptable risk of being caught and a desirable amount to gain—then the individual should decide in favor of committing the crime. On the other hand, increasing the perceived likelihood of capture and the unpleasantness of the expected penalty should reduce crime—this is the deterrence hypothesis.

In their strong form, such theories of normative rationality predict that potential criminals will gather information relevant to risks and benefits and combine this information according to the expected utility formula (the sum of outcome values multiplied by probabilities of occurrence). We have every reason to believe, from theory and research, that this strong form of rationality is wrong.

Limited Rationality

From a theoretical perspective, the highly influential views of information-processing psychology argue that human rationality is seriously limited by biological constraints (e.g., Newell and Simon, 1972). Herbert Simon received the Nobel Prize in Economics in 1978 for his concept of "bounded rationality." Drawing upon this work, behavioral decision theorists (Slovic et al., 1977; Kahneman et al., 1982; Einhorn and Hogarth, 1981) have produced a coherent body of research showing that people fail to behave consistently with normative rationality, but instead make simplifications and shortcuts that are reasonable but may produce inferior outcomes.

Empirical research in criminology confirms these results. Criminals do not seem to acquire the kind of information about crime (certainty and severity of objective sanctions) implied by rational models. For example, the Assembly Committee on Criminal Procedure (California) studied knowledge of criminal penalties and concluded, "It appears that knowledge of penalties cannot act as deterrents since these are unknown until after a person has committed a crime or become a prisoner" (1975:78). Paternoster et al. (1982) reported a panel study showing that behavior more strongly determines perceptions of risk than perceptions influence behavior. Research that has manipulated the amount of gain, likelihood of gain, severity of punishment, and likelihood of punishment in hypothetical crime situations found that subjects are sensitive to these variables but do not combine them into the interaction terms (representing expected risks and payoffs) that are necessary for computing expected utility (Carroll, 1978; Feldman, 1977; Krauss et al., 1972; Rettig, 1964; Rettig and Rawson, 1963; Stefanowicz and Hannum, 1971).

The above research tested the rational model that criminals first gather information, then code it and combine it according to the expected utility rule. Although this model seems incorrect, perhaps a weaker version of rationality is possible whereby criminals are sensitive to risks and payoffs but do not combine this information optimally. In such a weaker model, changes in deterrence variables would still affect criminal behavior.

Of the studies cited above that tested the rational model, one has some interesting data bearing on the weaker version of rationality. Carroll (1978) presented subjects with hypothetical crime opportunities in the form of gambles that independently varied four dimensions: likelihoods of gain and loss, amount to gain, and severity of punishment. Subjects included incarcerated adults and juveniles as well as adult and juvenile noncriminals. Each subject was given a complete set of crime opportunities, so that the responses of each subject to every aspect of the hypothetical situations could be evaluated. Subjects' responses were essentially additive across the four dimensions, not multiplicative as required in the strong form of the rational model. However, there were further deviations from even the weaker model of rationality: Only 41% of subjects were responsive to the likelihood of capture, 60% to the likelihood of success, 67% to the penalty, and 84% to the available money.

These results did not substantially differ across subject types. Many subjects focused on only one dimension and either ignored the others or made minor adjustments based on one or two other dimensions. These data suggest very strong "dimensional preferences" (Slovic and Lichtenstein, 1968) and a tremendous difficulty in combining multiple pieces of relevant information into a single judgment. The policy implications of such conclusions should be clear: Some deterrents work some of the time with some potential criminals.

Criminal Expertise

Although these laboratory results portray a very weak version of rationality, other criminological research suggests a different view, namely, that experienced criminals have a great deal of technical and interpersonal skill and knowledge relevant to specific crime opportunities. Interviews with experienced criminals suggest that certainty and severity of punishment are not static properties of a crime (e.g., a burglar in London has a particular probability of getting caught) but are under partial control of the criminal. Criminals are experts at controlling or minimizing risks. The criminal's skill in leaving no evidence that will stand up in court, in manipulating the legal system through bargains and bribes, and in setting up and carrying out crimes and disposing of the gains is indicative that an experienced criminal faces different opportunities and sanctions than does an amateur (Inciardi, 1975; Letkemann, 1973).

This apparent contradiction between the uncomplimentary view of criminals portrayed in laboratory studies and the complimentary view emerging from sociological interviews can be resolved in several ways. First, the laboratory studies could be misleading. The information provided in those studies could be irrelevant to how criminals actually think (e.g., too abstract) or fail to engage their expertise because it is not "real," or the laboratory studies may not have selected criminals who were expert enough. Alternatively, the interviews could be misleading: Criminals may be better at "snowing" the naive social scientist than at making good judgments. Finally, it could be that both are right: Criminals may have a great deal of knowledge *and* be unable to consider many pieces of information at one time. Carroll (1982) suggested that criminals may extend the decision process over time in such a way that features are sequentially incorporated into decisions and behavior. Thus, the criminal uses considerable judgment and knowledge in evaluating a particular opportunity but at any one moment is only making limited use of simple information.

For example, one of Letkemann's interviewees remarked, "When I was down to a certain level I would go out" (1973:22). Lack of money was one factor initiating a search for a good opportunity. Another interviewee provided a sequential ordering of decision factors:

Usually, the assessment of economic value precedes the assessment of risk. A safecracker may, while on legitimate business, spot a particularly "easy" safe. He may then assess the probable economic value of the safe's contents. Whether the value is high or low, if the risks are low, he may "make" the safe. On the other hand, if both are high, he may also attempt the job. (1973:151)

This simple contingent process model (Payne, 1973) can be interpreted as:

1. Assess money in pocket (if high, no crime; if low, go to Step 2);
2. Assess certainty of success (if low, no crime; if high, go to Step 3);
3. Assess amount of gain (if low, go to Step 4; if high, go to Step 5);
4. Assess risk (if high, no crime; if low, go to Step 5);
5. Commit crime (a step that itself would consist of substeps in the planning, selection of techniques, and execution of the crime).

This viewpoint suggests that planned crimes, spontaneous crimes, and crimes of passion will differ in the number of features that are considered because of the progressive limiting of time for judgment. Criminals seem to realize that "some crimes are committed in a deliberate and rational manner, others, such as those generated by frustration, may be done impulsively" (Letkemann, 1973:22). Financial need may keep a criminal from examining crime opportunities in a leisurely manner. When money is acutely needed, "he may deliberately need to find a spot, dispense with careful planning, and proceed quickly and at high risk." Thus, "crimes committed shortly after release from prison, when the exconvict is out of money, are the most risky" (1973:143).

Thinking about criminals as "experts" requires that we adopt an understanding of expertise consistent with recent studies of experts in various domains. These studies suggest that experts utilize past knowledge organized systematically and strategically, but not necessarily in ways that correspond to optimal performance (Johnson, forthcoming; Larkin et al., 1980). Drawing upon these studies of expertise, we would expect that experienced criminals will perceive crime opportunities using a large set of perceptual patterns that serve to index not only factual knowledge but also information about strategies and actions. They should more actively and rapidly search out and develop crime opportunities (Cook, 1980), whereas novices may respond only to obvious opportunities and spend considerable time thinking them over because each opportunity is novel.

If we can conclude that the thought processes of potential criminals are indeed interesting to study, and potentially important to policy as well as theory, what then is the best way to study such mental events? We turn to the question of methods in the next section.

Appropriate Methods

Crime Statistics

For the most part, the deterrence hypothesis has been investigated with studies that aggregate information across offenders and offenses. For example, the effect of deterrents on crime might be investigated by studying arrest rates (number of arrests for a type of offense divided by the known number of offenses of that type) and crime rates in a sample of jurisdictions. A negative correlation would be interpreted as evidence for deterrence, namely, that crime is less frequent where punishment is more certain.

The conclusions from such studies range from the dramatic statement that "an additional execution each year... may have resulted, on average, in seven or eight fewer murders" (Ehrlich, 1975:414) to the definitively ambiguous statement by the National Academy of Sciences that "we cannot yet assert that the evidence warrants an affirmative conclusion regarding deterrence" (Blumstein et al., 1978:7). The latter authors express several concerns about aggregate data: (a) the direction of causality is ambiguous—crime rates are not simply caused by sanctions but also change sanctions, as when increasing crime rates crowd prisons and result in lower sentences; (b) errors in measuring crime rates can bias results, because jurisdictions with underreporting of crime will appear to have low crime rates and high clearance rates; and (c) apparent deterrent effects can actually be due to incapacitation, because longer sentences also remove offenders from crime opportunities.

Interviews

Observations of the behavior of individual offenders would be very useful if that information allowed us to assess behavior patterns and their objective and subjective precursors. However, methodological concerns exist regarding the ways criminals have been observed. First, in studies of the responses of criminals to hypothetical crime situations (e.g., Carroll, 1978), we have little confidence that offenders are behaving the same way they would in an actual crime situation. The hypothetical situations may be missing crucial features of real situations, and offenders may respond in a much more casual fashion in the absence of real consequences. Second, in accounts of prior crimes given by criminals, there is no simple way to check the truthfulness and accuracy of the accounts. There are well-known biases introduced by limitations and distortions of recall (Ericsson and Simon, 1980; Nisbett and Wilson, 1977) and the social situation of the interview (Orne, 1972). These biases may make it difficult to determine the time order of reports of perceptions of risks and benefits versus reports of criminal activities (cf. Paternoster et al., 1982).

Verbal Protocols

The omnipotent observer would presumably want to know what criminals "really" think about at the time they are considering actual crime opportunities. Although this sounds like a farfetched goal, researchers in other domains have obtained detailed portrayals of ongoing mental operations in naturalistic settings through the collection of verbal protocols (Ericsson and Simon, 1980; Newell and Simon; 1972; Payne et al., 1978). In this procedure, subjects provide continuous verbal reports by "thinking aloud" about their perceptions, thoughts, and feelings while performing the behavior of interest. Verbal protocols have been used in both laboratory settings and in such real-world contexts as stock portfolio selection (Clarkson, 1962), supermarket shopping (Payne and Ragsdale, 1978), and medical diagnosis (Johnson et al., 1982).

Thus, we believe the study of criminal thought processes should ideally require actual criminals, actual crime opportunities, and procedures for observing perceptions and judgments in vivo. To achieve a uniform and practical real-life crime situation with actual criminals, we selected the crime of shoplifting. Shoplifting is frequent, nonviolent (for researchers' safety), public, and a serious crime concern. It has been estimated that between 2% and 8% of customers engage in shoplifting (Barmash, 1971; Rosenbaum et al., 1980; Shave, 1978). Faria (1977) estimated that store theft accounts for about 25% of all dollar crime loss in the United States and shoplifting accounts for about one half of that amount (Shave, 1978). In the next section we describe an empirical study using the verbal protocol method in real-life shopping situations, additionally comparing experienced and novice shoplifters.

A Study of Shoplifters' Thoughts

Finding Shoplifters

Any procedure for recruiting shoplifters would probably result in a biased sample. Our first thought was to work through stores or the courts to identify apprehended shoplifters and solicit their cooperation. This could bias the sample toward those who shoplift a great deal or those who are relatively incompetent. In our own study of a downtown Chicago department store (Rosenbaum et al., 1980), we followed randomly selected shoppers through the store and estimated that 7.8% of them shoplifted, yet the same store was apprehending only a few people each day. Our second thought, on the heels of the first, was to advertise in newspapers. This could bias the sample toward those who have spare time and lack any fear of us, probably to the exclusion of the true professional shoplifter. For convenience, we decided to try the latter technique first.

Advertisements were run in several newspapers in our area of Chicago for several weeks. The ads asked for volunteers, both nonshoplifters and shoplifters, to participate in a study of shoplifting. The ad identified the study with Loyola University, offered to pay volunteers $4.00 an hour for their time and reimbursement for travel, and gave a phone number for response. A steady trickle of calls resulted. Each caller was given a description of the study, assured that everything would be anonymous (code names were suggested), and asked to report his or her history of shoplifting, if any.

Subjects with the most extensive self-reported histories of shoplifting were considered "experts," whereas those with lesser histories were considered "novices." Thirty-one experts were called back and asked to come for the study, of whom 17 actually agreed and appeared. The median expert claimed to have shoplifted 100 times in his or her life and 10 times in the past year. Twenty-eight novices were asked in, of whom 17 appeared; the median novice had not shoplifted at all. The no-shows did not differ significantly from participants in age, sex, or shoplifting history. There were 20 males and 14 females in the final sample, ranging in age from 18 to 62; sex and age did not differ across the expert and novice groups.

Procedure

Subjects were met individually by a graduate student experimenter of the same sex. Because thinking aloud is unnatural for many people, subjects were given practice with verbal protocols using a booklet of store advertisements. When they seemed ready, subjects were asked to take the experimenter on a shopping trip, preferably to a store or stores in which they normally shopped. Upon arrival at the store, subjects were reminded of the "think aloud" procedure. In addition, 10 experts and 8 novices (randomly chosen) were asked to form an intention to shoplift, but were cautioned not to actually remove anything without paying for it. The shoplift intention instructions were intended to simulate situations in which shoplifting was planned rather than precipitated in the store, and also to ensure at least some shoplifting thoughts in return for our efforts. Each subject carried a microcassette tape recorder concealed in his or her clothing, with a small lapel microphone. Subjects were allowed to walk through the stores for as long as they wished, which was usually about 1 hour. If the subject paused between verbalizations for a long time, neutral prompts from a prepared list were given (e.g., "Say what you are thinking now").

As the subject walked through stores, the experimenter coded each department visited on a number of characteristics, including security devices (e.g., mirrors, cameras), store layout (e.g., height of aisles), item protections (e.g., locked cases, chained items), and people (e.g., number of salesclerks).

Coding of Verbal Protocols

The resultant protocols were first broken down into short phrases, each consisting of a single idea or thought (Newell and Simon, 1972; Payne et al., 1978). Protocols consisted of approximately 300 phrases. Coders identified statements referring to shoplifting, which comprised 41% of the statements of experts, 5% of the statements of novices asked to form an intention to shoplift, and 0% of the statements of novices who were simply shopping. An important result of these simple analyses was that experts were far more efficient in analyzing shoplifting possibilities: They used approximately 6 statements in considering an item to shoplift (the median expert considered 7 items for shoplifting), whereas novices used approximately 11 statements per item considered (the median novice in the shoplift intention condition considered 2 items for shoplifting).

These phrases were coded into four main categories (perceptual, motivational, judgmental, and extraneous) and subcategories of the first three. For example, the statement "They have a couple of mirrors in the back" was coded as a perceptual statement about security devices, "I like that shirt" was coded as motivational attraction, and "Sometimes I wonder about the consequences of what would happen to me if I got caught" was coded as judgmental risk. Table 2.1 gives a complete list of categories and the frequencies of statements by subjects, for statements referring to shoplifting.

The results portrayed in Table 2.1 are interesting but not dramatic. Experts made proportionately more perceptual statements than did novices (32% versus 11%), whereas novices had a greater proportion of motivational statements than did experts (33% versus 21%). Differences between experts and novices within these three categories were not significant. However, experts asked to form an intention to shoplift differed from experts asked to shop in the judgment subcategories. Those experts asked to form an intention to shoplift made more statements about specific tactics, risks (of being observed, caught, arrested, or punished), and explicit decisions to take or not to take an item, and made fewer statements proportionately about the feasibility of shoplifting. This seems consistent with their instructions: The experts asked to form an

TABLE 2.1. Number and percentage of shoplifting statements made for each statement type by condition[a]

	Shoplifter Type and Instructional Condition		
Statements	Expert/Shoplift (N = 10)	Expert/Shop (N = 7)	Novice/Shoplift (N = 8)
Perceptual			
Store personnel	18 (2.2)	10 (2.0)	0 (0.0)
People	8 (1.0)	6 (1.2)	5 (3.2)
Security guards	19 (2.0)	23 (4.8)	0 (0.0)
Security devices	38 (4.6)	44 (9.1)	0 (0.0)
Store layout	6 (0.7)	15 (3.1)	0 (0.0)
Size of item	15 (1.8)	17 (3.5)	3 (2.0)
Price of item	8 (1.0)	18 (3.7)	3 (2.0)
Naming item	77 (9.3)	50 (10.4)	4 (2.6)
Orienting/location	31 (3.8)	15 (3.1)	2 (2.0)
Motivational			
Attraction	65 (7.9)	34 (7.0)	21 (13.5)
Use/need	49 (5.9)	14 (3.0)	8 (5.1)
Examination of item	50 (6.0)	21 (4.4)	15 (0.6)
Price too high	1 (0.1)	5 (1.0)	3 (2.0)
Store service/policy	3 (0.4)	2 (0.4)	0 (0.0)
Intention to shoplift	13 (1.6)	4 (0.8)	2 (2.0)
Searching for item	12 (1.4)	3 (0.6)	1 (0.6)
Shopping method	0 (0.0)	3 (0.6)	2 (2.0)
Judgmental			
Feasibility (takeable)	84 (10.2)	87 (18.0)	14 (9.0)
Tactic/method	140 (17.0)	61 (12.7)	29 (18.6)
Risks	96 (11.6)	24 (5.0)	21 (13.5)
Justifications	7 (0.8)	0 (0.0)	6 (3.8)
Take/not take	85 (10.3)	26 (5.4)	17 (10.9)
Total	825	482	157

[a]Percentages of column total are in parentheses.

intention pursued the consideration of opportunities further toward their logical result.

Strategies for Evaluating Crime Opportunities

Statements were also examined to focus on specific aspects that we thought would be important a priori. First, shoplifting thoughts were coded not only for content but also for whether the statements referred to a specific item or more generally to the department within a store or the store in general. We hypothesized that shoplifting thought processes would be hierarchical; that is, subjects would mention characteristics of the store, then of the department, and lastly talk about particular items. Novices made only seven statements directed at the store or department level and thus showed little evidence of hierarchical processing. Experts did seem to think in a hierarchical fashion: 66% of the items considered by experts were preceded closely (i.e., within a few statements) by an assessment of either the store or the department. Often more than one item was considered within a specific hierarchical assessment. The "higher level" thoughts about the store or department generally consisted of statements about security devices, feasibility, risks, and strategies for shoplifting.

The more strategic behavior of the experts is also revealed by their tendency to talk about possible strategies for shoplifting apart from the consideration of specific items. Ten of the 17 experts disclosed strategies they have used in the past or might use in the future; novices made no mention of shoplifting strategies unless they were considering an item. The following excerpt discusses a strategy not to use:

I, ah, you know, I back away from bagging things. That's real obvious. That's real familiar. You know security is very familiar with that technique. You're roaming through the store with a bag, you're going to be watched.

Second, subjects often mentioned what would and would not deter them from shoplifting an item. Although these statements overlap with the content codes of Table 2.1, they are in fact quite different, since we are restricting this analysis to factors subjects themselves label as favorable or unfavorable for shoplifting. The major deterrents to shoplifting were the presence of security devices, item inaccessibility (e.g., too large), the possibility of being observed and caught, the presence of store personnel, and negative feelings such as guilt. The lack of these deterrents, as well as a store layout conducive to shoplifting (e.g., high counters that impede observation) were considered facilitators. Experts differed substantially from novices in what they mentioned and how they reasoned about these factors. Experts considered item inaccessibility (38% of statements referring to deterrents and facilitators) and security devices (32%) as primary deterrents to shoplifting, but novices paid less attention (23% and 10%). For example, one expert said, "Aha, most of the cases have deadbolt locks." Novices thought frequently about the chance of being observed or caught (39%), but experts did not (16%). Novices also expressed noticeable amounts of negative feelings (10%), but experts did not (2%). When considering some earrings, one novice said, "...it would be, you know, against the law, and I guess that's where my mom comes in my head saying what right is it of yours to take."

Perhaps the most interesting observations refer to the pattern of deterrents and facilitators that emerged in consideration of those items that subjects explicitly decided to take or not to take. Examining the subset of items novices considered for shoplifting in which a decision was verbalized, we found that novices always mentioned one facilitator but no deterrents when they decided to take an item ($N = 11$ items). However, when they decided not to take an item ($N = 6$), they always mentioned at least one deterrent along with facilitators. Thus, one deterrent was sufficient to stop novices from taking an item. The following excerpt illustrates this rule:

This would be the kind of place. There's no cameras that you can see, doesn't look like there's any twoway mirrors. There's too many people to handle. The only thing that would stop me probably is that it just doesn't seem like it's worth the risk to put something that only costs a dollar in your pocket. On the other hand, if it was really expensive, it wouldn't be worth the risk because you could get in real trouble.

Experts seemed to be following a different strategy in their decisions either to take ($N = 67$) or not to take ($N = 14$) an item. In contrast to the novices, the mention of a deterrent was often followed by mention of a facilitator among items chosen to take. In effect, experts discounted deterrents by talking about how to get around them. The following excerpt illustrates this strategy:

Belts, leather. It's got denim running through it, yeah. Once again I would say if there would be any attempt I think something like this would be sufficient, and probably relatively simple to do. It's only a saleslady around, and she's not paying much attention anyhow.

Thus, if the deterrents could be discounted, overcome, or balanced by facilitators, experts seemed prepared to take the item.

One additional way in which experts and novices differed emerged quite unexpectedly from the protocols. Experts began their consideration of items for shoplifting by naming the item ("Oh, gloves"). Those in the shoplift condition named a median of 42% of their items; those in the shop condition named a median of 33% of their items; nonshoplifters named a median of 0%. We believe this naming reflects the knowledge experts have about particular items: When an item is named, prior knowledge is being recalled to aid in the evaluation of that item.

Environmental Influence on Shoplifting Thoughts

A final set of analyses was directed at establishing connections between shoplifting thoughts and attributes of the store and subject. Three indices of shoplifting activity were used for each store: (a) number of items considered for shoplifting, (b) proportion of statements devoted to shoplifting, and (c) final decision to shoplift. Predictors entered into multiple regression analyses included characteristics of the store (such as numbers of mirrors and cameras, height of aisles, numbers of salesclerks and shoppers present, presence or absence of security personnel, and visibility indices of percentage of time the subject was visible to shoppers, clerks, and security) and background variables (including store type, time of day, and the age, sex, and shoplifting experience of the subject).

Number of items considered for shoplifting and proportion of items decided to take were both related to only one predictor: type of store. Department and drugstores seem to have more items of interest and more "takeable" items than did grocery stores or other stores. This was true for both experts and novices. These results seem to support the validity of the study because they are consistent with other accounts of shoplifting activity which find that department and drugstores suffer more crime (Bickman et al., 1979; Kraut, 1976; Morton, 1975).

The proportion of statements devoted to shoplifting was predicted by four factors: (a) sex, with males talking proportionately more about shoplifting than females; (b) visibility of salesclerks, with statements about shoplifting decreasing as salesclerk visibility increased; (c) past shoplifting experience, with experienced shoplifters talking more about shoplifting; and (d) age, with younger subjects talking more about shoplifting. These results are subject to multiple interpretations. Males may talk more about shoplifting to impress their (male) experimenters, but females may talk less about shoplifting to avoid revealing socially unacceptable behavior, and females may find it easier to talk about nonshoplifting thoughts in the presence of another female, which would decrease the proportion of thoughts devoted to shoplifting. Salesclerk visibility may decrease shoplifting thoughts, but it may only decrease shoplifting verbalizations. The other results are consistent with the types of people who actually shoplift (Bickman et al., 1979).

Generalizations

We began this chapter with the issue of rationality in judgments of crime opportunities. That will be the principal focus of this section, with additional comments on the differences between expert and novice shoplifters, the implications for deterring shoplifting, and the validity and utility of the verbal protocol procedure for investigating the thought processes of criminals.

Rationality

To assess the rationality of shoplifters' judgments, we would need to consider: (a) the rationality of outcome, that is, did the subjects make decisions about shoplifting consistent with a normative economic model of optimal decisions? and (b) the rationality of process, that is, did the subjects go about deciding in a rational way, collecting relevant information, carefully weighing it in a systematic and effective manner, and acting consistently with their decisions? Our data, rich as they are, do not allow such judgments in much detail.

In terms of the rationality of outcomes, we have no information on the alternatives our subjects might have considered were they not in a store; we can only look at their taking or not taking a particular item and implied preferences across items. We have no information on their preferences among consequences they may have faced such as social ostracism or criminal penalties unless these were mentioned and evaluated (which they very rarely were). We have only sketchy information on the assessment of uncertain risks; no probabilities of capture for given individuals in given cases can be generated without heroic assumptions. We therefore cannot say whether any of the decisions made by our experts or novices was "correct" in the sense of maximizing their own expected (or objective) utility consistent with their preferences. All we can suggest is that it is rational for expert shoplifters to be more likely to shoplift than novices because they are more skilled and therefore face less risk.

In terms of the rationality of process, it seems apparent that subjects are sensitive to many features of crime opportunities that are objectively important for assessing the value of items and the risks involved. It also seems apparent that considerations at the point of decision are extremely abbreviated. Only a few features of the crime opportunity were evaluated by subjects. Motivated by either attraction to or need for an item, subjects made brief assessments of risks and then considered strategy.

The decision process for expert shoplifters seemed to involve the selection of strategies to overcome deterrents and minimize risks. They operated in a search or proactive mode, actively scanning the store for information on risks and opportunities before considering items for shoplifting. Thoughts during consideration of items drew upon extensive past knowledge (the naming of items by experts suggests accessing prepackaged information) and were directed at specific strategic issues such as the size of the item, the presence of security devices, and the chance of being observed. Few experts considered the distal consequences of shoplifting: arrest, trial, fines, or jail. This makes a great deal of sense psychologically, because the strategic issues are immediate, concrete, and partially controllable, whereas the distal consequences are vague, usually not experienced, and generally uncontrollable. This is "rational" in a very local sense, but irrational in that changes in the distal consequences may not be appropriately considered if potential criminals generally ignore those factors.

A greater degree of rationality can be retrieved if we conjecture that the distal consequences are considered when deciding to become a shoplifter, that is, to become the sort of person who looks for shoplifting opportunities in stores. Thus, someone who goes around shoplifting and thinking about shoplifting may have made a (tacit) prior decision that shoplifting is worth the risk of the distal consequences. A salient change in those distal consequences such as a highly publicized change in the law or a personal experience of arrest (cf. Tyler, 1980, for a discussion of salience in the context of fear of crime) may prompt a reevaluation of this orientation; such a reevaluation is not likely to happen in considering a specific item for shoplifting.

The preceding speculations are consistent with our data on novices. Novices seem to be deficient in strategic knowledge, so they must spend time thinking over what to do in shoplifting an item. They do not spontaneously look around a store in the way experts do and thus must reason "from scratch" when they consider an item for shoplifting. However, they also spend time thinking about justifications, experiencing negative feelings such as guilt and fear, and thinking about the consequences of getting caught. Finally, they are deterred by any sign of risk. These results suggest that novices have not made a decision to act like a shoplifter and have not thought over the risks involved. They see the strategic issues as essentially uncontrollable (at their level of skill they are right!) and therefore avoid any sign of risk when forced by our instructions to consider shoplifting. When thinking about shoplifting, the novices not only produced a mixture of thoughts including clumsy attempts to reason out strategies, but also included decisions about being a shoplifter that experts presumably have made affirmatively in the past. This seems to reflect what Cook (1980) discussed as degree of involvement in crime and to capture the reasoning of Clarke and Cornish (1985) that separate decision models may have to be developed for entry into a crime, selection of specific opportunities, and exit.

Overall, this analysis (and conjecture) suggests a fairly high degree of rationality in the decisions of both experts and novices. Both pay attention to a lot of information that pertains to the consequences of their acts. However, this process appears to occur normally over an extended period of time, with different considerations at different points in time, each consideration being quite simple and manageable. The sequence is similar to the distinction between first choosing to have an academic career and later choosing to apply for a job or accept a particular job offer. Different factors may be considered or ignored during these separate considerations. This decision process is most aptly labeled heuristic rather than normative or optimal. It lacks the systematic form and proper multiplicative combination of uncertainties and consequences of the normative economic model. It could be sensitive to many of the same features, but not necessarily in the same way. For example, proper evaluations of attributes previously considered may be more difficult.

These speculations and theoretical proposals, although consistent with our data and those of others studying crime perceptions (e.g., Claster, 1967; Kraut, 1976; Waldo and Chiricos, 1972), are still based on assumptions about what shoplifters thought about before they entered this study. Any study of such earlier decision making would require another study, and one even more difficult to implement.

Deterrence

The implications of our results for deterring potential shoplifters at the point of theft are reasonably clear and very different for novices and experts. Novices can be deterred by almost anything, but busy stores and alert store employees seem to effectively engender a fear of being observed. This may be superfluous, because novices hardly think about shoplifting and experience guilt and fear quite readily when they do. Any credible threat should deter novices, but it is possible that less believable threats about the consequences of shoplifting may do more harm than good by directing attention to the possibility of shoplifting.

Experienced shoplifters seem more like wolves when compared to the sheeplike novices. They act against the environment, bring in knowledge about shoplifting tactics and opportunities, and develop means for negating deterrents. The various deterrents employed by retailers such as cameras, large packaging, and inaccessible items help create an overall atmosphere of difficulty associated with the store that should reduce shoplifting. However, these deterrents tend to be static; shoplifters readily adjust their strategies to overcome them. Newer technologies may prove more difficult to overcome, but at present the most dynamic aspect of stores is store personnel. Sales personnel can change their behavior to interfere with shoplifters' strategies, at the same time appearing to offer attentive service (cf. Bickman et al., 1979). Thus, there seems to be a pitched battle in the aisles between expert shoplifters and retailers; the frontline for retailers is held by the store employees. Their activity and commitment seem more important than what police or courts may threaten, at least in the point-of-theft considerations we observed.

Research Evaluation and Directions

Our study of shoplifting provides some preliminary information about how expert and novice shoplifters think about crime opportunities. The verbal protocol method was successful in revealing criminal thought processes including information salience and decision strategies. We were able to describe the strategies and knowledge of experienced criminals and the environmental determinants of criminal thought processes. The sensible differences between experts and novices, the consistency of results with other styles of research, and our general impression that subjects were serious and motivated offer some evidence of validity.

Our interpretations of the results have emphasized that a fuller understanding of shoplifting may require conceptualizing criminal thought processes as a sequence of different judgments extended over time. At a simple level, we may distinguish the decision to be a shoplifter from the decision to shoplift a specific item (cf. the analysis by Clarke and Cornish, 1985, of residential burglary). A verbal protocol analysis of this extended sequence seems impractical, but a clever researcher may find a way around the logistical problems. One alternative is to rely on retrospective accounts provided in interviews. Such self-reports can be valuable and may be accurate under some circumstances (Ericsson and Simon, 1980). Research that proceeds with a variety of methods is most likely to capture the complexity of criminal thoughts. We regret not having interviewed our shoplifters and nonshoplifters about their prior thoughts after going to the trouble of locating willing subjects. Research ideas grow gradually, and the verbal protocol procedure seems a valuable tool for the study of criminal thought processes, deterrence, and decision making in unstructured, visually rich, and realistic situations.

References

Assembly Committee on Criminal Procedure (California)
    1975   "Public knowledge of criminal penalties." Pp. 74–90 in R.L. Henshel and R.A. Silverman (eds.), Perception in Criminology. New York: Columbia University Press.
Bandura, A.
    1977   Social Learning Theory. Englewood Cliffs, NJ: Prentice-Hall.
Barmash, I.
    1971   "Retailers stem their inventory shrinkage." New York Times, February 22.
Becker, Gary S.
    1968   "Crime and punishment: an economic approach." Journal of Political Economy 76:169–217.
Bickman, L., D. Rosenbaum, T. Baumer, M. Kudel, C. Christenholz, S. Knight and W. Perkowitz
    1979   Phase I Assessment of Shoplifting and Employee Theft Program: Final Report—Programs and Strategies. Report submitted to the National Institute of Law Enforcement and Criminal Justice, Law Enforcement Assistance Administration, U.S. Department of Justice.
Blumstein, A., J. Cohen and D. Nagin (eds.)
    1978   Deterrence and Incapacitation: Estimating the Effects of Criminal Sanctions on Crime Rates. Washington, DC: National Academy of Sciences.
Carroll, J.S.
    1978   "A psychological approach to deterrence: the evaluation of crime opportunities." Journal of Personality and Social Psychology 36(12): 1512–20.

1982 "Committing a crime: the offender's decision." Pp. 49–68 in V.J. Konecni and E.B. Ebbesen (eds.), The Criminal Justice System: A Social-Psychological Analysis. New York: Freeman.

Clarke, Ronald V. and Derek B. Cornish
1985 "Modeling offenders' decisions: a framework for research and policy." Pp. 147–85 in M. Tonry and N. Morris (eds.), Crime and Justice, Volume 6. Chicago: University of Chicago Press.

Clarkson, G.
1962 Portfolio Selection: A Simulation of Trust Investment. Englewood Cliffs, NJ: Prentice-Hall.

Claster, D.S.
1967 "Comparison of risk perception between delinquents and nondelinquents." Journal of Criminal Law, Criminology, and Police Science 58:80–6.

Cook, P.J.
1980 "Research in criminal deterrence: laying the groundwork for the second decade." Pp. 211–68 in N. Morris and M. Tonry (eds.), Crime and Justice: An Annual Review of Research, Volume 2. Chicago: University of Chicago Press.

Ehrlich, I.
1975 "The deterrent effect of capital punishment: a question of life and death." American Economic Review, 65:397–417.

Einhorn, H. J. and R. M. Hogarth
1981 "Behavioral decision theory: processes of judgment and choice." Annual Review of Psychology 32:53–88.

Ericsson, K.A. and H.A. Simon
1980 "Verbal reports as data." Psychological Review 84:231–59.

Faria, A.J.
1977 "Minimizing shoplifting losses: some practical guidelines." Journal of Small Business Management 15, No. 4.

Feldman, M.P.
1977 Criminal Behavior: A Psychological Analysis. New York: Wiley.

Inciardi, J.A.
1975 Careers in Crime. Chicago: Rand McNally.

Johnson, E.J.
"Expertise and decision under uncertainty: performance and process." in M. Chi, R. Glaser and M. Farrer (eds.), The Nature of Expertise. Hillsdale, NJ: Erlbaum.

Johnson, P.E., F. Hassebrock, A.S. Duran and J.H. Moller
1982 "Multimethod study of clinical judgment." Organizational Behavior and Human Performance 30:201–30.

Kahneman, D., P. Slovic and A. Tversky (eds.)
1982 Judgment Under Uncertainty: Heuristics and Biases. New York: Cambridge University Press.

Krauss, H.H., F. Robinson, W. Janzen and N. Cauthen
1972 "Predictions of ethical risk taking by psychopathic and non-psychopathic criminals." Psychological Reports 30:83.

Kraut, R.E.
1976 "Deterrent and definitional influences on shoplifting." Social Problems 23:358–68.

Larkin, J., J. McDermott, D.P. Simon and H.A. Simon
  1980 "Expert and novice performance in solving physics problems." Science 208:1335–42.
Letkemann, P.
  1973 Crime as Work. Englewood Cliffs, NJ: Prentice-Hall.
Morton, R.
  1975 Crime and Retailing. Washington, DC: U.S. Department of Commerce.
Newell, A. and H.A. Simon
  1972 Human Problem Solving. Englewood Cliffs, NJ: Prentice-Hall.
Nisbett, R.E. and T.D. Wilson
  1977 "Telling more than we can know: verbal reports on mental processes." Psychological Review 84:231–59.
Orne, M.T.
  1972 "On the social psychology of the psychological experiment: demand characteristics and their implications." Pp. 233–46 in A.G. Miller (ed.), The Social Psychology of Psychological Research. New York: Macmillan.
Paternoster, R., L.E. Saltzman, G.P. Waldo and T.G. Chiricos
  1982 "Causal ordering in deterrence research: an examination of the perceptions behavior relationship." Pp. 55–70 in J. Hagen (ed.), Deterrence Reconsidered: Methodological Innovations. Beverly Hills, CA: Sage.
Payne, J.W.
  1973 "Alternative approaches to decision making under risk: moments versus risk dimensions." Psychological Bulletin 80:439–53.
Payne, J.W., M.L. Braunstein and J.S. Carroll
  1978 "Exploring predecisional behavior: an alternative approach to decision research." Organizational Behavior and Human Performance 22:17–34.
Payne, J.W. and E.K.E. Ragsdale
  1978 "Verbal protocols and direct observation of supermarket shopping behavior and some findings and discussion of methods." Pp. 571–7 in H.K. Hunt (ed.), Advances in Consumer Research, Volume V. Ann Arbor Michigan: Association for Consumer Research.
Petty, R.E. and J.T. Cacioppo
  1981 Attitudes and Persuasion: Classic and Contemporary Approaches. Dubuque, IA: W.C. Brown.
Rettig, S.
  1964 "Ethical risk sensitivity in male prisoners." British Journal of Criminology, 4:582–90.
Rettig, S. and H.E. Rawson
  1963 "The risk hypothesis in predictive judgments of unethical behavior." Journal of Abnormal and Social Psychology 66:243–8.
Rosenbaum, D., T. Baumer, L. Bickman, M. Kudel, J.S. Carroll and W. Perkowitz
  1980 Phase I Assessment of Shoplifting and Employee Theft Program: Final Report—Field Feasibility Assessment of New Measurement Strategies. Report submitted to the National Institute of Law Enforcement and Criminal Justice, Law Enforcement Assistance Administration, U.S. Department of Justice.

Shave, P.L.
  1978   Shoplifting in the State of Washington: The Crime and Its Prevention.
         Seattle, WA: Division of the Attorney General's Office.
Simon, H. A.
  1957   Models of Man. New York: Wiley
Slovic, P., B. Fischhoff and S. Lichtenstein
  1977   "Behavioral decision theory." Annual Review of Psychology 28:1–39.
Slovic, P. and S. Lichtenstein
  1968   "Relative importance of probabilities and payoffs in risk taking."
         Journal of Experimental Psychology Monographs 78(3, part 2):1–18
Stefanowicz, J.P. and T.E. Hannum
  1971   "Ethical risk-taking and sociopathy in incarcerated females." Cor-
         rectional Psychologist 4:138–48.
Tyler, T.R.
  1980   "The impact of directly and indirectly experienced events: the origin of
         crime-related judgments and behaviors." Journal of Personality and
         Social Psychology 39:13–28.
Waldo, G.P. and T.G. Chiricos
  1971   "Perceived penal sanction and self-reported criminality: a neglected
         approach to deterrence research." Social Problems 19:200–17.

3
Victim Selection Procedures Among Economic Criminals: The Rational Choice Perspective

DERMOT WALSH

Editors' Note

There are three chapters dealing with robbery in this volume, and we are now beginning to know almost as much about this crime as about burglary. In this chapter Dermot Walsh performs two important tasks: First, he contrasts the decision-making activities of commercial burglars and robbers, and second, he paints a vivid picture of the nature of the criminal's sources of information and the way in which this is handled during the processes of assessment and planning which precede the criminal event. His starting point is the distinction between normative and bounded rationality, which is a persistent theme throughout this volume. Walsh goes on to report on the results of his retrospective interviews with imprisoned burglars and robbers about their techniques of victim/target selection and rejection. Although his data indicate differences in decision making both within burglary and robbery as broad crime categories, and between burglars and robbers—results that bear out the need for crime-specific analyses—some of his most interesting findings relate to characteristics common to both. He provides a fascinating sketch of the subterranean "knowledge market" where "leakmen" and "knowledge brokers" peddle information about likely opportunities to supplement that already gathered by the criminal through personal observation during his or her daily routine and via the social networks of family, work, or leisure. Walsh's description of the stages of assessment and planning—the emergence of potential schemes and the exploration of their viability through negative thinking and flaw hunting—have much in common with the methods adopted by Carroll and Weaver's expert shoplifters to discount situational deterrents by immediately itemizing facilitators. More generally, these techniques suggest the operation of information-processing strategies (the "editing" activities of prospect theory; contingent processing; "satisficing") discussed in part 2 of this volume. The discussion of attitudes to risk, the importance of previous experience, and the roles of luck and fatalism provide pointers to how sudden hazards during commission of the crime (and prior anxieties about these possibilities) may be handled. Similar proportions of Walsh's samples of commercial burglars and robbers undertook some degree of planning (cf. also Feeney, this volume), but robbers claimed significantly more determination than burglars (54% to 11%) to carry out a particular crime; this finding may explain the fact that twice as many of the former (48% to 24%) admitted to having been drunk or drugged at the time of their offenses.

Introduction: Contrasting Attitudes to Rationality

When the robbers and burglars interviewed for the present study were discussing their crimes what was very noticeable was that those who felt that they had behaved quite irrationally in their last crime were happy to say so and did not try to conceal their foolishness. For example, in a case of robbery and kidnap:

We were on the way home, coming out. He was coming out of the Kentucky Fried Chicken, took him to the beach four to five hundred yards away. Knew we should not do it, but we were that far gone . . . no masks . . . told him my name! Took him to the beach, right by a Securicor security place.

There were others, however, who were operating on quite a different basis, apparently as rationally as possible:

Knew what I was going for. Securicor van . . . carry a maximum of £15,000 in one bag . . . by deduction . . . weigh the factors. Watch different supermarkets in turn, area, availability of transport, access, number of people. Where their weak link is, one bag traveling at a time, shop floor or just before they come out of the shop. Right set of circumstances occur two to three times a week, firms don't bank every day. Going over everything I've planned, looking for possible failures, trying to come up with new plans if necessary.

Differing Conceptions of Rationality

By rationality is meant activities identified by their impersonal, methodical, efficient, and logical components. Perhaps it would help to start by specifying three of the typical law enforcement assumptions about the rationality of economic criminals as opposed to those who commit personal crimes, where the object is not primarily financial gain. One assumption is that such criminals operate on a utilitarian basis of pleasure and pain calculation. Hence increasing the pain through severity of legal sanction must surely diminish the prevalence of the activity, implying that economic criminals can be manipulated by a clinical calculation of sanction. Two other assumptions are, however, inconsistent with this: (a) that such criminals are not always rational (if they were, it is argued, they would not be content with the small gains they so often make through crime); and (b) that they are not rational because they get caught (if they were rational they would supposedly get away with the crime). This then typically leads on to a discussion of the supposed rationality of those who evade capture, seeing them as a quite separate, more intelligent category. Yet it is possible that such people, far from being a superior, separate group, are in fact merely part of the wider whole who evade capture at timepoint A and fail to do so at timepoint B.

Generally in criminological theorizing a hard typological line has been drawn in the past (for example, Clinard and Quinney, 1967; Gibbons, 1968) between the rational criminal and the irrational one; this distinction is usually made on the basis of type of target opted for. Thus, Letkemann's (1973) safebreakers, Sutherland's (1956) professional thieves, Einstadter's (1969) armed robbers, and Laver's (1982) terrorists are seen as highly rational and calculating in comparison with drunks, vandals, shoplifters, or joyriders, and we are invited to accept a division between professionals and thrillseekers.

In contrast, most of Maguire's (1982) house burglars were seen as neither professional nor amateur, but what he termed "middle-range" (1982:167) criminals, characterized by short-term specialization. Maguire also pointed out (1982:81) that professionalism is not always associated with specialization (competent habitual offenders may vary their activities), and he concluded by saying that the language used gives a false impression of rationality, and that gambling is a better model to use to describe burglary than formal rationality.

Bennett and Wright (1984) described the offender as aware of choosing to offend and commonly planning the offense, but only rational in the limited sense of what seems reasonable to the offender at the time, given the predicament he or she is in. (One might ask whether this is not all that might be expected.) Bennett and Wright argued that costs and rewards are not balanced in the case of any particular offense, nor in the case of alternative courses of action—for example to stay in, or to go out and burgle—and they pointed out that this does not match up with what the doctrine of deterrence requires. Bennett and Wright prefer the concept of limited rationality, in which it is not presumed that offenders weigh *all* the relevant factors every time an offense is contemplated, and in which other factors (moods, motives, moral judgments, perceptions of opportunity, laziness, alcohol and narcotics consumed, the effect of others, and their attitude to risk) apparently unrelated to the immediate decision often take over. They concluded (1984:152) that offenders are behaving rationally as they see it at the time, but that what might be perceived as rational on one occasion might not be so perceived on another.

There is an obvious confusion here (cf. Bennett and Wright) between utilitarianism as a doctrine on the one hand, and rationality as a means on the other. For example, it is perfectly possible for someone to be behaving rationally, that is, methodically, efficiently, impersonally, and so on, and yet not be behaving in a utilitarian way. Bennett and Wright are denying that burglars use utilitarianism, and they make an implicit distinction between (a) what is objectively rational (which would automatically exclude burglary), and (b) rationality as defined by the actor at the time. They argue that burglars exhibit only the latter and hence are to be accused of "limited rationality." Such a distinction denies the salience of an individual's assessment to himself or herself, whereas, of course, in the sociology of deviance it has long been accepted that actors nearly always see their own behavior as rational; it is merely the adjudicators who disagree.

Rationality and Risk

Much more, however, has to be said about the nature of the risk that the economic criminal is up against. It may well be that even with the use of great rationality many would still be caught (and commonly, because of this, be seen as irrational), because of the nature of the risks, accidents, and errors that are an inevitable feature of planned nonconformity.

If we ask how far can risk be controlled by rationality, the answer is not "totally," but only, "quite well." The human predicament remains uncertain, and rationality does not invariably work in the ordinary noncriminal world, for example, in business and commerce. Making a parallel with the intense rationality of modern army special service groups such as the Commandos, the Parachute Regiment, and the Special Air Service, we notice frequent mission failures due to the nature of the risks built into the objective. For example, the use of glider-borne troops against occupied Norway in 1942 (Operation Freshman) failed totally despite tight planning and resulted in all personnel being killed. Yet such failure does not mean we deny rationality. We are instead prepared to accept the role of risk (weather conditions, pilot error, and so on) in this type of event.

From Wellington and Napoleon onward, military commanders have realized that rationality is not always enough and have attached great importance to such things as luck and boldness. Following this parallel a trifle further, one risk-handling technique in small-scale military attacks, apart from rationally engineering the element of surprise, is to wait for an opportunity and snatch at it (this is the kind of behavior exhibited by those who win the Victoria Cross or the Distinguished Service Order).

Present Research: Aims and Methods

I have previously written on shoplifting and house burglary as examples of economic crime, both to draw attention to the threefold interaction between offender, victim, and event in the production of crime and to highlight the process of victim selection (Walsh, 1978, 1980). The present investigation further pursues the issue of victim selection, but for more serious economic crimes (commercial burglary and robbery), drawing more heavily on offenders' verbatim accounts.

Commercial Burglars

Two small groups were drawn from a local prison at an interval of 6 months. The men chosen were all those in the prison at the time whose last offense was for burglary of commercial premises (not houses). Those who agreed to take part and were interviewed totaled 45. Significantly, the refusal rate varied depending upon who asked for the offender's cooperation. When a prison staff member made the request with the first sample, the refusal rate was 59%. With the second sample, the investigator did the asking, and there were no refusals. The focus of the interview was on how victims were chosen; that is, what characteristics and attributes a suitable victim should have, and what characteristics and attributes were seen as making a victim unsuitable and hence subject to rejection. Discussion of an aerial photograph of an industrial estate, together with a chart showing the nature and use of its buildings, formed part of the interview.

Robbers

Men from a local and a regional prison were interviewed. After a list was made of all those with current convictions (from the Nominal Index cards arranged by region of origin, as with the burglars), it was again decided to interview all of them. All were Category B (medium security), and 31 were seen in the local prison, and 38 in the regional. As with the burglars, the men were asked if they were prepared to be interviewed and were given guarantees of anonymity and confidentiality. They were given the opportunity to refuse, first in their own quarters and later in the interview room. There were 10 refusals to staff at the first stage and 3 to the interviewer at the second stage—a refusal rate of 14%. As with the burglars, the interview focused on victim selection, and 16 postcard-size photographs of potential victims in different categories (male/female, young/old, white/West Indian, and so forth) were used to stimulate discussion.

Results

The Knowledge Market

So what in fact is the nature of the risk that economic criminals are up against, and how far does the use of rationality minimize it? For rationality to be total, how many and which pieces of information must be acquired and scanned? The list is infinite rather than finite, and in both a military special service situation and in an economic crime, beyond a certain point the planners cease to try for more information, realizing that the aggressor always has the advantage, accepting risk, and justifying the outcome by the gain only.

It is highly doubtful that economic criminals could ever have access to the mass of information needed to make either victim selection or the crime itself totally rational. Besides the potentially limitless list of hard, factual target information, there are also the hazards of the event (such as the eccentricities of the target custodian returning unexpectedly or being on the premises in the dark developing negatives, and so forth), a trip-up on any of which might be (wrongly) considered to be evidence of irrationality by outside armchair assessors, especially if the error was allegedly foreseeable.

Beginning at the beginning, what kind of knowledge market are offenders in? (There will of course be more than one in practice.) What kind of knowledge comes their way and is accessible to them? Here are some examples from the robbers: "Lived near the post office," "Knew he [a mobile shop owner] had a round [circular route visiting regular customers] on the estate," or "In lodgings, he'd been done for it before, said it was easy, he wanted the money." Some information will be derived from the social network of friends and acquaintances, and much will be occupation based, derived from somebody's job and somebody's friends.

Examples of network-derived knowledge are: "It [a payroll heist] had been done before, pretty easy, knew all about the geezer, out drinking with him," "[A jeweller's shop] sussed out by one of the other two," or "Friend of my cousin, same pub, same circle of friends, he said do I fancy doing a robbery?" Examples of occupation-based knowledge are: "I had somebody working for me who had been inside . . . he'd known about the job through someone else . . . approached me to do it with him, he was originally going to do it with them," "Co-defendants suggested it, one of them used to work there," or "It was a sex shop, I used to work there as a manager."

Commonly such knowledge will come from men and women at the grass-roots level of the work force with whom the criminal has contact: drivers, porters, cleaners, and so on. Such is the "knowledge pool" the criminal inhabits, which determines what kind of knowledge is instantly available and accessible. Other kinds of knowledge do not appear so commonly to be actively sought out.

Of course there are tipsters or "leakmen" who leak a trickle of usable information, sometimes without realizing who they are leaking it to: "People talk about their workplace . . . cash [amount] an idea forms, without them knowing, you case the place . . . went a few times to the place." There are also tipsters working at the prospective target who know full well to whom they are talking. Sometimes tipsters are talking less to future criminals than to middlemen, "knowledge brokers" who will pass the information on to a likely taker in general conversation, or to curry favor or for money ("a drink") or for status (evidence of mental acuity and being in the mainstream of life). For example: "Got set onto him," "Opportunity put our way, decided to have a go ... put onto it, I'd give them a drink if it came off ... I did." Apart from the "passing on," the advice of known knowledge brokers may be actively sought on likely targets. "One come to me and asked me if I knew anything [places]. I said yes ... knew it already, I used to run past [jogging] every night, knew his [jewelry shop owner's] movements." The contact points are characteristically the cafe, the pub, the workplace, and the home. An acceptable broker must have a good pedigree and reputation, and of course relatives are preferred to others.

Assessment and Planning

When we discuss the preliminaries to the decision to commit the crime we are not talking so much about direct choice as about a general discussion, with a possibility emerging, a target, and a means. This may or may not be sparked off by proffered knowledge coming from a leakman via a broker, but may instead relate to Brantingham and Brantingham's (1984) concept of "awareness space," that is, the area that a person is familiar with by virtue of his or her daily movements, together with its opportunities for crime.

The putative scheme may come from a leakman, a broker, or a general review of the situation. However it originates, the scheme is then scrutinized and assessed with free-ranging negative thinking, in which a catalogue of objections are itemized and considered. There is then a phase of flaw hunting, searching for chinks in the "impregnable" security system that protects the target (for example, realizing that "banditproof" glass can be shattered with an industrial rivet gun), and looking for what might in the broadest sense be termed "the window of vulnerability"—the one feature the target custodians have neglected to provide for.

Locating this window is a very rational process. It will certainly determine the method (whether burglary or robbery, for example), the modus operandi, and, in turn, usually the day and the time. A preliminary plan will then generate a further, more specific, negative-thinking, flaw-hunting session. If the draft plan can stand up to this test, then it will be used, once the right team can be assembled and doubts and reservations about the reliability of newcomers overcome.

Flaw hunting as a total process uses fuzzy logic with elided syllogisms. That is, the values contained in the propositions that make up the syllogism are not always precisely quantifiable. (An example of such a value might be any item that is vague in itself, but which nonetheless has to be taken into the reckoning, e.g., ground-floor target defenses.) Although in its normal form a syllogism might be, "If A = B and B = C, it follows that A = C," in a criminal situation an offender will often just say in effect, "A = B, therefore A = C," eliding the middle proposition, B = C, usually because of its obviousness to those who habitually make this kind of assessment. For example:

First proposition: "On this warehouse there are alarms of such-and-such a type."

Second proposition (which is elided): "Type such-and-such can be neutralized by electromagnets."

Final proposition: "Therefore take the magnets to neutralize the alarm system."

Conclusions are often stated first, and the middle reasoning is left out to suit the customary form of such assessments, so that as speech the example above becomes, "Take the magnets—there are alarms" or words to that effect. Merit marks are awarded for excessive pessimism and suspiciousness, and a generalized paranoia is used to look for "catches." It is a tentative, leisurely, suspicious approach.

As the plan evolves it entails weaving through the barriers set up by the target custodians. The mean pathway through the obstacles is sought. This planning has three characteristics: (a) direction—it is purposeful; (b) evasion—avoiding rather than confronting hurdles and big locks head-on; (c) breadth—a maximum breadth compatible with overreaction to obstacles, evading them on the assumption that they will be there. For example, a statement such as, "It's bound to be locked" entails giving that feature a wide berth.

Intuition and Experience

The final check, which can be employed right up to the last second before the crime but is usually done sooner, is that derived from intuition, past experience, and hunches. Bruner and Postman's directive state theory (Allport, 1955) would imply that people never confront totally new situations, that there are always a history and a background that supply the actor with working hypotheses which are continually subject to revision as he or she grapples with reality. The past experience that economic criminals bring to their next crime, whatever its origin—from the media, from folklore, or from personal experience of similar actions—may be of high quality, salience, and perceptivity. Such operators know when a set of circumstances "does not feel right," for some intangible, intuitive reason. They similarly know when it feels very suitable indeed. From an armed robber:

It is like playing a game where, although the odds are against you, something inside you says you're going to win anyway. If you're giving the cards out and know what the cards are, the other person hasn't got a chance.

Effectively this is conceding that rationality is not enough ("something inside you"). If we ask how do such people react when their rationality does not work, even when bolstered with intuition, the answer usually emerges in terms of luck and fatalism.

Luck and Fatalism

Fatalism is represented by the use of the slang phrase "come on top," which means sudden chaos and imminent hazard to the offender. Fatalistically it is accepted that things may come on top for any reason, and this is not seen as either in the control of the offender or due to lack of foresight, but just "one of those things."

Back lanes give plenty of cover, roof windows, they're rarely belled up [equipped with alarms], you could use the roof. If it come on top, plenty of ways to run away, plenty of ways in and out.

Errors and accidents are accepted as part of the general injustice of life, so prevalent as not to be deserving of further comment. Two robbers robbing a shop wore crash helmets with tinted visors to frustrate identification. Only in the shop did they discover that they could not hear each other talking because of the helmets. After wounding the shop owner with an axe, they fled because of their communication difficulties. The man who had inflicted the axe wound made no comment about his feelings about the discovery of his temporary deafness.

Those who were drunk or drugged at the time of the robbery saw the errors that then ensued as being an inevitable part of living such a life, and they seemed to find comfort in the fact that although they were not proper robbers, others were; there were other men who did robbery properly according to the rules. In the robbery sample, 48% were drunk or drugged at the time of the offense, compared with 24% of the commercial burglars.

Commercial Burglars as Rational Offenders

How much rationality can be sieved out from these accounts? Or is the rational robber or burglar merely a myth to reassure the irrational?

The commercial burglars were shown an aerial photograph of an industrial estate, together with a chart identifying the nature and use of each building, and were asked to comment on which of the 49 premises shown were likely in their view to be selected as targets. From the results of this exercise three findings are of interest. There was a stated preference for edge as opposed to center targets, confirming Brantingham and Brantingham's (1975) findings. There was also a strongly identifiable concentration on the issue of surveillability, confirming Bennett and Wright (1984). Finally, 53% of men gave responses showing logical and methodical assessment as opposed to the intuitive feelings and emotional reactions displayed by the rest. For example:

No, because it is open ground and [car] lights passing over it might silhouette you. No, they wouldn't leave it open if there was anything worth taking; no, except the stores, it's isolated, metals are profitable."

Consideration must be given here to what at first seems a small point. The use of rationality imposes a greater strain on the criminal than the use of intuition or hunch, in that one's self-esteem is put on the line if, using rationality, the attempt still fails. With hunch-crime, however, if the criminal is caught, failure can be explained by saying that on this occasion he was not really trying. When the criminal really is trying, knows it, and fails, the result is to be instantly confronted with one's own inadequacy. This seemed to show with commercial burglars in that those using rationality were conscious that it restricted them more (perhaps to a time, for example, or a method), and they experienced much more fear and anxiety during the crime than the criminals working on a hunch.

Robbers as Rational Offenders

Although Petersilia, Greenwood, and Lavin (1978) discovered that about a quarter of their sample could be described as planning robbers, within this group 52% had planned their robberies, and of these 25% had planned for months or years, with days or weeks being the commonest planning time. Significantly, too, the robbers in general showed a much greater determination to carry out the robbery than did the commerical burglars in relation to their crimes. Of the burglars, only 11% said that nothing would put them off, compared with 54% of the robbers. The typical way for all robbers to choose their victim was through knowledge acquired through employment, residence, observation, or gossip (47%). The second most popular way was by intuition. More planners used knowledge than did opportunists, and more opportunists than planners used intuition.

With regard to planning in robbery it must be accepted that if robbers admit in court to having planned their offenses, longer sentences are more likely to be awarded. It may then be that admitting to having planned is similarly concealed in the interview context for verisimilitude. Those who have planned and still failed would also perhaps prefer to classify themselves as opportunists.

When discussing target choice and related matters, the form of the comment and the reasoning, too, differ from those used by the commercial burglars. There appears to be less reasoning and a greater concentration on social rather than technical issues. For example, "Third party who suggested it had gone to the chemist's and the guy opened the side door to him. He said if you knocked on the side door he'd open it," "His boy used to work there at the supermarket, he knew the actions that was taken; son told the father who involved me," or "Planned it, it was a shop, first the getaway route, then I worked backwards [to a suitable victim]."

Conclusions

Methodological Problems

Interviewing offenders appeared to be the most useful technique for assembling data on commercial burglary and robbery for several reasons. Because offenders are the source of the crime it would seem absurd not to avail oneself of their versions of what they were doing and why. Linked with this, other methods of data collection, valuable as they may be, would seem to both skirt the issue and generally be impractical for crimes characterized by great secrecy and brief commission time. Finally, there appeared to be a general dearth of information about offenders who do these crimes, but many unexamined assumptions.

Captive offenders were chosen rather than those at liberty because of the twin difficulties with the latter of obtaining sufficient numbers and sufficient privacy for realistic interviews free of audience effect. A choice of either group has attached to it a similar list of problems: (a) potential unrepresentativeness of the subjects; (b) subject response difficulties such as that of coherently summarizing complex (and possibly emotional) events and the possibility that materially quite different accounts would be given to different interviewers; (c) recall problems in discussion of past events (condensing, distorting, rationalizing, and so forth); (d) reticence concerning disclosure of trade secrets; (e) the deliberate use of deceit; (f) an analysis problem of the nature of patterns perceived in such data.

Although none of these problems was glaringly apparent, equally it was not to be expected that in their nature they would be. In any event it was felt that the invisible distortions implied by such problems would be far outweighed by the general gain accruing from letting offenders tell their own story. Large differences, or patterns of questionable validity, are in any case always subject to close scrutiny and cross-checking by later studies, particularly in an area where so little has so far been established. However, on the specific issue of rationality it may be that although men would talk in highly rational terms when interviewed in the privacy of a prison cell, they might very well not do so if they were selecting a target for a live operation.

Extent of Rationality Displayed

Reading all the target selection comments from the interviews together, we find that each man mentions rational facts, and if we read the comments as a whole we get an impression that all the angles are covered. Yet closer examination shows that rather than each criminal covering all the points for his crime, considering area, target, victim defenses, and so on seriatim, what is happening is that each man has bees in his bonnet about particular items and disregards others totally. We do not know whether this is because he has not thought of them, although this is unlikely, or that his past experience suggests they can be disregarded and he has not mentioned them for this reason, but if he is lucky enough even operating on this basis, he still "wins."

The concept that we are fumbling for from Bennett and Wright is perhaps limited, temporal rationality. Not all these men are highly intelligent, and few are equipped to calculate Bentham-style, even supposing the information were available. Yet it is very common for rationality to be used. Of course it is partial and limited rather than total, but at the time the actor feels he has planned enough and weighed enough data. Not all the statements about logic and method can be dismissed as bogus rationality. These men are doing their best to calculate, but in the end, risk and imponderables mean that they will often fail. Many of the other group, which includes drunk and drugged people, may also by their own lights, holding the influence of intoxicants constant, be feeling at the time that they are behaving rationally, too.

Offending as Rational Behavior

We are in danger of assuming that an absurdly stringent definition of rationality would be usable in crime by the men who actually do it. In the nature of the task, the kind of rationality used by the civil engineer will not be discovered. To say this, however, is not to imply that no rationality is used at all. It is a matter of degree, and it would be well to spend less time dwelling on supposedly irrational features than on rational ones, but not to expect that rationalism and utilitarianism are the same thing.

Supposedly the small gains of many economic criminals are proof of irrationality, but there are two alternative explanations. One emphasizes the difficulties inherent in making predictions of exact gains in advance; the other emphasizes that, small though the sums may be, they may still be adequate for the offender's immediate requirements and hence subjectively much larger than they appear. Gunn and Gristwood (1976) in a general comparison of robbers with other criminals serving long sentences found few differences between the two groups, but they made the point that for all those serving long sentences a high prevalence of early family problems or psychiatric illness is found, and this of course would be expected to detract from the rationality of such men.

Rationality in the sense of being logical and methodical is commonly present apparently among economic criminals, but it is not a pure distillate. Although where it is used it is seen by the operator to be working utilitarianism, it is far from being pure utilitarianism. The use of a rationality that seems at the time adequate, but may subsequently be seen by the offender to be in error, differs from purer forms in that the boundaries that are set to the problem of victim selection are much narrower than pure rationality requires. If certain critical factors have adequate perceived outcomes, this is a sufficient basis for action; the net is not broadly spread. What usually erroneously convinces assessors that there is less rationality than there is, is the presence of accidents and errors. However, many of these would still occur even if the purist forms of rationality were used, because of the risk element.

Implications for Further Research and Policy

This type of study seems to indicate that criminal decision making is both patterned and exposable; moreover, such research is inexpensive. It would then seem desirable to conduct repeat studies with refined methods with different interviewers to see if the patterns persist.

Policy signposts based on a single study must be highly tentative. Having said this, those emerging would include: (a) offenders for these crimes vary in rationality from outright "senseless" behavior to being as rational as circumstances permit; (b) high-rationality offenders are usually activated by target-relevant knowledge about one specific victim (people or premises) originating in employment, residence, or social network (local connections seem most common, and the perpetual flow of such detailed local knowledge must be accepted); (c) high-rationality offenders can be seen as relentless flaw hunters seeking and commonly finding vulnerability in even the most complex security system.

References

Allport, F.
  1955 Theories of Perception and the Concept of Structure. New York: Wiley.
Bennett, T. and R. Wright
  1984 Burglars on Burglary. Aldershot, Hants, England: Gower.
Brantingham, P.J. and P.L. Brantingham.
  1975 "The spatial patterning of burglary." Howard Journal 14:11–23.
  1984 Patterns in Crime. New York: Macmillan.
Clinard, M.B. and E.T. Quinney
  1967 Criminal Behavior Systems: A Typology. New York: Holt, Rinehart & Winston.
Einstadter, W.J.
  1969 "The social organisation of armed robbery." Social Problems 17:64–82.

Gibbons, D.C.
  1968   Society, Crime and Criminal Careers. Englewood Cliffs, NJ: Prentice-
         Hall.
Gunn, J. and J. Gristwood
  1976   "Twenty-seven robbers." British Journal of Criminology 16:56–62.
Laver, M.
  1982   The Crime Game. Oxford: Martin Robertson.
Letkemann, P.
  1973   Crime as Work. Englewood Cliffs, NJ: Prentice-Hall.
Maguire, M.
  1982   Burglary in a Dwelling. London: Heinemann.
Petersilia, J., P.W. Greenwood and M. Lavin
  1978   Criminal Careers of Habitual Felons. Washington, DC: U.S. Govern-
         ment Printing Office.
Sutherland, E.H.
  1956   The Professional Thief. Chicago: University of Chicago Press.
Walsh, D.P.
  1978   Shoplifting: Controlling a Major Crime. London: Macmillan.
  1980   Break-Ins: Burglary from Private Houses. London: Constable.

4
Robbers as Decision-Makers

FLOYD FEENEY

Editors' Note

The interviews with 113 Californian robbers that form the basis of Floyd
Feeney's chapter were undertaken in 1971 and 1972 as part of a wider
study of robbery. The material has been reanalyzed here to explore the
rational components of robbery, which Feeney finds to be substantial,
provided that a broad definition of rationality is employed. Feeney's
results, backed up by a rich store of verbatim quotes, offer a number of
unanticipated insights into criminal decision making: for example, that
over half the robbers claimed to do no planning, that robberies can be
quite opportunistic and casual affairs (passengers waiting outside a store
in the robber's car were sometimes unaware of what he was doing
inside), and that some robbers were strangely reluctant to consider
committing burglary. It is surprising that robbery, which is so seriously
regarded by society, should frequently be embarked upon with such
apparent lack of deliberation on the part of the offender, and that the
more experienced the robber the less he seems to plan the offense or to
worry about being caught. Although this lack of explicit planning may
be more apparent than real (as Feeney remarks, experience may well
provide a substitute), the lack of fear seems well founded: The sample
included one individual who, in spite of having committed over 1,000
robberies by the age of 26, had been convicted only once. Such examples
graphically illustrate the difficulties of deterrence or prevention, although Feeney's final paragraph contains the tantalizing suggestion that
devices that make money difficult to obtain, such as no-cash systems on
buses, may be more effective in preventing robberies than measures such
as TV surveillance, which rely on deterrence. Finally, the fact that a
number of differences were found between those who robbed commercial enterprises and those whose targets were individuals suggests, as
with burglary, the importance of adopting an even more crime-specific
focus in relation to types of robberies.

Because of its suddenness and its potential for serious injury or death,
robbery is one of the most feared of all crimes. It is the most frequent
stranger-to-stranger crime involving violence, and its rapid increase over

the past several decades has been a major corrosive force in contemporary urban life in the United States and to a lesser extent in Britain and Europe. The prevention and control of robbery is consequently an important item on the social agenda on both sides of the Atlantic.

As a legal term, *robbery* covers a fairly broad spectrum of criminal activity, from the Great Train Robbery worth millions of pounds to schoolyard bullies taking lunch money from their classmates—a kind of robbery that is often not reported. As a practical matter most robberies dealt with by the police and the courts fall into a narrower range largely consisting of two categories: muggings and other attacks on individuals on the street and holdups of commercial establishments. This chapter addresses the question whether it is useful in developing policies for the control of robbery to focus on how decisions about robbery are made by the robbers themselves. The conclusion is that this is a useful perspective for addressing the robbery problem, although obviously not the only approach that may be fruitful.

This chapter is based primarily on interviews with 113 northern California offenders charged with robbery and convicted of robbery or an offense related to robbery. Although this means that the offense of conviction is in some instances not a robbery, this sample was thought to be more representative of persons doing robberies than one based wholly on persons convicted of robbery itself. The sample was stratified to include both adults and juveniles, blacks and whites, offenders involved in commercial and in individual robberies, and offenders given both long prison sentences and shorter local sentences. As robbery is largely a male enterprise, only males were interviewed. The interviews were conducted in 1971 and 1972 (Weir, 1973) and were reanalyzed for the purpose of this chapter. The discussion is based on unweighted figures. Northern California had a very high robbery rate during the period of the interviews.

Like other human beings, individuals who commit robberies make many decisions. For all but the most prolific robbers, most of these decisions concern everyday life and have nothing to do with robbery. Of those that do involve robbery, some are strategic, career-type decisions such as the decision to get involved in crime, to commit a first robbery, to continue robbing, or to desist. Others are much more tactical, such as how to choose a victim, whether to use a gun, and how to escape. It is not possible to discuss all these different kinds of decisions here, but an attempt will be made to cover some of the more important decisions and to give the flavor of the decision-making process. Some of the argument that follows is based on solid empirical evidence. Where necessary, however, this has been supplemented with impressions and fragmentary evidence.

Logically the decision to rob is a very complex matter involving the whole past of the individual considering the crime as well as that person's present situation. As robbery is generally thought of as an economic crime, it might be expected that the typical individual considering a robbery goes through some kind of mental calculus to determine whether he has a need for money and what the legitimate opportunities for getting money are—whether through work or from family or friends. If these calculations indicate a need that cannot be satisfied through legitimate means, consideration might then be given to committing a crime to acquire the money, and if so, to which crime is the most suitable. Presumably in making this calculation the individual considers the relative financial gains that might be expected from the various kinds of crimes possible and the relative risks of getting caught or otherwise harmed. Presumably also the individual considers what actions he will be required to perform in committing the crime and how he feels about undertaking these actions.

Because robbery is a serious crime with severe penalties and significant possibilities for getting hurt, individuals considering robbery might be expected to pay particular attention to these matters, and those deciding to commit the crime might be expected to give careful thought to the choice of a target and the development of a plan for reducing the chances of apprehension. It is surprising therefore to find that the northern California robbers studied do not fit this description very well. Fewer than 60% stated money as the primary aim of their robbery, over half said they did no planning at all, and over 60% said that before the robbery they had not even thought about being caught.

The Decision to Rob

The decision to rob begins with some kind of desire. As previously indicated, fewer than 60% of the robbers said they wanted money. Twenty-four percent wanted something other than money, and 19% were involved in what might be called "accidental robberies" burglaries, fights, or other acts that were not originally intended to involve both theft and violence but which came to do so as events unfolded, as shown in Table 4.1.

Nearly a third of those seeking money wanted it for drugs, and almost as many wanted specific things such as clothes or a car. The remainder seeking money needed food or shelter or just had a general desire for money. Most of those who wanted drugs were adult heroin addicts. Some said that their habits required only a few dollars a day, whereas others said they needed $100 a day or more. Many stressed the difficulty of their situations:

But see, I would have been able to support my family if I wouldn't have had to pay for the heroin, so it didn't matter which way you split the money—whether it went

TABLE 4.1 Motivations for committing robbery (expressed in percent)[a]

Motivation	Adults (n = 82)	Juveniles (n = 31)	All Offenders (n = 113)
Money	(64)	(35)	(57)
For drugs	22	3	17
For food and shelter	11	0	8
For other specific things	18	10	16
General desire for money	13	23	16
Other than money	(22)	(32)	(24)
For excitement, to relieve boredom or general unhappiness	6	6	6
Out of anger, upset	5	10	6
To impress or help out friends, to prove subject could do it	4	13	6
Not sure why, drunk or on drugs at time	7	3	6
Not really a robber	(13)	(32)	(19)
Recover money owed	7	0	5
Interrupted burglary	0	13	4
Fight turned into a robbery	0	13	4
Partner started a robbery without prior knowledge	6	6	6
Total	100	100	100

[a]Percentages may not add to 100 because of rounding.

for the heroin or whether it went to the family. I mean it was still for the heroin, because if it wasn't for the heroin I wouldn't have had debts to make money for. Well, I had a family to take care of and the heroin got to the point that I didn't keep food in the refrigerator and the rent paid and bills paid, phone bill, electric bill, and it was hard to handle both things, and that's when I got into robberies.

Many of those who wanted specific things had current problems or financial needs. Several wanted money to leave the state to avoid arrest. Another was trying to pay traffic tickets to avoid being put in jail. Several juveniles had run away from a juvenile camp and wanted to leave town. Another adult had given money to his roommate for several months to pay the rent. The roommate used the money for other things, however, and suggested a robbery when the manager demanded the back rent. The offender was not earning enough at his job to cover the loss and reluctantly agreed.

Those who wanted food and shelter were generally not destitute, but their circumstances were often poor. One was in a very low-paying job:

I had a little $1.65 job working 20 hours a week, which wasn't very much, but I was still trying to make it on the legit side, but there just wasn't nothing open to me. I don't mind working, but $1.65 is kind of ridiculous.... [Robbing] was the only thing open to me at the time.

Others had no jobs but were looking for work. One adult with a good employment record was trying to find a new job. Finally he tried robbery—his first—when he ran out of other places to turn:

I needed the money for food. I tried welfare. I tried to borrow all the people that I could borrow from. Nobody else that I could borrow from. I didn't have any sources of money. I was just flat broke. I was getting it out of the savings and borrowing money from my mother, but I was getting kind of run out because she was starting to need more. I didn't even think about how much I wanted to get. I just felt that anything I got would help. It was better than nothing.

Another explained that he had a family:

There wasn't no food in the house, you know. Scrounging. And I'm forced into having to do something like this. I knew I was desperate. Besides, I was going out stealing anything I could get a hold of, get a little money to get some food.

Many in the group who said they just wanted money were not really able to explain why:

I have no idea why I did this. Well, I guess it was for money, but I didn't have no money problem, really, then. You know, everybody got a little money problem, but not big enough to go and rob somebody. I just can't get off into it. I don't really know why I did it.

The large number of juveniles who said they just wanted money were particularly vague. One apparently wanted to avoid the inconvenience of going to the bank:

For the money. I think that being involved I could use, at that time I could use the money. Yeah. I was accumulating money. Many reasons. 'Cause I got low on my pocket and I needed some pocket money. 'Cause I didn't want to go to the bank.

Over 40% of the offenders indicated that money was not the real purpose of the robbery. A quarter of these were involved in arguments or fights. One became angry at a racial slur:

I was mad at Mom. This old broad had made me mad. I seen the lady coming out of the store. I said, "Help," you know. And she said something, she mumbled something but all I know was "black." I hear that. So I got mad.

Another took a wig from a young woman who had rejected his attempt to pick her up. He did it:

Because I felt she was disrespecting me, kind of. I did it 'cause I seen fear in her. So I knew if I took this, she might start acting right ... to punish her the way she was talking.

A drunk juvenile got mad when the victim bumped into him:

It was just a sudden thing. I didn't really mean to do it. I didn't plan or nothing; it just happened. Just like that. Because he offered it to me. There's no reason. I just took it. I beat him up, you know. I was happy I beat him up. I was going to walk away and leave him there but he gave me $4. He thought I was going to cut his throat. He gave it to me. I wouldn't cut his throat. I didn't want to get busted for murder.

Some were just generally angry—one because his apartment had just been "ripped off." Another was mad at everyone:

I was mad and I had to do something to get it out of my system. I was mad at my cousins and my girlfriend. I was mad at my mom at the time.

Both also had other reasons, however:

I get a kick out of it really. Watch people's faces when they see you. They scared. I robbed because he gave me a smart answer. [Did several robberies that same evening.]

I don't know. It sounded easy and I guess we needed the money. We didn't really need it but we wanted to do something. Something to do. I don't know.

A surprising number of offenders got involved primarily because of partners. One, who had done no previous robberies, tried to help a friend and wound up in prison:

Because he asked me to help him out. He done a favor for me before. I didn't really want the money. It was an emotional thing more than anything else. Like the guy did me a hell of a favor.

Juveniles often cited the influence of friends. Several were just trying to prove they could do robberies. One had $265 in his pocket but robbed to show that he was not "scared." Another said, "People got to prove things to people. My partner didn't think I could do it."

Six percent of the offenders said their partners started something and they just went along:

Oh, in a simple sentence, I was either going to take part in the robbery then or, you know, stay there and be a part of it already as far as my mind was going then. It might have been an irrational thing because I was with the gentleman, and if the guy would have turned to me, well, I would have been caught, and blamed and made to give it up anyway. Well, we was. I felt a part of it, you know, when he [partner] committed the act, right then. I know it sounds silly, but that's the way my mind was going then.

Another sizable group of offenders simply wanted excitement or a change of some kind in their lives:

Just to cause some trouble. Well, we just wanted to try that, you know. Goof around, you know, have some fun—jack up somebody.... We thought we were really big and stuff like that.

I don't really have any fear of prisons or things like that. I always sort of felt like I was going back someday. [I was] disillusioned with myself . . . and with some of the compromises I was forced to make in life. And "capering" appealed to me.

I did it because I didn't care. I felt I didn't have anything to live for anyway so what the heck's the difference.

Another group did not think of themselves as trying to rob at all. They were attempting to recover money they claimed was either theirs or owed to them. Their motivation was to get what they thought belonged to them. A number had money with them or at home.

There was little difference between blacks and whites in the motivations expressed for committing their current robberies. They were about evenly divided between those saying that money was the primary reason and those saying that reasons other than money prompted the robberies.

Surprisingly, one fourth of the adult commercial robbers said that money was not their primary motivation. All of those who said they were disillusioned or depressed were commercial robbers, as were the adults who were primarily interested in excitement and a number of the adults who just went along with their partners.

Planning

Most of the robbers appear to have taken a highly casual approach to their crimes, as Table 4.2 indicates. Over half said they did no planning at all. Another third reported only minor planning such as finding a partner, thinking about where to leave a getaway car, or whether to use a weapon. This minor, low-level planning generally took place the same day as the robbery and frequently within a few hours of it. The longest lead time was generally that needed to get a weapon if one was not already available.

Fewer than 15% or so had any kind of planned approach. The largest number of these (9%) simply followed an existing pattern for their offenses. They did little new planning for their current offenses because they already had an approach that they liked. Fewer than 5% of the robbers planned in any detail. These robbers—all adults and all involved in commercial robberies—stole getaway cars, planned escape routes, detailed each partner's actions, evaluated contingencies, and observed the layout of prospective targets. As might be expected, commercial robberies were planned more often than those of individuals (60% versus 30%).

The robbers varied greatly in the number of robberies committed. Forty percent of those seeking to commit a robbery said they were committing their first robbery, 26% said they had committed 2 to 9 robberies, 24%

TABLE 4.2 Amount of planning undertaken before committing robbery (expressed in percent)[a]

Type of Robber	None	Minor	A Lot	Pattern Only	Number (n)
First-time robbers	56	44	0	0	(36)
Committed 2–9 robberies	46	33	0	21	(24)
Committed 10–49 robberies	27	50	9	14	(22)
Committed 50 or more robberies	56	11	11	22	(9)
Accidental robbers	100	0	0	0	(21)
Overall	55	33	3	9	(112)
Overall minus accidental robbers	46	40	3	11	(91)
Adults	52	33	4	11	(82)
Juveniles	63	32	0	3	(30)
Individual	69	25	0	5	(59)
Commercial	40	42	6	13	(53)
Black	62	29	0	10	(63)
White	47	39	6	8	(49)

[a]Percentages may not add to 100 due to rounding.

reported 10 to 49 robberies, and 10% reported 50 or more robberies. The repeat offenders had many fewer arrests than the number of robberies mentioned, and virtually all said the police did not know about the offenses for which they had not been arrested.

Generally the amount of planning increased with the number of robberies committed. None of those not fully intending a robbery did any planning, and none of the first-time robbers did any planning other than minor planning. Twenty-one percent of those who said they had committed 2 to 9 robberies did some planning beyond the minor variety, as compared with 23% of those who reported 10 to 49 robberies and 33% of those who reported 50 or more.

The impulsive, spur-of-the-moment nature of many of these robberies is well illustrated by two adult robbers who said they had passengers in their cars who had no idea that they planned a robbery. One passenger, who thought his friend was buying root beer and cigarettes, found out the hard way what had happened. A clerk chased his robber-friend out the door and fired a shotgun blast through the windshield of the passenger's car. Other robbers, who had no transportation of their own, persuaded friends to drive them to robbery sites. In most of these incidents the friends dropped the robbers off and drove on, wholly unaware of what was about to happen.

The generally casual approach to the crime is also illustrated by the approach of many offenders to the possibility of apprehension. Over 60% of the robbers said they had not even thought about getting caught before the robbery, as Table 4.3 shows. Another 17% said that they had thought about the possibility but did not believe it to be a problem. Only 21%

TABLE 4.3 Extent to which robbers thought about being caught (expressed in percent)[a]

Type of Robber	Not at All	Thought Not a Problem	Thought Was a Problem	Number (n)
First-time robbers	56	14	31	(36)
Committed 2–9 robberies	61	22	17	(23)
Committed 10–49 robberies	55	25	20	(20)
Committed 50 or more robberies	67	11	22	(9)
Accidental robbers	80	10	10	(20)
Overall	62	17	21	(108)
Adults	63	13	24	(79)
Juveniles	59	28	14	(29)
Individual	74	11	16	(57)
Commercial	49	24	27	(51)
Black	68	13	18	(60)
White	54	21	25	(48)

[a]Percentages may not add to 100 due to rounding.

considered the possibility a risk to be concerned about. Some, who had given no thought to getting caught before the robbery began, said that they did think about it during or immediately after, particularly when things started going wrong or they became involved in hot-pursuit chases. A few began to worry only after they had already escaped. The greatest concern was shown by the first-time robbers. A quarter of this group thought the risk of apprehension was a problem.

Decisions Concerning Means

Only 22% of the robbers indicated that they considered doing some crime other than robbery as a means of accomplishing their ends. Of those who did consider other crimes, burglary was the crime most frequently considered and shoplifing the second. A number of robbers were also selling drugs.

Most of those who considered burglary preferred robbery. Some did so because there was more money or no need to fence the loot, some because they thought robbery was safer or because they were fearful about going into houses. Others had been caught doing burglaries. One drug user had been shoplifting to support his habit but had moved to a town where the price of the drugs was twice what he had previously been paying. He decided to rob stores because the money was better and faster:

That's the reason I went into robbing the stores. [When I came here] my habit immediately jumped to $100 a day, just the difference in dope. The dope down there and the dope up here was that different. So I said, "I can't be running around boosting and beating people on the head and doing whatever, $100 a day, man. That's crazy."

Another had been dealing drugs but quit because the police were getting suspicious. A few preferred burglaries but decided on impulse to try robbing. Three incidents began as burglaries but turned into robberies when the victim returned home unexpectedly. One shoplifting turned into a robbery in much the same way.

Fewer than 10% of those whose objective was something other than money considered any other crime. Half, however, of the highly active robbers responsible for 50 or more robberies considered some other crime. Many of those who said they did not consider any other crime had a prior arrest record for burglary or shoplifting. Although the offenders did not say so, it is possible that this prior history affected their decision to rob.

No systematic information is available as to how many offenders considered satisfying their needs through legitimate opportunities. Many of the robbers mentioned their inability to find work as a factor in their general situation, however. None of the juveniles and only 20% of the adults who robbed for money had jobs at the time of the robbery, and most of these were in low-paying or part-time jobs. White adults who robbed for money were more often working than black adults. About half of those who robbed for something other than money were working.

One of the most important tactical choices that a robber must make is whom to rob. In line with the general lack of planning, the robbers' comments as to how they chose victims were much more matter of fact than expected. Over 20% said that they chose their victims because of convenience, 15% said that the victim appeared to have money, and another 15% chose their victims because a fast getaway was possible or the risk otherwise appeared to be low. Others gave mixed reasons or did not know why they had chosen. Some typical comments as to convenience:

Just where we happened to be, I guess. Don't know.

Nothing else open at 2:00 a.m. Had been there before.

We thought it would be the quickest, you know, it's a small donut shop.

Another important tactical choice concerns the location of the robbery. A nearby site obviously is the most convenient and familiar but also carries the highest risk of recognition. Despite this risk over a third of the robbers attacked victims in their own neighborhoods and over 70% in their own towns. Moreover, only half of the 30% who robbed in another town had gone there for the purpose of committing a robbery. Fifteen percent just happened to be in the other town. Some were visiting friends or relatives; others were passing through when they decided to do a robbery.

Even when in another town for the purpose of committing a robbery, most apparently were there for reasons other than the idea that going out of town was the best approach. One was in a town 15 miles away simply because that was the only place where he could find a gas station open after midnight. Another was driving around looking for a motel to rob, and most of the motels in the area were outside the town where he lived. His partner had suggested one closer to home, but the robber rejected it as a target because he knew one of the employees. Of the adults who went to another town to rob, only one went to a town other than one contiguous to the town in which he lived. The one exception was a fairly well-planned robbery at a major resort which involved traveling several hundred miles.

One of the juveniles who was out of town for the purpose of doing a robbery wandered around for nearly 150 miles before selecting a robbery site; another drove 100 miles from home, and a third, 50. All had decided to do the robberies on the same day and apparently were attempting to ensure success by getting a long way from home.

Decisions Concerning Weapons and Force

Eighty percent of the offenders used some kind of weapon: 53% used guns, 19% knives, and 8% other weapons. Most said they were trying to intimidate their victims and gain control over the situation rather than to harm or dominate the victims. Most felt that showing the weapon was enough to accomplish their purpose but were prepared to use force if the victim resisted or the police came by.

A surprising percentage had qualms about the use of the weapons they carried, however, and made deliberate decisions to forego some of their advantage. Nearly 30% of those who used a "gun" used a weapon that was either not loaded or that was simulated. Sixteen percent carried guns that were not loaded, 7% simulated weapons, and another 5% toy weapons. Most wanted to be sure that no one was hurt and explained that if they had no bullets in the guns, there was no chance that they could accidentally shoot anyone:

I didn't want a real gun because I might get jittery or something. Or if I would jam somebody that got out of line. I don't know. I wouldn't shoot nobody.

It couldn't have been loaded. I made sure of that. I just didn't want it loaded. I didn't want to hurt nobody. Just wanted to more or less scare them to give me some money.

Others used a simulated weapon or kept their weapon hidden in the belief that the penalty would be less severe if they were caught:

I felt that if I got caught it'd be a lot lighter on me if I didn't have a gun than if I did.

[Gun not displayed.] Yeah, we told her we had a weapon, but we didn't show it to her. She didn't believe it because we didn't show it to her. We didn't want to hurt anyone. Man, we'd been in jail for life if we'd got caught.

For a few offenders the decision was hasty and pragmatic rather than deliberate. One explained his unloaded gun: "Probably because I didn't have any bullets handy for it." Another simulated a gun because he didn't have one but wanted the money.

Ninety percent of the commercial robbers used a weapon of some kind, and 80% used a gun. Of those who used a gun, nearly 80% used a loaded gun. Seventy percent of those who robbed individuals also carried weapons. Only a third carried guns, however, and only half of those used a loaded gun.

Eight percent of the offenders used weapons other than a gun or a knife: a screwdriver, a lug wrench, a metal bar, a pool cue, a shovel and a board, some dog spray, or a broken beer bottle. In almost every instance the weapon used was something handy when the need arose rather than an instrument carried by careful design.

Sixty percent of those who did not use weapons failed to do so because the robbery itself was an impulsive act and no weapon was readily available. Whether they would have chosen to use a weapon if they had taken more time is not known.

A few offenders deliberately chose not to use a weapon for moral or legal reasons:

I couldn't see using a weapon on a lady. I figured I could catch her off guard and grab her purse and run.

I tried to make it nonviolent. I figured if I had to go [was caught], I would go on as less as I could.

One third of the robbers or their partners hurt someone during the robbery for which they were convicted. One additional adult reported that he had shot at a victim but missed. Robbers of individuals hurt their victims more than twice as often as the commercial robbers. Juvenile offenders harmed their victims more often than did adult offenders.

Most of the offenders who hurt victims said they did so because the victims resisted. Most chose to hit their victims with their fists or a weapon rather than to shoot or cut the victim. A sixth of those encountering resistance did, however, take drastic action: shooting, cutting, or spraying liquid into the eyes of their victims.

Around 15% of the robbers used physical force right at the outset, usually to establish initial control over the situation and usually striking without warning. One said he attacked in this way because the victim "was big." Another said it was his first robbery and that he wasn't sure what to do. He got a tire jack out of the truck, and:

See, first I think, "Well, if I hit him in the head that might kill him," so I hit him on the shoulder.

A juvenile used force to flee a burglary when the house occupant unexpectedly returned.

Around 10% of the offenders hurt their victims unintentionally. In one the victim ran into another room slamming the door behind him. When the robber chased after him, the door hit the robber's gun hand, causing the gun to fire. The bullet accidentally struck the victim. Another robber deliberately pointed his gun away from the victim and sought not to fire. The gun fired accidentally, however, and the bullet struck the victim after ricocheting off a wall. In other cases one victim suffered a heart attack, and another jumped out of a moving car. The robbers were concerned because they had neither intended nor foreseen the possibility of harm to the victims.

A quarter of those who hurt somebody did so in an attempt to recover money they had some claim to. A number of these arose out of drug-selling and gambling situations. Another victim had refused to "spot" a good location for a burglary after being paid to do so. Although these victims were certainly not asking to be robbed or hurt, they were certainly not totally innocent either. In every instance in which there was an attempt to recover money someone was hurt. Whether this was because the offenders were angry or because they met resistance is not clear.

Overall, the robbers did not generally appear to use gratuitous force. In some instances the force applied was greater than necessary, but generally the robbers did not appear to take any abstract pleasure in hurting people. Only one reported the use of force for its own sake. He said that after he had hit the victim with a lug wrench, his partner then hit the victim several more times. In commenting on why his partner had done this, he said, "Knowing him, he did it for meanness. He likes to hurt people."

Learning and Decisions to Continue

The process by which some of those committing one or two robberies become highly active offenders committing 50 or more robberies is obviously important. For some offenders this progression seems to involve an escalation from shoplifting to burglary to robbery. Several of the highly active robbers studied, however, went much more directly into robbery and at a very early age.

The information in this study is too limited to be more than suggestive. There are strong hints, however, that the key transitions take place very early. Most of the first-time robbers indicated that they felt fear and apprehension as they approached their robberies. Most also tended to be very tentative about the robberies. Many reported that they would have considered leaving the money if the victim said he would lose his job or that he needed the money for rent. The more experienced robbers, however, were much more hardened. They were much less tentative and fearful, were unmoved by any difficulties that the crime might create for the victim, and tended to view victims as objects rather than persons. This harder kind of outlook was generally present after only a few robberies.

Seventy percent of the robbers said that they did not plan to commit another offense, 14% said that they might, and 4% said that they probably would, as Table 4.4 shows. The remaining 12% said that they did not know whether they would or not. Thus a total of 30% of the offenders were willing to give some overt indication that they might commit further robberies. These indications show greater realism and honesty than might have been expected.

TABLE 4.4 Will you do more robberies? (expressed in percent)[a]

Answer	Adults ($n = 81$)	Juveniles ($n = 30$)	All Offenders ($n = 111$)
No	68	80	71
Maybe	15	10	14
Probably	2	7	4
Don't know	15	3	12
Total	100	100	100

[a]Percentages may not add to 100 due to rounding.

Rationality

Many of the decisions described are clearly rational in the sense used by Clarke and Cornish (1985). The individuals making these decisions had desires and needs that they chose to satisfy by committing robberies. Whether they were generalists who also committed other crimes or specialists who concentrated on robbery, they definitely had made robbery a deliberate part of their repertoire. Although these decisions would seem more rational if they involved more planning and more concern about the possibility of apprehension, the decisions nonetheless easily meet the standards of minimum rationality. There is clearly a thinking process involved. It is not Benthamite, but it is not much different from what people do in their everyday lives. This is particularly true for the decisions made by highly experienced robbers. Although these robbers frequently say that they undertake no planning, their experience is in a sense a substitute. Many of these robbers seem to feel that they can handle any situation that arises without specific planning.

Many of the decisions involved in robberies committed for reasons other than money also seem rational in this sense. Taking property from someone you are fighting with can be instrumental in accomplishing the aims of the fight. Going along with your friends or trying to recover property can also be instrumental acts. Some of the decisions described do not meet this kind of rationality test, however. Impulse decisions to commit serious crimes while loaded on drugs or alcohol cannot easily be called rational. Even these acts can be instrumental, however, in accomplishing goals that the actor—in his stupefied state—wants. Whether it is useful to treat these as rational for the purpose of developing theories of explanation, prevention, or control is not altogether clear. It is worth noting, however, that the criminal law often does so (LaFave and Scott, 1972).

Implications for Research

Whatever the scientific validity of the rational actor model for the purposes of developing criminological theory, the model is clearly useful for many purposes. It provides an excellent framework for analyzing and understanding the decision-making process used by offenders and puts a healthy emphasis on gaining information from offenders and on dealing with specific crime problems.

The emphasis on obtaining information directly from offenders is particularly important. Detailed discussions with offenders about their crimes and their methods of thinking and operation have already had considerable payoff in recent years, in the fine work on burglary and crime prevention that has been done in Britain (Bennett and Wright, 1984; Clarke, 1983; Maguire, 1982; Walsh, 1980), in the contribution that self-report studies have made to the study of criminal careers, and in the excellent new work in this volume. This kind of work is in its infancy, however, and there is a great deal more to be learned.

The greatest payoffs are likely to come from increased attention to the strategic decisions made by offenders and the learning process involved—the decision to rob, to continue robbing, and to desist from robbing. Studies in the past decade (Chaiken and Chaiken, 1982; Farrington, 1979; Greenwood, 1982; Wolfgang et al., 1972) have taught us a great deal about the importance of criminal careers, but we need to understand more than just the number of offenses and the sequences involved. We need to understand the thought processes and the decisions as well. In this context "decision" should not be defined too narrowly. Often there may be no single "decision" to begin robbing, to continue robbing, or even to desist from robbing. Rather, the offender has a whole thought process and belief system that ultimately lead to some kind of conclusion.

There are also likely to be substantial payoffs to further gathering of information about tactical decisions and the factual contexts as seen by the robbers. If headway is ever to be made in dealing with crime, we must access the information that offenders have and use this for purposes of prevention and control. Robbers know a lot about themselves and about robberies that no one else knows. A foreign journalist who tried to project the course of future events in Berlin in 1932 by studying only voting returns and demographics, to the exclusion of *Mein Kampf* and the Nazi platform, would today be considered very foolish.

The emphasis on particular crime problems is also timely and helpful. There are no doubt purposes for which it is useful to aggregate thinking about the Brighton hotel bombing, pilfering from the neighborhood market, and marijuana sales. For most practical purposes, however, it is much more useful to treat these as separate problems. If the solutions that emerge from separate analyses suggest some greater aggregation, that will be the appropriate time to have greater aggregation.

Implications for Policy

The studies to date tell us some useful and important things about the decision-making process employed by robbers and help point the way toward the more sophisticated research needed to obtain a fuller picture. The extent to which this information has implications for policy in its present fragmentary state is less clear.

The robbers themselves had some ideas, as Table 4.5 shows. The most frequent suggestion they made as to ways of preventing robberies was to supply jobs or job-training programs to persons like themselves. This suggestion was made by 37% of the robbers. Fourteen percent of the robbers, however, said that it was not possible to stop people from robbing and that nothing could be done. Other suggestions made by a few offenders each included more counseling, more drug programs, target hardening, and letting offenders know the penalties in order to improve deterrence.

Some of the study findings tend to confirm the traditional police concern with apprehension. Whereas many offenders said that they did not think about being caught, some also said that they chose to rob rather than to burgle or shoplift because of prior apprehensions for those crimes. One chose to rob because he was on probation for burglary and was fearful of getting caught for that again.

There are some hints that the aversive effect of apprehension is strongest for first-time offenders who are still learning how to rob. This suggests that if apprehension could be made to take place early in the offender's career, it might be possible to interrupt the learning process and steer the offender away from robbery. This might be a gain even if the offender continued to commit some other crime such as shoplifting. The

TABLE 4.5 What to do to keep guys from robbing (expressed in percent)[a]

Answer	Adults (n = 82)	Juveniles (n = 31)	All Offenders (n = 113)
Can't stop people from robbing	13	16	14
Jobs, job training, social welfare programs, education	34	45	37
Improved rehabilitation programs, counseling	5	3	4
Drug programs, get rid of drugs	2	3	3
Deterrence, let them know the penalties	1	6	3
Target hardening	1	3	2
Don't know, but punishment won't stop them	2	0	2
Other, mixed comments	21	13	19
Don't know, no answer	20	10	17
Total	100	100	100

[a]Percentages may not add to 100 due to rounding.

learning curve for robbery appears to be very rapid, however, and it is easier to describe the possible effects of early apprehension than to make early apprehensions. In any event, it would be useful to have more information from offenders about the effects of apprehensions and nonapprehensions at the various stages of their careers.

A more practical possibility is that of obtaining more convictions of offenders when valid arrests are made. This is particularly important in the United States where 30% to 60% of all robbery arrestees are not convicted, usually for reasons of evidence rather than innocence (Feeney et al., 1983; McDonald, 1982). This is one of the few areas in which rapid progress might be possible if the political will to address the issue existed. Its importance is indicated by the experience of one offender in the study. This offender began robbing and shooting heroin at age 13. By age 26 he had plausibly and conservatively committed over a thousand robberies without a conviction until his present sentence. He had been arrested on five occasions, but in each instance the charges were dropped. Is it any wonder that he did not worry too much about being caught?

The findings on decision making could also have implications for sentencing. If the reports that even the most active robbers do relatively little planning and rarely think about getting caught are accurate, this weakens the appeal of deterrence as a strategy for controlling robbery. Steep penalties are unlikely to deter those who do not believe they will be caught. Such penalties may, however, deter others, who then decide not to commit robberies. The fact that some offenders leave the bullets out of their guns because of the possible penalties suggests that some offenders worry about penalties more than they indicate. This may be particularly true for first offenders. The relative ineffectiveness of deterrence on those who actually rob strengthens the case for incapacitation, as incapacitation provides some measure of control over the impulsive as well as the calculating robber.

The findings suggest that, to be at all successful, prevention efforts must be very selective and highly targeted. There are some indications that robbers who plan little and act on impulse can be successfully thwarted by prevention schemes that make obtaining money more difficult and more time consuming, such as no-change bus fares and the holding of limited cash at gasoline stations (Misner & McDonald, 1970). There are also indications, however, that robbers are much less affected by prevention devices, such as bank cameras, which essentially operate on deterrence principles.

References

Bennett, T. and R. Wright
    1984   Burglars on Burglary. Aldershot, Hants, England: Gower.
Chaiken, J. and M. Chaiken
    1982   Varieties of Criminal Behavior. Santa Monica, CA: Rand.
Clarke, R.
    1983   "Situational crime prevention: its theoretical basis and practical scope."
           Pp. 225-56 in M. Tonry and N. Morris (eds.), Crime and Justice: An
           Annual Review of Research, Volume 4. Chicago: University of Chicago
           Press.
Clarke, R. and D. Cornish
    1985   "Modelling offenders' decisions: a framework for research and policy."
           Pp. 147-85 in M. Tonry and N. Morris (eds.), Crime and Justice: An
           Annual Review of Research, Volume 6. Chicago: University of Chicago
           Press.
Farrington, D.
    1979   "Longitudinal research on crime and delinquency." Pp. 289-348 in N.
           Morris and M. Tonry (eds.), Crime and Justice: An Annual Review of
           Research, Volume 1. Chicago: University of Chicago Press.
Feeney, F., F. Dill and A. Weir
    1983   Arrests Without Conviction. Washington, DC: U.S. Government Print-
           ing Office.
Greenwood, P.
    1982   Selective Incapacitation. Santa Monica, CA: Rand.
LaFave, W. and A. Scott
    1972   Criminal Law. St. Paul, MN: West.
Maguire, M.
    1982   Burglary in a Dwelling. London: Heinemann.
McDonald, W.
    1982   Police-Prosecutor Relations in the United States. Washington, DC: U.S.
           Government Printing Office.

Misner, G. and W. McDonald
   1970   The Scope of the Crime Problem and Its Resolution. Volume II of
          Reduction of Robberies and Assaults of Bus Drivers. Berkeley, CA:
          Stanford Research Institute and University of California.
Walsh, D.
   1980   Break-Ins: Burglary from Private Houses. London: Constable.
Weir, A.
   1973   "The Robbery Offender." Pp. 100–211 in F. Feeney and A. Weir (eds.),
          The Prevention and Control of Robbery, Volume I. Davis, CA:
          University of California.
Wolfgang, M., R. Figlio and T. Sellin
   1972   Delinquency in a Birth Cohort. Chicago: University of Chicago Press.

5
The Decision to Give Up Crime[1]

MAURICE CUSSON AND PIERRE PINSONNEAULT

Editors' Note

Maurice Cusson's book, *Why Delinquency?*, represents one of the most thoroughgoing attempts to explain crime as rational conduct. In the present chapter he and a colleague, Pierre Pinsonneault, employ the same approach to explore the neglected topic of desistance from crime. Their material is drawn from interviews with 17 ex-robbers in Canada as well as some ex-offenders' biographies. The main factors they see as involved in desistance—"shock" resulting from some aversive experience when committing robbery, "delayed deterrence" involving recognition of the inevitability of capture, a reduced ability to "do time," fear of imprisonment, an overall increase in the anxiety connected with a life of crime, and a reevaluation of criminal life and its pointlessness—are neatly summarized in their diagram. Also included in this diagram is the concept of "backsliding"—the result of temptation—which would be a useful addition to our own speculative desistance model reproduced in the Introduction. Cusson and Pinsonneault's analysis illustrates, therefore, how the rational choice framework presented in this volume is likely to be refined and improved as a result of new empirical research. A methodological note: It also provides an example of the degree of care needed in interpreting interview material. As the authors observe, having a worthwhile job seems to be important in desistance, but it was not spontaneously mentioned by the men they interviewed.

It is an understatement to say that the relationship between age and crime is fairly close. Let us recall three facts: First, the rate of arrests according to age starts a sharp decline at the end of adolescence. Second, among adult recidivists a reduction in criminal activity takes place with aging (Glueck and Glueck, 1937). Third, according to Blumstein and Cohen (1982:50), the total duration of the career of persons convicted for index crimes and who started crime at 18 years of age was 5.6 years. We must add, however, that this average hides important variations: There

---

[1]Translated by Dorothy R. Crelinsten.

are offenders who start their adult career at 18 and end it in their forties.

These findings would be inconceivable if desistance from crime were not a frequent occurrence. Offenders give up crime almost as often as they get into it. To die a criminal, one would almost have to die a violent death.

Dropout rates from criminal careers are rather variable. Blumstein and Cohen (1982:38) noted three periods: from 20 to 30 years of age, from 30 to 42 years, and from 43 to 60 years. Between the ages of 20 and 30 the dropout rates are fairly high; they are fairly low between 30 and 42, and from 42 to 60 they become quite high again. The physical wear and tear, it seems, forces people to retire.

We know that most offenders give up crime eventually. But what else do we know? What makes a person decide to stop committing crimes? What are the reasons behind such a decision? What are the circumstances? The timing? Interviews with ex-offenders are essential if we are to understand the decision-making process that puts an end to a criminal career. Very few researchers have done this, and understandably so. It is not easy to trace, contact, and interview ex-prisoners who have been out of the system for several years. It was only after some difficulty that we succeeded in interviewing a small group of 17 ex-offenders and asking what made them put an end to their criminal activities. These men had all committed armed robbery. They were recidivists. They were between 30 and 40 years of age and had not been arrested during the course of the 5 preceding years. Later we learned that almost all of them had committed their last crime between the ages of 20 and 30.

There are further signs that our interviewees had really given up crime. First, before the interview, we told our subjects that the topic would be the abandonment of crime; second, what they told us of their present life convinced us that they had actually given up crime. A detailed description of the methodology and of the data has been published elsewhere (Pinsonneault, 1984).

Our findings are mainly based on the statements of these men. However, to complete this source, which we must admit is far from being comprehensive, we have consulted a number of autobiographies written by ex-offenders. We also refer to a few studies on the subject.

Shock

The decision to give up crime is generally triggered by a shock of some sort, by a delayed deterrence process, or both (see Figure 5.1). Conwell's remark in *The Professional Thief* is still valid: "It is generally necessary for the thief to suffer some shock or jolt before he will face the future seriously" (Sutherland, 1937: 182).

It was often during the commission of their last crime that our subjects

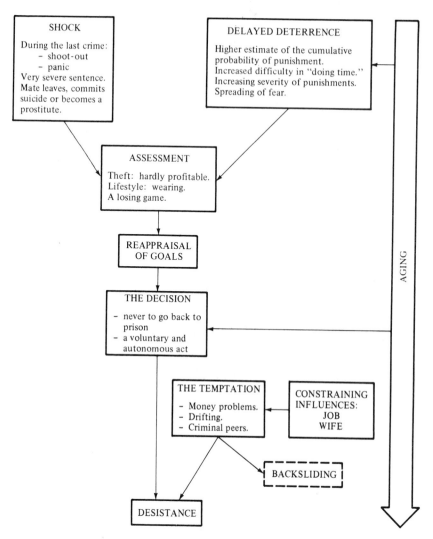

FIGURE 5.1. The decision-making process in desistance from crime.

suffered this shock. One of them was wounded by the police during a shoot-out as he was leaving a bank. Another saw his partner killed by police bullets. A third told us that his accomplice had tried to kill him to get his share of the loot.

It frequently happens, too, that the crime that precedes the decision to stop takes place in a climate of intense fear that culminates in sheer panic. In his autobiography, Malcolm Braly (1976) tells the story of his last attempt at burglary. It is so apt that it is worth citing even though it is a bit long.

I went broke and convinced myself it would be a small risk to take something easy, just enough for food and rent, and I was out in the night, prowling a nursery and garden-supply house, when the lights of a squad car washed over me, and I was sure they had spotted me crouched there in the underbrush. I bolted in an instant panic to run stumbling and frequently falling across a large empty lot, expecting at any moment to see spotlights ahead. I would be snared from the darkness like a terrified rabbit.

The last time I fell I landed in a small stand of underbrush, and crawled deeper into this thin cover to lie gasping with exhaustion. My throat burned with a deep and painful fire and I was far more alarmed at the erratic hammering of my own heart than I was at the possibility I might be questioned by the police.

How grotesque I seemed to myself. The boy who had climbed the sides of buildings with such a reckless heart was gone, and in his place had appeared this middle-aged man who knew only one way to fail. . . .

I decided that night on the boldest move I thought possible and I wrote Knox Burger asking him to loan me the fare to New York, to the Magic City, and this good man telegraphed me the money within an hour of receiving my plea for help. Once more I set off in pursuit of my real life. (Braly, 1976: 372)

Other times, the shock takes the form of a very severe sentence and all that goes with it. The man condemned to a long prison sentence loses not only his freedom; he can also lose someone dear to him. Alone in his cell he learns one day that his wife is unfaithful, that she has become a prostitute, that she has asked for a divorce, or that she has committed suicide. Some of the men we interviewed had in fact lost either a wife or an intimate girlfriend.

A French armed robber who had killed a policeman during a shoot-out was condemned to death and spent 13 months in the death cell before being reprieved. This experience, he writes, made him a different man: "I began to ask myself questions about life, death, the mystery of creation" (Guillo, 1977: 210). A few years later, his wife, who had refused to ask for a divorce, died of cancer, and he was unable to get out of prison to go and see her.

Delayed Deterrence

The men began to see the entire criminal justice system as an apparatus which clumsily but relentlessly swallows offenders and wears then down. (Shover, 1983: 212)

At first glance, multirecidivists are living examples of the ineffectiveness of punishment. Yet there seems to be a relationship between the fear of punishment and the abandoning of crime. Men who for years could not be intimidated despite many severe punishments end by deciding to go straight mainly because they do not want to go back to prison.

Delayed deterrence is the gradual wearing down of the criminal drive caused by the accumulation of punishments. In the long run, the succession of arrests and incarcerations do have their effect. They engender a pervasive fear, which over the years becomes acute and makes acting out more and more difficult.

This delayed deterrence has four components: (a) a higher estimate of the cumulative probability of punishment, (b) the increasing difficulty of "doing time," (c) an awareness of the weight of previous convictions on the severity of the sentences, and (d) a spreading of fear.

Higher Estimate of the Likelihood of Punishment

It is clear that, with age, criminals raise their estimates of the certainty of punishment. They come to terms with the simple fact that the more crimes they commit, the greater the cumulative probability of arrest. This fact is often overlooked; people seem to think that the probability that an offender will be arrested is equal to the probability of being arrested for a single crime. This obviously does not apply to the career criminal. What must be considered in the career criminal's case is the cumulative probability of punishment—that which is calculated on the total number of his or her crimes. Young delinquents generally do not realize that each new crime increases the probability of their being caught. On the other hand, all the ex-convicts that we met agreed that those who commit crimes regularly sooner or later run the risk of finding themselves behind bars. There is a term for this in Canadian penitentiaries: "the law of averages" (also noted by Letkemann, 1973, p.37). As expressed by one of our interviewees, "Every time you commit one, you risk being arrested. The law of averages is against you; the prisons are there to prove it." With age, the criminal comes to the conclusion that theft is a bad risk: "If you steal, you'll find yourself inside fast enough, because the odds are against you. You're known to the cops; you may have more experience, but you're not as quick."

Increasing Difficulty of Prison Life

The ex-offenders that we met were unanimous in acknowledging that, with age, it is more and more difficult to do time. (Maguire, 1982:8, made the same observation that with age the prison seems to be "more painful than in the past.") As they grow older they can no longer stand prison life and the company of other inmates. Even more important, they feel very keenly that they are wasting time and ruining their lives. Braly (1976) experienced this feeling while serving his last sentence. "I had seldom pulled time as hard as this. I had always had my real life to look forward to. Now it seemed it might well be behind me. The waste of this precious time appalled me" (1976:362). Shover (1983:211) likewise said of the men he interviewed, "Most of the men became acutely aware of time as a diminishing exhaustible resource." One of his subjects, speaking of prison, said, "It's just knocking time out of my life!"

Fear of Longer Sentences for Repeat Convictions

We know that the more active a defendant's criminal file, the greater the risk of a long sentence. Criminals know this as well. The majority of our subjects told us that the fear of incurring a long prison term the next time had an influence on their decision to stop.

Increased Fear

Gradually, fear infiltrates every aspect of the criminal's life. The armed robber, once he has the money, is afraid to leave the bank in case the police are waiting outside to shoot him. He lives in daily fear. He feels under constant stress, paranoid: "You're always on edge, on pills." "It's a strange life, too. You're always nervous. Cause there's always something they can pin on you. You never know what's gonna happen. That makes it exciting too, but it gets you after a while" (West, 1978:186).

Assessment

Thus, there comes a time when the recidivist's will to continue in crime is weakened by the corrosive action of delayed deterrence or by a shock of some sort. The offender then enters a period of crisis. Anxious and dissatisfied, he takes stock of his life and his criminal activity (Cormier et al., 1959:40; Shover, 1983:210). The conclusions he arrives at, on the whole, will be (1) that theft does not pay enough considering the risks involved ("Is it worthwhile doing 4 to 5 years for a couple of thousand dollars?")[2] and (2) that the whole criminal way of life has become a problem. The following is a statement made by Maguire (1982):

> The impetus to think seriously about retirement from crime altogether seemed to come in many cases from a gradual disenchantment with the criminal life in its totality: the inability to trust people; the frequent harassment by the police; the effects on wives and children when the offender is in prison. (Maguire, 1982:89)

Our interviewees arrived at a point where their way of life seemed senseless: "I lost my taste for spending $300 to $400 a night just to show

---

[2] Let us say in passing that theft is not judged in moral but in strictly utilitarian terms. Our subjects feel no guilt and do not take the harm caused their victims into consideration when they decide to abandon crime; it is the cost/benefit angle that counts.

off." They also had plenty of problems with their peers: conflicts over women, arguments over the sharing of loot, fights with rival gangs, and the like. Furthermore, it seems that at a certain age there is no longer any desire to associate with disreputable, coarse, untrustworthy, and violent people. "You can't have an intelligent conversation with those people." One comes to see the underworld as a dead end.

It is not hard to understand, then, that by the time they retired from crime, most of our subjects had come to believe that they would always be the losers if they continued along the same path. This feeling of failure was noted by Cormier et al. (1959:44) by Irwin (1970:156), and by Shover (1983:211).

A Reevaluation of Goals

Having made this assessment, the offender tries to envision the future and see what awaits him. What does he see? A long succession of incarcerations that will end only when he is old enough to receive his old-age pension. Or he sees deterioration, alcoholism, and suicide. The prospect of dying in prison seems to him the ultimate failure. "I would probably end in one of the small graveyards that are part of every prison reservation" (Braly, 1976:336; see also Carr, 1975:180, and Shover, 1983:211).

The glimpse of the future, then, forces the criminal to change his course, even if it means giving up his past aspirations. As Herbert Simon (1955:111) observed, the level of aspirations tends to adjust to the realm of possibility. The person who does not succeed in getting what he wants will lower his aspirations. This is somewhat the case for the offender who decides to retire. He decides to give up the affluent life, to do without his Cadillac and be satisfied with a more modest income. (See also Cormier et al, 1959:44; Irwin, 1970:209; Shover, 1983:212.)

The Decision

What does the decision to give up crime mean exactly? Our subjects described it as the decision never to return to prison: "I couldn't say that I would never start again. It could still happen. But I put my life on the line; I don't want to go back inside, I would rather shoot myself." What is essential is to avoid another incarceration. It is not so much a positive decision, the desire to go straight, but a negative one, never to go back to prison.

Furthermore, our subjects stressed the fact that their decision was voluntary and autonomous. They claimed total responsibility and maintained that they alone made the decision to retire: "I didn't go to see anyone else, I decided on my own." "You can't count on others to decide this sort of thing." The decision is not made easily: "To stop, a fellow has to want to get out of it with all his heart." "When a fellow wants to, he can. It's wanting to that's difficult."

Aging

Hirschi and Gottfredson (1983) convincingly made the point that there is a direct connection between age and crime. In the case of those individuals who stop committing crimes at the end of adolescence, one can speak of normal maturation. For those who stop during their thirties, Cormier et al. (1965:10) and the Gluecks (1974:169) put forward the concept of late maturation. There comes a time when the offender acquires the ability and control required to keep him from committing further crimes.

At the point when they gave up their criminal careers, the men we met had the impression of having become more realistic, more prudent, and more mature. Their temporal perspectives were broadened. They had evolved to a point where their life ceased being a matter of drifting into a series of disconnected episodes to become oriented toward the future.

According to these men, the process of maturation that takes place with age was accelerated by a number of experiences, some of which had taken place in prison: the discovery of reading, studying, learning a trade, and so on. Reading had been an important factor in the maturing process for some of our respondents. To alleviate the boredom, they used to read in their cells. This broadened their perspectives and made them think.

Backsliding

In some cases, the ex-offender is tempted to commit new thefts. When this occurs it is often because of money problems. Some of them lose their jobs; others do not regulate their expenditures properly and begin to accumulate debts. Sometimes a new crime is committed when the ex-prisoner is idle, bored, and despondent. Many of our respondents told us they tried to avoid meeting former inmates. One of them had even decided to live in the country in order to avoid all contact with the underworld: "Downtown, it's too easy to start again; you meet fellows from the former gang: 'Want to do a job that pays real money?' "

Women and Jobs

Concerning the influence of women, there is no connection between marriage in itself and desistance (West, 1982:101–104). It is rather the type of woman involved. Some of our respondent's wives were real Penelopes, waiting faithfully for their husbands throughout all the years of their imprisonment. We were struck by the fact that certain men, at the time they gave up, were looking for a woman whom they described as "responsible." They wanted to marry someone serious enough and strong enough to prevent them from getting into trouble. Moreover, some of these men had found what they were looking for. They had married rather authoritarian women who assumed a large part of the responsibility for the family. In one case the ex-prisoner had married a woman with children of her own. This suited him perfectly because he said, "Having children makes a person more responsible."

We are still slightly perplexed with regard to the connection between having a job and giving up crime. Our respondents did not broach the subject, but when we asked them, the large majority of them told us that they had an interesting job and that it played a role in the decision to put an end to their dubious activities. Clearly, it appears that having an interesting and fairly well-paid job helps a person considerably to persevere in obeying the law. Our interviewees discovered that work is a better solution than crime. "Honest work pays more than stealing TV's worth $800 and selling them for $200. On the other hand, you get fewer "vacations.""

The same thing can very likely be said about the family as about employment. Neither has an important role in the decision to stop, but they help the ex-offender a great deal in his effort to resist the temptation to commit new crimes. An interesting job and satisfying family ties give meaning to life and provide an incentive for respecting the law. One avoids acting out in order to keep one's family and one's job.

Conclusion

It is somewhat paradoxical that in this analysis we rediscover some key concepts in criminology: aging, deterrence, the bond, differential association. The study of the abandonment of crime calls for recapitulation of the genesis of criminal habits in reverse. Like rolling a film backward, we see the aging offender take the threat of punishment seriously, reestablish his links with society, and sever his association with the underworld.

Considering the narrow confines of our empirical data, it is scarcely necessary to point out that this analysis is rather speculative. To our knowledge there is not one quantitative research study on the reasons for desistance. By contrast, studies on the origins of crime number in the hundreds. We should take cognizance of our ignorance of a question that, after all, has both theoretical and practical importance. Any assistance offered an adolescent enjoying the full glory of delinquency is bound to fail. Its chance of being accepted would be much greater at the point where the adult offender is already considering retirement. In the latter case, we are not fighting against the odds. A burglar Maguire (1982) interviewed gave evidence of this:

A 34-year-old man bitterly pointed out the ironical fact that, when younger, he had been given probation or other "rehabilitative" sentences, but having no wish to end his criminal career, he treated them as a joke. Now, when he was thinking more seriously of retiring from crime, he was "written off" by the penal system as a habitual criminal and "automatically" given prison sentences for relatively minor offences, receiving no help or encouragement from anybody. (Maguire, 1982:89)

Obviously, the decision we have described here is not the only one. Our analysis refers to the man deeply involved in crime who, around the age of 30, finds the strength and resources to change his way of life. There could be other eventualities—that of the occasional offender who drifts effortlessly out of crime just as he drifted into it; that of the burglar who, after a succession of misadventures while doing jobs, becomes disgusted and quits (Clark and Cornish, 1985); that of the aging recidivist, tired and worn out, who nearing his fifties, gives up and gradually deteriorates; that of the author of a crime of passion—in which case the question of abandonment does not arise, for such a tragic event can hardly become a habit.

It has become quite fashionable lately to do research on criminal careers, and it is encouraging to see a rediscovery of the fact that crime does have a temporal dimension. This means that there is a story to tell about criminal lives. A good part of these stories are bound to be sad, portraying the struggle of losers. The criminal scene does have some positive sides, however. As we saw, it happens more often than not that these stories have a happy ending.

References

Blumstein, A. and J. Cohen
   1982   The Duration of Adult Criminal Careers. Final report to the National Institute of Justice, Pittsburgh.
Braly, Malcolm
   1976   False Starts: A Memoir of San Quentin and Other Prisons. Boston: Little, Brown.
Carr, James
   1975   Bad, The Autobiography of James Carr. New York: Dell.
Clarke, Ronald V. and Derek B. Cornish
   1985   "Modelling offenders' decisions: a framework for research and policy." Pp. 147–185 in M. Tonry and N. Morris (eds.), Crime and Justice, Volume 6. Chicago: University of Chicago Press.

Cormier, B.M., M. Kennedy, J. Sangovicz and M. Trottier
   1959   "The natural history of criminality and some tentative hypotheses on its
          abatement." The Canadian Journal of Correction 1(4):35–49.
Cormier, B.M., M. Kennedy, J.M. Sangovicz, R. Boyer, A.L. Thiffault and A.
Obert
   1965   "Criminal process and emotional growth." Pp. 3–41 in E. Cameron (ed.),
          Forensic Psychiatry and Child Psychiatry. Boston: Little, Brown.
Glueck, Sheldon and Eleanor Glueck
   1937   Later Criminal Careers. New York: The Commonwealth Fund.
   1974   Of Delinquency and Crime. Springfield, IL: Charles C Thomas.
Guillo, F.
   1977   Le p'tit Francis. Paris: R. Laffont.
Hirschi, T. and M. Gottfredson
   1983   "Age and the explanation of crime." American Journal of Sociology
          89(3):552–84.
Irwin, J.
   1970   The Felon. Englewood Cliffs, NJ: Prentice-Hall.
Letkemann, P.
   1973   Crime as Work. Englewood Cliffs, NJ: Prentice-Hall.
Maguire, M.
   1982   Burglary in a Dwelling. London: Heinemann.
Pinsonneault, P.
   1984   L'abandon de la carrière criminelle. Montreal: Centre International de
          Criminologie Comparée, University of Montreal.
Shover, N.
   1983   "The later stages of ordinary property offender careers." Social Problems
          31(2):209–18.
Simon, H.A.
   1955   "A behavioral model of rational choice." Quarterly Journal of Eco-
          nomics 69:99–118.
Sutherland, E.H.
   1937   The Professional Thief. Chicago: University of Chicago Press.
West, D.
   1982   Delinquency: Its Roots, Careers and Prospects. London: Heinemann.
West, W.G.
   1978   "The short-term careers of serious thieves." Canadian Journal of
          Criminology 20(2):169–90.

6
A Decision-Making Approach to Opioid Addiction

Trevor Bennett

Editors' Note

Too few rational choice analyses of crime have dealt with other than such predatory offenses as shoplifting, burglary, and robbery. As these are among the most obviously "rational" crimes, this has meant that the more general utility of rational choice explanations is still in question. For this reason Trevor Bennett's discussion of opioid use is especially welcome, the more so because he concludes that a rational choice perspective provides a useful way of ordering and understanding the relevant empirical data. On the basis of his review of the literature and his own interviews with 135 opioid users, he argues that offender choices and decisions govern in important ways the initiation into opioid use, its continuation, and its cessation. Among his conclusions are that opioid users frequently decide to try drugs at some point prior to the first usage, that this decision may reflect a conscious desire to become part of the "drug scene," and that active recruitment by professional "pushers" may be largely a myth, most initial experimentation being the result of mild encouragement from friends. Bennett's data suggest that it usually takes more than a year to become addicted and that, even when addicted, the opioid user is frequently able to control his or her habit. Some addicts come off the drugs for days, weeks, or even years; others avoid using opioids when this conflicts with other leisure or work goals; and many take opioids for the positive benefits conferred (a sense of well-being, confidence, etc.). Cessation, too, seems to be a much more frequent occurrence than the popular view of addiction would suggest. Situational factors such as a change of job or abode sometimes play a part, but some addicts also appear to tire of the life (echoes here of Cusson and Pinsonneault's findings about desistance from robbery). In short, Bennett's analysis suggests that users are much more in control of their lives than the conventional picture of the addict as a socially deprived or psychologically damaged individual tends to imply. He concludes by speculating on the possible link between a changing view of the addict— now viewed increasingly as at least partially responsible for his or her actions—and a changing official response to addiction which, in Britain at least, has recently become more punitive. It would be interesting to see whether the focusing of such rational choice analyses on other specific (i.e., named) forms of drug abuse and their extension where relevant to the elucidation of the circumstances surrounding drug-taking "events"— that is, the acquisition and/or consumption of specific drugs—would provide data that might inform control policies still further.

Recent developments in a number of academic disciplines suggest that it is profitable to explain human behavior in terms of rationality and choice. Traditional theories based on the positivist precepts of pathology and disposition are seen as offering inadequate or only partial explanations of the way in which people behave. Examples of explanations based on rationality and choice can be found in psychology in studies of decision making and risk assessment (Slovic, 1972), in sociology in phenomenological and radical approaches to deviance (Cicourel, 1968; Quinney, 1970), in economics in studies of subjective evaluation (Witte, 1980), and in criminology in the situational approach to criminal behavior and crime prevention (Clarke, 1980). In each of these disciplines the gradual change in perspective from dispositional to rational theorizing has been noted by at least a small number of commentators. A similar shift in perspective has occurred in the study of drug abuse and addiction, although this development has not received as much attention.

Before examining these developments it is necessary to identify the nature of the explanations characteristic of the rational choice perspective. The key concepts of this approach are "rationality," "decision making," and "choice." Rationality conveys reason, meaning, and calculation. Williamson, for example, explains delinquency as the result of "a rational assessment of its benefits and drawbacks" (1978:333). Decision making refers to judgment and the cognitive processes that determine action. Clarke and Cornish have described decision making as "the conscious thought processes that give purpose to and justify conduct, and the underlying cognitive mechanisms by which information about the world is selected, attended to, and processed" (1985:147). Choice refers to freedom of action, discrimination, and self-determination, as revealed in the observation by Clarke that people "are usually aware of consciously choosing to commit offences" (1980:138).

In addition to these three main concepts, the literature on rationality and choice is permeated with other, related notions. In a recent review of the literature, Clarke and Cornish (1985) identified various assumptions on which such explanations are based. Behavior that is viewed as abnormal in positivist accounts is viewed as normal and mundane in accounts that stress rationality. Deviance is viewed as purposive rather than meaningless, intentional rather than compulsive, and episodic and self-limiting rather than continuous and enduring. Deviants are viewed as self-determining, deliberative, and responsible for their actions.

The first part of this paper comprises a selected review of both traditional and recent explanations of drug abuse in an attempt to identify evidence of rationality, decision making, and choice. Many of the theories outlined are of a general nature and apply to all kinds of drug use. Where possible, however, the debate will be confined to the topic of opioid (e.g., opium, heroin, and methadone) use and addiction. The second part presents the findings of a research project based at the Institute of Criminology, Cambridge, England, on patterns of drug taking among opioid users in three English towns. The paper concludes with a discussion on the implications of a rational choice perspective for the control and treatment of addiction.

Searching for Causes: A Look Backward

The majority of explanations relating to drug abuse fall under the heading of a search for causes. By looking backward, such explanations have emphasized the development of dispositions to take drugs. Etiogical explanations of addiction can be divided into two main types: (1) those focusing on individual factors, and (2) those focusing on social factors.

Individual Factors

Most theories of addiction based on individual characteristics derive from the works of psychiatrists and members of the medical profession who have been involved in the treatment of addiction. Consequently, the predisposing cause is often identified as some kind of metabolic or psychological pathology.

The concept of addiction as a metabolic disease is implicit in the early methadone treatment programs (Dole and Nyswander, 1965). It was argued that the reasons for taking the initial doses of heroin might be psychological in nature, but the later craving for heroin is the result of the drug leaving an imprint on the user's nervous system. Some writers have claimed that addicts are deficient in the neurotransmitters that are responsible for generating a feeling of well-being. Heroin or other opioids are used to supplement this deficiency (Martin et al., 1977). Others have argued that addiction can be the result of a hypersensitive nervous system. Sufferers become overwhelmed by the level of stimuli in the environment and experience dysphoria as a result. This discomfort can be eased by blunting their perceptions with soporific drugs (Jonas and Jonas, 1977).

A widely held view of addiction is that it is the result of a psychological weakness or abnormality within the individual. The typical format of this kind of explanation is that some kind of psychological pathology generates a problem in coping with everyday existence which, instead of being solved by conventional means, is solved by the use of drugs. Gold and Coghlan (1976), for example, argued that some people are unable to cope with the conflicts and anxieties of normal life and turn to opioids as a means of reducing this anxiety. Greaves (1974) suggested that addicts have lost their ability to create natural euphoria. Instead of obtaining pleasure from everyday pursuits, they seek a passive euphoria through drug taking. The concepts of automedication and adaptation are central to these accounts. Khantzian (1975), for example, stated that addicts suffer from a maladjusted ego organization and sense of self, and become predisposed to use drugs when they fail to develop effective adaptive solutions to the problems created by this condition.

Few of these accounts move beyond listing personal inadequacies that predispose a person to drug use, and the link between predisposition and use is rarely considered. However, some writers do consider the link. A distinction is sometimes made, for example, between predisposing causes of addiction and precipitating factors. A person might be primed to drug taking by predisposing factors, but might only take drugs in response to particular situational stimuli. Some psychologists have stressed the importance of mediating constructs, for example, which link the predisposition to the act (see Gold and Coghlan, 1976). Nevertheless, such notions are rarely developed in this literature, and the bulk of these accounts focus on factors that affect the development of "addiction-prone" personalities.

The search for factors in users' past histories is not necessarily incompatible with a rational choice approach. It is recognized in this approach that a person's immediate decision making can be shaped by past experiences (see Clarke, 1980). Unfortunately, there is very little evidence that addicts are psychologically any different from nonaddicts. Stevenson et al. (1956) compared a sample of Canadian heroin-dependent prisoners with a sample of non-drug-dependent prisoners of similar social and criminal histories and found that although heroin users were slightly less stable, objective, and purposeful than other prisoners they did not differ significantly in terms of basic personality characteristics. They reported that few heroin-dependent prisoners had any kind of psychiatric disorder and concluded that "addicts are basically ordinary people." Gendreau and Gendreau (1970) compared a sample of Canadian heroin addicts with a control group matched for age, intelligence, socioeconomic status, criminal experience, and opportunity for drug use and found that the two groups did not differ significantly on 12 personality scales. This result led them to reject the concept of the "addiction-prone" personality.

Social Factors

The search for causes among social factors has been conducted mainly by sociologists and social psychologists. Such explanations give greater weight to immediate situational factors but continue to focus on dispositions and pathologies.

A number of theorists have devised explanations of drug abuse based on Merton's concept of anomie (e.g. Misra, 1976; Robins, 1973). Merton (1957) viewed drug dependence as a "retreatist" adaptation to the discrepancy between society's culturally defined goals and the socially prescribed means for achieving those goals. He argued that individuals unable or unwilling to achieve these goals might renounce both the goals and the legitimate means for achieving them and "retreat" or escape through alcoholism, mental illness, vagrancy, or drug addiction.

Social psychological theories of the causes of drug dependence note the relationship between personality variables and interpersonal relations. Chien et al. (1964), for example, observed that juvenile drug abusers were often from less cohesive families, were less likely to have someone to help them with their personal problems, and were subject to disturbed relations between family members. Relationships between family members have been noted as important in the genesis of drug dependence by other writers. Coleman and Davis (1978) drew upon family systems theory to explain the way in which unresolved conflicts within the family can lead to stress. Heroin addiction is a possible method of coping with this stress. Kaplan (1975) argued that some individuals cannot deal with self-rejecting attitudes that occur during group interaction and may turn to drugs as a recourse.

Some sociological and psychological explanations of drug use do include concepts characteristic of the rational choice perspective. Subcultural theorists such as Cloward and Ohlin (1960) contend that the meanings and motives for drug use develop in the context of group membership. Behavior that is defined as pathological by outsiders is defined as normal within the group. Social learning theorists such as Becker (1963) argue that people take drugs only after they have developed a set of ideas and beliefs about drug use and have learned the methods of experiencing their effects in group interaction. Drug-taking groups generate methods of rationalizing and normalizing their behavior and develop an independent culture within which drug taking is learned and made acceptable. Generally, however, sociologists and social psychologists have focused their attention on the process by which people acquire deviant dispositions. Their accounts do include notions of rationality, meaning, and normality, yet little attention is paid to decision making and choice.

Research that has compared addicts and nonaddicts in terms of social variables generally has failed to support the contention that drug users are in any important way socially "different" from nonusers with similar backgrounds. The study by Stevenson et al. (1956) cited earlier found no differences between heroin-using and nonusing prisoners when compared in terms of family life or cultural attitudes and beliefs. In another

Canadian study, Murphy and Shinyei (1976) found no difference between matched drug-dependent delinquents and nondependent non-delinquents in terms of such factors as ethnic background, religious affiliation, father's or mother's education, absence of the father from the family, whether or not the mother worked, or vocational or educational ambitions.

Neither individual nor social theories of the causes of drug use offer wholly satisfactory explanations for the phenomenon of drug use. Without additional knowledge about the ways in which predispositions are converted into drug taking, such explanations are of limited value.

Understanding Drug-Taking Careers: A Look Forward

Over the last two decades an alternative approach has emerged which focuses on the developmental process of addiction. Greater explanatory weight is given to the role of immediate situational factors in the development of addiction and to the individual's perceptions, beliefs, and decision making. The approach centers on the concept of the drug-taking "career."

The concept of a deviant career was popularized in the early 1960s by Becker (1963). According to Becker, a deviant career is characterized by a series of clearly defined stages or statuses through which individuals must pass if they are to progress through the career structure. A deviant career is similar to an occupational career in that members are able to understand their progression from one stage to another and share a perspective, influenced by the routinized methods of solving problems relating to their occupation, which gives meaning to their actions. Movement from one position to another in the career structure is not inevitable but dependent upon various career contingencies such as individual motivation and the influence of situational factors.

Since Becker's work, considerable interest has been shown in the concept of drug taking as a deviant career. Over the last decade or so research has focused on the three stages that have been identified as key points in the development of such a career: initiation, continuation, and cessation. An important product of this research is a major shift in perspective from conceiving of the drug taker as determined and pathological to one who is self-determining and (within the context of the drug-taking group) rational and essentially normal.

Initiation

Escalation or "stepping-stone" theories are based on the assumption that initial opioid use is preceded by, and to some extent the result of, an earlier progression through a range of "soft" drugs. It was widely believed in the United States, for example, that the apparent increase in heroin use after the Second World War was a product of marijuana use leading to a craving for "hard" drugs (see the Final Report of the Commission of Inquiry into the Non-Medical Use of Drugs, 1973). The introduction of new drugs of abuse during the 1960s helped broaden the notion that experimentation with one drug inevitably led to experimentation with others. Various arguments were presented at the time to explain the stepping-stone phenomenon. One of the most common was that the initial excitement produced by a drug eventually wore off, and as a result of tolerance or boredom users searched for more powerful substitutes.

There is little support for the escalation hypothesis in the findings of research. Although it is acknowledged that many opioid users take other drugs, relatively few cannabis or other soft-drug users ever consume opioids. A study by Plant (1975), for example, found that only 15% of a sample of 200 cannabis users had ever consumed heroin or other pharmaceutical opioids. Although the majority of the users had consumed other drugs, there was little evidence of escalation. In fact, the evidence pointed to de-escalation. Initial periods of experimentation with a wide range of drugs typically were followed by longer periods of specialization in just one or a small number of nonopioid drugs.

The belief that most or many addicts are pressured into taking their first opioid by pushers keen to expand their outlets is not supported by the research. Studies focusing on the initiation of opioid use have stressed the importance of group interaction. There is almost complete agreement among studies that opioid use is typically initiated in the company of friends. Chambers et al. (1968) found that 89% of a sample of 155 black addicts treated at the Public Health Service Hospital in Lexington, Kentucky were introduced to heroin by a peer. Stephens and McBride (1976) discovered that three quarters of their sample had been initiated to opioid use by friends or groups with whom the individual identified.

Social groups are also believed to be important in the development of a range of values, attitudes, beliefs, and justifications supportive of drug taking. Such a view dismisses the pathological nature of initiation by placing it in the context of the social setting. The Commission of Inquiry into the Non-Medical Use of Drugs, for example, argued, "Once one is open to a drug experience, however, his actual use of the drug is more likely to occur in an aleatory—although natural—rather than deliberate fashion" (1973:710). Sadava (1969) similarly pointed to the naturalness of the process once it is placed in context: " . . . drug using behavior . . . is not [usually] a sudden dramatic change in the individual's life and values, but develops as a natural, i.e. not surprising, process within the sociocultural context" (quoted in the Final Report of the Commission of Inquiry into the Non-Medical Use of Drugs, 1973:710). A sense of rationality and normality in first opioid use is also apparent in the explanations that the users themselves give. Studies based on interviews with drug takers almost always cite curiosity as the main reason for first drug or first opioid use (Craig and Brown, 1975; Plant, 1975; Brown et al., 1971). Another frequently noted reason is influence of friends. Elaborations of this usually reveal that the individual was a willing participant in a situation where opioids or other drugs were available.

There is one important exception to the general finding that first opioid use typically occurs in the company of other users. Members of the medical profession who have access to opioid drugs and who are familiar with their properties occasionally self-prescribe. A study by Winick (1962) of 98 physician-addicts found that not one of them had been introduced to opioids directly by others. In this case, however, the individuals had acquired a substantial body of knowledge about the effects of these drugs in much the same way as nontherapeutic users acquire knowledge through interaction with addicts.

The findings of research based on both individuals who had learned the benefits of opioid use through social group interaction and members of the medical profession who had learned about their benefits through their medical practice strongly suggest that the decision to consume the first opioid, whether for self-medication or for recreational purposes, is a product of individual choice. There is little evidence of compulsion, irrationality (in the context of the user's social group culture), or mindlessness in the decision to take the drug.

Continuation

Much of the literature on the continuation of opioid use provides evidence supportive of the rational choice perspective. In this section are listed some of the areas of thinking and research on the development of opioid addiction that lend support to the principles of this approach.

First, opioid users do not progress from first use to regular use very rapidly. A study by Gardner and Connell (1971) found that approximately half of a group of users attending a drug dependency clinic in London, England, took over a year to become addicted, and almost one fifth of them took 2 years or more. Accounts from addicts suggest that addiction can be a slow process. The time taken to become addicted was described by Burroughs:

It takes at least three months shooting twice a day to get any habit at all. It took me almost six months to get my first habit and then the withdrawal symptoms were mild. I think it no exaggeration to say it takes about a year and several hundred injections to make an addict. (1969:11)

Second, progression from occasional use to regular use is not inevitable. The argument that the opioid drugs are so powerfully addictive that once tried the user will inevitably become addicted, as exemplified in the title of a book by Smith and Gay (1972), *It's So Good,*

Don't Even Try It Once, is given little support in the research literature. Many individuals choose to remain at the level of occasional use. Robins (1973), in a study of United States servicemen returning from Vietnam, revealed that 35% had tried heroin while in Vietnam and 19% had become addicted. Two years later the men were reinterviewed. Only 8% had used heroin during the 2-year period, and fewer than 2% had used it on a daily basis. Blackwell (1983) found in a study of 51 opioid users that one third of the sample were in a state of "drift" and were not committed to opioid use.

Third, not all users who progress from occasional to regular use continue to use drugs regularly. Many addicts periodically abstain from drug use for periods ranging from a few days to years. Stimson and Oppenheimer (1982), in their study of a representative sample of addicts attending a drug dependency clinic in London, found that over two thirds had abstained for a period of 1 week or more since they became addicted. Over half of the group had abstained for at least one period of 9 weeks or longer. In a study of 422 addicts in treatment facilities in New York City, Waldorf (1976) found that 40% had voluntarily abstained from heroin for 3 months or longer and 21% for 8 months or longer. DeFleur et al. (1969) estimated that addicts are voluntarily abstinent for approximately one fifth of the time that they are addicted.

Fourth, there is evidence of controlled drug use. Many addicts refrain from consuming opioids every day in order to reduce costs or to control their level of tolerance and addiction. Johnson et al. (1979) studied the economic behavior of heroin addicts and reported that most heroin users did not take heroin every day. In addition, he found considerable variation in daily dosages. He concluded:

The concepts of physical dependence, tolerance, and habit size were not particularly useful in helping to understand the varied patterns of daily use. These terms . . . imply a degree of stability in daily use or steady escalation in heroin dosage that is not present in the case histories of these research subjects. (1979:24–25)

Fifth, addicts' reasons for continuing to consume opioids after the initial experimentation show that there is a purpose in their actions beyond combating the immediate effects of withdrawal. Chien et al. (1964) reported that addicts gave as their reasons for continued heroin use a desire to maintain social poise and to ease social interactions. Addicts' accounts of their reasons for continuing to take opioids refer to self-medication. Stimson and Oppenheimer (1982) reported that some of the addicts they interviewed claimed that they used heroin as a way of coping with depression or anxiety.

Dispositional theories are ill equipped to explain the kinds of variations in drug use described above. A satisfactory explanation of opioid addiction must make such variations comprehensible. The literature on the continuation of opioid use takes some steps in this direction by acknowledging that individuals are capable of rationally choosing to pursue such life-styles. Explanations of addiction need to account, however, not only for initiation and continuation, but also for the cessation of drug use.

Cessation

Theories that identify biological, psychological, or social pathologies as the cause of opioid addiction have difficulty in explaining why some addicts cease drug use. The belief that "once an addict always an addict" was challenged by Winick (1962), who popularized the concept of "maturing out" of addiction, a concept previously confined to the study of criminal behavior and associated in particular with the work of Glueck and Glueck (1940). Winick's study was based on an analysis of data compiled by the Federal Bureau of Narcotics on 7,234 addicts who had not used narcotics for at least 5 years. He found that the average length of the period of addiction was 8.6 years. The later the age of onset of narcotic use, the shorter the total period of addiction. The average period for users who commenced after the age of 50 rarely exceeded 5 years.

Winick presented independent confirmation of the limited nature of addiction in a study of addicts released from the U.S. Public Health Service Hospital in Lexington, Kentucky. Almost two thirds of the group aged over 30 years remained abstinent for at least 5 years following release. Other research findings have lent support to this contention. A study by Thorley et al. (1977) found that about one third of a group of 128 British heroin addicts had remained abstinent for 7 years following treatment in a drug dependency clinic. The study cited earlier by Robins (1973) of Vietnam returnees showed that only about one tenth of those who were previously addicted to heroin continued to use the drug during the 3-year period following their return.

There are obvious methodological problems associated with follow-up studies. It can never be certain that addicts did refrain from use for the entire follow-up period. Winick argues, however, that it is unlikely that regular users of narcotics can avoid eventually coming to the attention of the authorities. It also can never be certain that former addicts will not return to drug use at some later date. Nevertheless, the findings of follow-up and longitudinal research show that addicts can cease opioid use for long periods of time. There is no evidence, therefore, that once hooked, users are determined to live out their lives as addicts.

Why do addicts cease taking drugs? One of the most popular types of explanation of cessation of opioid use stresses the importance of changes in immediate situational factors that directly affect the individual. The Commission of Inquiry into the Non-Medical Use of Drugs, for example, noted from a review of the evidence on opioid use that, "Termination or reduction of drug use may thus occur with graduation from school, change of residence or neighbourhood, a new job, marriage, parenthood or a number of events in the life of an individual" (1973:739). Other studies have identified such factors as finding satisfactory employment (Bowden and Langenauer, 1972) and feeling a sense of responsibility for family members (Haslem, 1964). Brown et al. (1971) asked addicts attending treatment facilities in the District of Columbia why they currently wished to come off drugs. The main reason given was an "effort to change life pattern." In particular they mentioned a desire to improve family relations. The Commission of Inquiry into the Non-Medical Use of Drugs provided further examples of situational factors that can influence the user's decision to continue taking opioids:

In some cases, abstinence will be initiated or sustained for personal reasons or because of chance factors. In one case, a fifty-pound weight gain was the reason given for not returning to heroin. Another individual was motivated to stop after his daughter was killed in a fire which he accidentally started while under the influence of heroin. (1973:744)

Winick's concept of maturing out suggests that addiction might be a self-limiting process. Individuals simply tire or grow out of the desire to take drugs. Waldorf (1976) offered some support for this hypothesis. He found that the strongest predictors of voluntary abstinence were age and number of years addicted.

Other explanations stress the importance of individual experiences and psychological reassessment. Ray (1961) discussed the role of "socially disjunctive experiences," which might precipitate abstinence. Decision making and freedom of choice characterize this process. Interactions with others might initiate "private self-debate in which he [the addict] juxtaposes the values and social relationships which have become immediate and concrete through his addiction with those that are sometimes only half remembered or only imperfectly perceived" (Ray, 1961:134). It has also been argued that addicts eventually refrain because the drawbacks of leading a life of addiction begin to outweigh the advantages. Gandossy et al. (1980) suggest that getting "ripped off" once too often by other users may encourage some addicts to reassess their life-style. Through these negative interactions with other members of the drug-taking group, the world of addiction may be called into question.

The Cambridge Study of Opioid Users

Between 1982 and 1984 six different samples of opioid addicts were interviewed as part of a study conducted at the Institute of Criminology, Cambridge, England, on users' choice of supply of drugs. One aim of this research was to investigate retrospectively the development of individual drug-taking careers. It must be stressed that the study was not designed primarily to examine careers, and the methods used were governed by the broader aims of the research. Nevertheless, the findings are relevant to this discussion and throw some light on the issue of rationality in drug taking.

Methods and Samples

One requirement of the study was that it should include the investigation of addicts using different sources of supply. In particular, it was necessary to select addicts currently receiving a prescription from a National Health Service (NHS) clinic, a general practitioner, a private practitioner and users who were currently dependent solely on black-market supplies. The final samples included two groups of addicts attending NHS clinics in Cambridge and Bristol ($n = 36$ and $n = 12$, respectively), one group receiving a prescription from a general practitioner in Bristol ($n = 11$), one group receiving a prescription from a private doctor in London ($n = 40$), and two groups dependent on black-market supplies only in Cambridge and Bristol ($n = 15$ and $n = 21$, respectively).

The main method used in the research was a combined structured and semistructured interview. Structured questioning involved reading questions directly from an interview schedule and writing the answers down by hand. Semistructured questioning involved extended conversations with the addicts to clarify the questions and discuss the answers. When this method was used the replies were tape recorded and later transcribed verbatim.

Results

The results can be broken down according to the three key stages of a drug-taking career: initiation, continuation, and cessation.

The majority of addicts in each of the six groups reported that they commenced drug taking with a nonopioid, usually cannabis or an amphetamine. Almost all had consumed at least one nonopioid before their first opioid, and the majority had experimented with three or more types of drug. Most of the addicts, therefore, had substantial experience in drug taking before they commenced opioid use.

One common belief, promulgated by the press in particular, is that individuals are pressured into using opioids by pushers bent on creating new sales outlets. The majority of four of the groups and a substantial minority of the remaining two reported that they obtained their first opioids from a friend. In many cases, this was a boyfriend or girlfriend. Most of the remainder said that they were introduced to opioids by an acquaintance (someone previously known to the user, but not considered a friend). Fewer than 10% of the total number of 135 addicts said that they obtained their first opioid from a stranger.

Only six addicts reported that they were in any sense pressured into taking their first opioid. In most cases, the source of the pressure was a boyfriend or girlfriend, and the nature of the pressure related to a sense of loyalty rather than to a fear of the consequences of refusal. Most of the addicts consumed their first opioid under conditions that could be described as congenial and free from pressure.

Approximately half of two groups of addicts and one third of the remaining four groups reported that the decision to try an opioid was made some time before they actually took one. Typically, the user explained that he or she had made a conscious decision to take opioids and had waited for, or sought out, an opportunity to do so. Although the decision was made more firmly and more consciously in some cases than in others, it was clear that a large proportion of the users had deliberated on the possibility of taking opioids some time before they actually took one:

I'd heard about heroin for as long as I could remember. I wanted to try it. I knew I'd take it, but I didn't know when. I took it at the first opportunity.

The most common reason given for first taking an opioid was curiosity. As noted earlier, this is almost a universal finding of research investigating reasons for initial drug use. The second most common reason was "to follow friends." Elaborations of this were various: Some users sought to become more integrated into their group, some wished to share the drug-taking experiences of their friends, and others sought to become involved in the addict life-style. It is interesting that some users admitted that, at the time of taking their first opioid, they wanted to become addicted in order to become part of the addict world:

Drugs fascinated me from an early age, especially the junkie culture. Let's put it this way: I wasn't worried about becoming an addict, I wanted to become one.

The process of becoming addicted was generally a slow one. The majority of addicts in all six groups said that it took in excess of 1 year for them to become addicted. Similarly, most of them reported that it took over a year to progress from first use to daily use. Between one third and one half of the addicts in each sample said that the gap between first use and perceived signs of addiction was in excess of 3 years. Many users claimed that they had long gaps without taking opioids between first use and addiction, whereas others described long periods of occasional use. There was little evidence in their accounts of compulsion or inevitability in the early stages of their opioid-using career. One user commented, "For the first three years I was only doing it once or twice a week and even then I only used a little bit."

Once users had reached the point of daily use the consumption of the drug became more regular. Nevertheless, many of them reported periods of abstinence lasting months or years. One addict reported that he usually gave up opioids during the summer months so that he could pursue his favorite sports. During the winter months he injected heroin on a daily basis. Other addicts spoke of a number of 1 or 2 year breaks during 10 or 15 year careers of regular opioid use. Such variations are not typical, but they suggest that users can control their drug taking even when they are ostensibly addicted:

I usually use every day for a couple of months and then I start cutting down. I have occasions when I dry myself out for three or four months. I don't want my habit to get too big.

Shorter term variations in opioid use were also apparent. All interviewees were asked to describe in detail their total drug use for the week before the interview. Between 30% and 90% of addicts who were receiving a daily prescription for heroin or methadone said that they refrained from using their prescription on at least one day. Between 25% and 55% reported that they refrained from taking any opioid at all (either prescribed or black-market drugs).

There was also evidence of daily variation in the amount consumed. Over the opioid-using days of the week prior to the interview the difference between the lowest and highest dosage exceeded 100% in about one half of the addicts. Between 10% and 40% of addicts reported a 300% variation in their daily consumption. The main reason given by addicts for varying dosages was that their need for opioids varied throughout the week. Addicts' needs included the desire to get high, the desire to perform well in specific social situations (e.g., attending the clinic), and the desire to treat particular psychological problems (e.g., depression or anxiety). As one interviewee put it, "I like a little high at the weekend. I like to have a couple of good days. I wouldn't get anything out of it otherwise."

When asked about their reasons for continuing to take opioids beyond the period of initial experimentation, very few addicts said that they did so solely to avoid the pains of withdrawal. As suggested earlier, many addicts voluntarily abstained for periods of 1 or more days and were used to experiencing the pains of withdrawal (which, incidentally, were rarely described as being any more unpleasant than a bad case of flu). Their reasons for continuing were generally more positive and purposeful than this. The most common reason given for continuing to use drugs was that they "liked them." Examples of this response were, "It's like being wrapped in an electric blanket," and "It makes me feel secure and confident." Other common reasons concerned self-medication and "to follow friends." The symbolic meaning of drug taking and the world of opioid use was an important motivating factor for many of these addicts.

All of the addicts interviewed were current users and by definition had not permanently abstained from opioid use. Nevertheless, they were all asked whether they would eventually cease, and if so, under what conditions. Of those who answered the question about half said that they did not want to abstain permanently and foresaw a lifetime of addiction. They argued that their lives were generally better on opioids, and they were comfortable with the prospect of continued addiction. The other half said that they would either conditionally or unconditionally cease within the next 10 years. Those who said that their decision was conditional most frequently cited entering into a stable relationship as the conditional factor: "I'm going to stop soon. I'm about to get married and I want to stop for my wife's sake." Others said that they would give up opioids if they or their social group moved out of the area. Another common condition, mentioned by the majority of the female respondents, was whether or not they became pregnant. There was little evidence of compulsion in addicts' accounts. In most cases the reasons given for continuing or refraining from opioid use suggested self-determination and individual control over their drug-taking behavior.

Summary and Discussion

It was suggested earlier that writings associated with the rational choice perspective are permeated with notions of purposiveness, meaning, planning, control, self-determination, deliberation, normality, mundanity, order, intentionality, and individual responsibility. A great deal of the recent literature on opioid addiction is also permeated with such notions. In addition, a great deal of research on drug-taking careers has provided evidence supportive of the key assumptions underlying the rational choice approach.

Our own research findings showed that users often consciously decided to begin taking opioids before they had an opportunity to do so. There was little evidence of coercion in arriving at this decision, as most users first took opioids when offered one by a friend. Within the social context of the drug subculture, the decision to try an opioid had both meaning and purpose. The reasons given for doing so were no different from those given by others to account for many kinds of nondeviant behavior. There was little evidence of compulsion or inevitability in the development from first use to addiction. The process was characterized by intentionality as the individual moved between periods on and off drugs and between periods of occasional and regular use. There was evidence of control in the variable nature of drug consumption when the user was addicted. Daily consumption was often variable, and addicts often voluntarily abstained for 1 or more days to manage their pattern of consumption. There was also evidence that, for some individuals, both their becoming addicted and their abstaining from addiction were intentional and planned. Permanently ceasing opioid use often had less to do with successful withdrawal—which addicts achieved on a regular basis during their periods of voluntary abstinence—than with complementary changes in their life-style which made nonaddiction both feasible and desirable.

There is much to be gained from a greater awareness of elements of rationality and choice in the development of addiction. Earlier theories, which stressed individual or social pathology and the compulsive and deterministic nature of drug use, offered only a partial and limited picture of the phenomenon of opioid use. Such explanations cannot account satisfactorily for variations in drug use, temporary and permanent abstinence, choice of drug, variations in dosages, the meaning of drug use, and the fact that some people predisposed to addiction never take drugs. A broader, more helpful theory of drug use and addiction would need to take note of individual perceptions and decision making.

Explanations based on the rational choice perspective are still in their infancy, and their application to drug abuse will necessarily be slow and tentative. However, the development of a career approach to addiction has provided a framework on which a rational choice approach might be built. It would seem unwise to attempt to generate a grand theory of addiction to explain all things. There are certain benefits to be gained from developing what Clarke and Cornish (1985) call "good enough" explanations. These may not be comprehensive or exhaustive, but they may provide a useful starting point from which to build a body of knowledge. A similar line of thinking can be found among the proponents of grounded theory (Glaser and Strauss, 1967). Working hypotheses can be used to give direction to research until evidence is found that refutes them. New working hypotheses can then be formulated to take account of the evidence and to give direction, once again, to research.

A Final Comment

Contemporary images of addicts, like contemporary images of criminals, play some role in shaping control policy. In Britain the image of the addict for most of this century has been one of someone who is suffering from a disease. Not surprisingly the official response has been to deal with addiction as a medical problem. This image remains, and recent policy has focused on medical treatment and control. In 1965, for example, a Ministry of Health Interdepartmental Committee (the Brain Committee) published a report reaffirming the existing belief that drug addiction was a medical problem: "[T]he addict should be regarded as a sick person, he should be treated as such and not as a criminal, provided he does not resort to criminal acts" (Interdepartmental Committee on Drug Addiction, 1965:8). Three main recommendations were made which formed the basis of the 1971 Misuse of Drugs Act and which shaped the treatment and control of addiction in Britain for the next decade. First, prescribing of heroin and cocaine was limited to a small number of licensed doctors as a means of controlling the availability of legally prescribed opioids. Second, specialized drug treatment centers were established and staffed by licensed doctors who were permitted to prescribe opioids to addicts (if necessary, indefinitely). It was hoped that competitive prescribing would not only undercut the black market but also attract addicts and draw them into the official net. Third, a system of notification of addicts was developed. It was argued that the notification of addiction was similar to the notification of infectious diseases under the Public Health Act: "We think the analogy to addiction is apt, for addiction is after all a socially infectious condition and its notification offers a means for epidemiological assessment and control" (Inter-departmental Committee on Drug Addiction, 1965:8).

Over the last few years there has been a marked shift in medical and governmental policy toward addiction. During the latter half of the 1970s the consultants in charge of the London drug treatment centers came to an agreement that they were not prepared to prescribe injectables or to prescribe opioids indefinitely to users as a means of controlling addiction. Most addicts attending these clinics are now offered short-term, reducing dosages of oral methadone for the purposes of withdrawal only. A recent publication outlining the government's long-term strategy on drug abuse, titled *Tackling Drug Misuse* (Home Office, 1985), places a new emphasis on the courts and the police in controlling addiction.

The treatment and rehabilitation of criminals is compatible with a conception of the offender as someone predetermined to act in an illegal way as a result of acquiring a disposition to offend. The treatment and rehabilitation of addicts is compatible with an image of the addict as someone who is suffering from an illness. It cannot be claimed that academic or popular conceptions of either criminals or addicts actually determine policy. Nevertheless, such conceptions are certainly drawn upon to account for and justify policies. The view of the criminal as a calculating individual who will weigh up the costs and rewards of crime has been used to justify deterrent and retributivist policies on crime. It is possible that a similar shift in perspective in relation to addiction could see a move further away from "medicalization" toward greater use of the police and the courts as a compatible control response in dealing with addiction.

References

Becker, H.S.
  1963 Outsiders: Studies in the Sociology of Deviance. London: Collier-Macmillan.

Blackwell, J.S.
  1983 "Drifting, controlling and overcoming: opiate users who avoid becoming chronically dependent." Journal of Drug Issues 13:219–35.
Bowden, C.L. and B.J. Langenauer
  1972 "Success and failure in the NARA addiction program." American Journal of Psychiatry 128:853–6.
Brown, B.S., A.B. Gauvey, M.B. Meyers and S.D. Stark
  1971 "In their own words: Addicts' reasons for initiating and withdrawing from heroin." International Journal of the Addictions 6:635–45.
Burroughs, W.
  1969 Junkie. London: New English Library.
Chambers, C.D., A.D. Moffett and J.P. Jones
  1968 "Demographic factors associated with negro opiate addiction." International Journal of the Addictions 3:329–43.
Chien, I., D.L. Gerard, R.S. Lee and E. Rosenfeld
  1964 The Road to H: Narcotics, Delinquency, and Social Policy. New York: Basic Books.
Cicourel, A.
  1968 The Social Organization of Juvenile Justice. New York: Wiley.
Clarke, Ronald V.G.
  1980 "Situational crime prevention: theory and practice." British Journal of Criminology 20:136–47.
Clarke, Ronald V.G. and Derek Cornish
  1985 "Modelling offenders' decisions: a framework for research and policy." Pp. 147–85 in M. Tonry and N. Morris (eds.), Crime and Justice: An Annual Review of Research, Volume 6. Chicago: University of Chicago Press.
Cloward, R.A. and L.E. Ohlin
  1960 Delinquency and Opportunity: A Theory of Delinquent Gangs. New York: Free Press.
Coleman, S.B. and D.I. Davis
  1978 "Family therapy and drug abuse: a national survey." Family Process 17:21–9.
Commission of Inquiry into the Non-Medical Use of Drugs
  1973 Final Report. Ottawa: Information Canada.
Craig, S.R. and B.S. Brown
  1975 "Comparison of youthful heroin users and non-users from one urban community". International Journal of the Addictions 10:53–64.
DeFleur, L.B., J.C. Ball and R.W. Snarr
  1969 "The long-term social correlates of opiate addiction." Social Problems 17:225–34.
Dole, V. and M.E. Nyswander
  1965 "Methadone treatment for diacetylmorphine (heroin) addiction." Journal of the American Medical Association 193:646–50.
Gandossy, R.P., J.R. Williams, J. Cohen and H.J. Harwood
  1980 Drugs and Crime: A Survey and Analysis of the Literature. Washington, DC: U.S. Government Printing Office.
Gardner, R. and P.H. Connell
  1971 "Opioid users attending a special drug dependence clinic 1968–1969." Bulletin on Narcotics XXIII:9–15.

Gendreau, P. and L.P. Gendreau
  1970 "The 'addiction-prone' personality: a study of Canadian heroin addicts."
        Canadian Journal of Behavioral Science 2:18-25.
Glaser, B. and A. Strauss
  1967 The Discovery of Grounded Theory: Strategies for Qualitative Research.
        London: Weidenfeld and Nicolson.
Glueck, Sheldon and Eleanor Glueck
  1940 Juvenile Delinquents Grown Up. New York: The Commonwealth
        Fund.
Gold, S.R. and A.J. Coghlan
  1976 "Locus of control and self-esteem among adolescent drug abusers:
        effects of residential treatment." Drug Forum 5:185-91.
Greaves, G.
  1974 "Towards an existential theory of drug dependence." Journal of Nervous
        and Mental Disease 159:263-74.
Haslem, P.
  1964 "The maturing process in addiction." Canadian Journal of Corrections
        6:28-30.
Home Office
  1985 Tackling Drug Misuse: A Summary of the Government's Strategy.
        London: HMSO.
Interdepartmental Committee on Drug Addiction
  1965 Second Report. London: HMSO.
Johnson, B.D., P.J. Goldstein and N.S. Dudraine
  1979 "What is an addict? Theoretical perspectives and empirical patterns
        of opiate use." Paper presented at the meetings of the Society for the
        Study of Social Problems, Boston. Quoted by P.J. Goldstein (p. 81) in
        J.A. Inciardi (ed.), The Drugs–Crime Connection. Beverly Hills, CA:
        Sage.
Jonas, D.F. and A.D. Jonas
  1977 "A bioanthropological overview of addiction." Perspectives in Biology
        and Medicine (Spring): 345-54.
Kaplan, H.B.
  1975 "Increase in self-rejection as an antecedent of deviant responses."
        Journal of Youth and Adolescence 4:281-92.
Khantzian, E.J.
  1975 "The ego, the self and opiate addiction: theoretical and treatment
        considerations." International Review of Psychoanalysis 5:189-98.
Martin, W.R. B.B. Hewett, A.J. Baker and C.A. Haertzen
  1977 "Aspects of the psychopathology and pathophysiology of addiction."
        Drug and Alcohol Dependence 2:185-202.
Merton, R.K.
  1957 Social Theory and Social Structure. Glencoe, IL: Free Press.
Misra, R.K.
  1976 "Drug addiction: problems and prospects." Drug Forum 5:283-288.
Murphy, B.C. and M.J. Shinyei
  1976 "Cons and straights: comparative free behaviour rates of 25 delinquents
        and 25 non-delinquents matched for age and legal occupation in British
        Columbia, Canada." Canadian Journal of Criminology and Corrections
        18:343-61.

Plant, M.A.
  1975   Drugtakers in an English Town. London: Tavistock.
Quinney, R.
  1970   The Social Reality of Crime. Boston: Little, Brown.
Ray, M.B.
  1961   "The cycle of abstinence and relapse among heroin addicts." Social
         Problems 9:132–40.
Robins, L.N.
  1973   The Vietnam Drug User Returns. Washington, DC: U.S. Government
         Printing Office.
Sadava, S.W.
  1969   "The social psychology of non-medical drug use: a review and analysis."
         Unpublished manuscript cited in Commission of Inquiry into the Non-
         Medical Use of Drugs (1973). Final Report. Ottawa: Information
         Canada.
Slovic, P.
  1972   "Information processing, situation specificity and the generality of risk
         taking behavior." Journal of Personality and Social Psychology 22:128–
         34.
Smith, D.E. and G.R. Gay (eds.)
  1972   It's So Good, Don't Even Try It Once: Heroin in Perspective. Englewood
         Cliffs, NJ: Prentice-Hall.
Stephens, R.C. and D.C. McBride
  1976   "Becoming a street addict." Human Organization 35:87–93.
Stevenson, G.H., L.P.A. Lingley, G.E. Trasov and H. Stanfield
  1956   Drug Addiction in British Columbia. Vancouver: University of British
         Columbia.
Stimson, G.V. and E. Oppenheimer
  1982   Heroin Addiction: Treatment and Control in Britain. London:
         Tavistock.
Thorley, A., E. Oppenheimer and G.V. Stimson
  1977   "Clinic attendance and opiate prescription status of heroin addicts over
         a six year period." British Journal of Psychiatry 130:565–69.
Waldorf, D.
  1976   "Life without heroin: some social adjustments during long-term periods
         of voluntary abstention." Pp. 365–84 in R.H. Coombs, L.J. Fry and P.G.
         Lewis (eds.), Socialization in Drug Abuse. Cambridge, MA: Schenkman.
Williamson, H.
  1978   "Choosing to be a delinquent." New Society, November 9, 333–5.
Winick, C.
  1962   "Maturing out of narcotic addiction." Bulletin on Narcotics 14:1–7.
Witte, A.D.
  1980   "Estimating the economic model of crime with individual data."
         Quarterly Journal of Economics 94:57–84.

Part Two   Theoretical Issues

7
On the Compatibility of Rational Choice and Social Control Theories of Crime

TRAVIS HIRSCHI

Editors' Note

In this witty excursion through the recent history of sociological thinking about crime, Travis Hirschi traces the checkered career of the rational choice perspective and discusses the reasons for its persistent failure to be granted status as a serious, testable, or even reasonable theory about human behavior. Hirschi ascribes these vicissitudes to the irreconcilable conflict of basic assumptions about human nature that underlies criminological theorizing—between those who hold to the image of human beings as social animals and those (social control, rational choice, and routine activities theorists) who perceive them as self-seeking. While recognizing the common ground between social control and rational choice theories, Hirschi proposes a division of labor, with social control perspectives providing a general theory of criminality or "involvement" (a theory of offenders), and rational choice providing a theory about specific criminal events (a theory of crimes). He sees two advantages in this division: First, it supplies the event theory with a suitably motivated offender; second, by retaining the concept of criminality—defined broadly as adherence to the pleasure principle—it enables other aspects of offending to be explained, such as its generalist nature and the stability over time of differences across people in their likelihood of arrest. Commenting that the rational choice perspective may overemphasize the intellectual sophistication of the offender, Hirschi suggests that social control theory, through its more realistic image of offenders as "losers," can provide a useful counterbalance. Similarly, it offers a partial corrective to rational choice theory's alleged lack of attention to those background factors commonly thought of as root causes of crime: Certain individual-level properties—such as age, body build, sex, gang membership—are, Hirschi proposes, situational rather than offender variables; that is, they are related to crime but unrelated to criminality. Although (cf. the Introduction) we believe that this division of labor unduly restricts the intended explanatory reach of the rational choice perspective as a general framework within which to think about crime and criminality (a concept about which we also have reservations), there are other ways of cutting the cake. One might be to propose a tripartite division of labor. In this multistage decision-making scenario, social control theory would address itself to factors influencing the degree of basic criminality and variations therein, whereas a rational choice perspective would concentrate on the decisions relating, first, to involvement in specific crimes (using, among other things, Hirschi's individual-level properties) and, second, to decisions relating to the commission of the crime itself.

Sociology and criminology emerged in the last quarter of the nineteenth century as part of the general revolt against the rational choice perspective. This revolt was driven by the widespread belief that the time had come to apply the techniques, assumptions, and findings of science to the study of human behavior. These techniques, assumptions, and findings did not seem to square with the rational choice model, which assumed that people pursue pleasure and avoid pain, that they can see the future, and that they therefore act to maximize their well-being. This model assumed that the legal power of the state was necessary to limit natural tendencies to use force and fraud in the pursuit of selfish interests. In fact, it often led to the conclusion that the fear of legal sanctions is the major deterrent to crime.

Neither sociology nor criminology treated the rational choice perspective as a testable, serious, or even reasonable theory of human behavior. Rather, they treated it as an obviously false theory, a theory contrary to the assumptions, findings, and techniques of science.

Because rational choice theory assumed that people are free to choose their course of action, it was at odds with the basic premise of science that events are caused by prior events. Because the theory assumed that people consider first their own profit or pleasure, it was at odds with the basic observation of science that humans are social animals found everywhere in naturally harmonious societies. Even the scientific techniques of measurement and experimentation argued against rational choice theory, since neither made sense if free will were at work.

Unfortunately for us, the assumptions of sociology and criminology were not as clear or explicit as those they rejected, and as a result we sometimes have trouble knowing what the fuss was about. Representing modern inductive science, these new disciplines felt free simply to dismiss the rational choice perspective and to excuse the vagueness of their own theories as the inevitable by-product of their grounding in observation rather than on abstract logical principles.

With the benefit of hindsight it is easy to see that these new disciplines were not so free of a priori assumptions. Linked initially to biology, criminology focused on human nature as that of an evolving social animal. Its logic therefore explained crime as the behavior of a *defective* animal. An emergent discipline in its own right, sociology stressed the social nature of human beings, and its logic therefore explained crime as the behavior of a moral animal caught between groups or in otherwise unfortunate or abnormal circumstances. When, in the first quarter of this century, criminology became a subfield of sociology, all it had to do to become compatible with its parent field was abandon the image of the criminal as defective. Sharing as they did the positivist's distaste for rationalistic, voluntaristic theories of human behavior, sociology and criminology got along very well for some 50 years, with little tension beyond that typical of field-subfield relations.

Given this history, it is easy to understand the concern within sociological criminology for possible contamination from the rational choice perspective. Given this history, it is remarkable how often the rational choice perspective has managed to work its way into sociological theory in general and sociological theories of crime in particular. Apparently, the idea of choice has some special affinity with the idea of crime. Apparently, too, the standard assumptions of the sociological perspective are inherently problematic when applied to an explanation of crime.

Perhaps the most instructive example is found in the work of Émile Durkheim. Durkheim devoted much of his scholarly effort to establishing sociology as an independent discipline. As part of this effort, Durkheim very cleverly refused to consider the individual apart from society on the grounds that such analytic exercises are contrary to nature, where the individual is always found *in* society. This was, of course, a variant of the standard positivistic procedure already described: Do not treat rational choice as an alternative theory. Instead, declare it contrary to nature and go about your business as though it did not exist. So far, so good. But what about such things as lust, greed, selfishness? Do they or do they not exist? Yes, said Durkheim, they do exist. They exist under conditions of egoism or anomie, which are unnatural conditions signifying the breakdown of society. This, too, came to be standard positivistic procedure: First declare the rational choice perspective contrary to nature; then assert that the rational choice perspective is applicable to the unnatural conditions of modern society. Many years after Durkheim, the American sociologist Robert K. Merton could be found asserting that "the image of man as an untamed bundle of impulses ... look[s] more like a caricature than a portrait" (1957:131). Later in the same paper Merton can be found saying that criminal behavior "presupposes that individuals have been imperfectly socialized" and, more directly to the point, that in the American society he was describing:

there occurs an approximation to the situation erroneously held by the utilitarian philosophers to be typical of society, a situation in which calculations of personal advantage and fear of punishment are the only regulating agencies. (1938/ 1957:149, 157)

Social Disorganization

Between Durkheim and Merton, rational choice thinking made an important incursion into American criminology by way of the concept of social disorganization. This concept, too, removed individuals from their natural or normal location in a smoothly functioning society and made them the rational calculators of classical or prescientific theory. Coming as it did from sociology, this perspective focused on the causes and consequences of social disorganization rather than on its own assumptions about human nature and society. The causes of social disorganization—mobility and heterogeneity (i.e., modern American society) follow the traditional pattern: The applicability of the rational choice model and the occurrence of crime presuppose a disruption of natural conditions. In any event, the social disorganization perspective borrowed much from the classical or rational choice perspectives. It assumed that freedom from social influence was an empirical as well as a logical possibility. It assumed that the wants of individuals exceed the means of satisfying them; that wants may be satisfied by illegal means, and that illegal means will be chosen by people when they conclude that the benefits are likely to exceed the costs (Kornhauser, 1978:24).

Although the term itself implies an unnatural or abnormal condition, this was not enough to protect social disorganization from sociology's distaste for rational choice theory. Indeed, the attack on social disorganization theory followed the usual lines: Its assumptions about human nature and society were contrary to fact; it mistook differences in social organization for defects in social organization; it incorrectly assumed that natural propensities are deviant; it therefore failed to provide a *positive* explanation of criminal behavior.

Practice makes perfect, and this second attack on the rational choice model led to theories of crime constructed better to minimize rational choice elements and better to conform to accepted standards of positive science. Before examining these theories, let me say something about the second major incursion of choice thinking into the sociology of crime.

Social Control Theory

The second major incursion came with the social control theories of the 1950s and 1960s. In social control theory, actors weigh the costs and benefits of alternative lines of action, legal and illegal, and choose those they consider most likely to maximize their pleasure. Specifications of the theory, such as my own (Hirschi, 1969), attempt to list the factors the actor takes into account in making this decision—such things as attachment to people or institutions, commitment to conventional lines of action, involvement in noncriminal activities, and belief in the moral validity of norms. In a more explicitly rational choice context, these same factors might be labeled interpersonal attachments, economic or pecuniary investments, time constraints, and moral considerations. In any event, the theory holds that to the extent these factors have large values the individual is likely to conclude that the costs of crime are not worth the benefits. In pure control theory, it is assumed that all people are capable of crime if the price is right, where price is defined as the product of crime benefits and the likelihood of detection. As a consequence, the theory, like standard choice theory, may be applied to crime anywhere it is found in the social system—as much to white-collar crime as to street crime, to drug use as to robbery or burglary.

Coming from sociology, control theory is not as clean or deductive as those rational choice theories found in, say, economics, but its assumptions seem to be much the same. Because control theories have been advanced by many sociologists (e.g., Reiss, Matza, Toby, Reckless, Nye, Kornhauser) and tests of such theories are reported frequently in the sociological journals, often with favorable results, it might appear that this time there is hope for reconciliation of rational choice and traditional sociological explanations of crime.

Integrated Theory in Sociology

Such optimism is not supported by recent work in the field. When Delbert Elliott reports that the emphasis in sociology in recent years has shifted from competitive tests of alternative theories to efforts to combine "elements of historically divergent theories into more inclusive and powerful theoretical models" (1985:123), the ecumenical spirit he describes does not extend to rational choice theory. On the contrary, rational choice assumptions are specifically eliminated from the integrated models constructed by Elliott and his colleagues, leading me to complain that they have adopted the terms and ignored the claims of control theory (Hirschi, 1979:34). My complaint was based on statements that will be recognized as derivations from the traditional sociological position: "[D]elinquent behavior, like conforming behavior, presupposes a pattern of social relationships through which motives, rationalizations, techniques and rewards can be learned and maintained" (Elliott et al., 1979:13); "We postulate that, in addition to weak bonding and the absence of restraints, some positive motivation is necessary for sustained involvement in delinquent behavior" (1979:15).

Such statements describe what Kornhauser has called the "automaton conformist of cultural deviance theory," an individual whose nature is "wholly passive, docile, tractable, and plastic," a wantless creature so good "he must *learn* to be willful, greedy, and cruel" (1978:35–36). In other words, these statements describe the social animal that nature gave sociology a hundred years ago to use against rational choice theories of crime, the animal with just the right mix of properties to assure the truth of certain brands of sociology and to deny scientific status to its competitors.

Evidence that this animal is still alive and well is found in a 1983 article in the *American Journal of Sociology* by Mark Colvin and John Pauly, who claim to recognize no less than seven major theoretical currents in sociology today: "learning theory, strain theory, control theory, labeling theory, conflict theory, radical criminology, and . . . integrated theory" (1983:516). Let us briefly look for rational choice content in each of these theoretical traditions as described by Colvin and Pauly.

As described, learning theory has virtually none. As described, it assumes human beings to be social animals who must learn to recognize the potential benefits of force and fraud, animals who engage in such activities only when they have the support of learned favorable evaluations of these activities or the support of important reference groups.

Strain theory, too, has no choice component. This is not surprising: The theory originated in opposition to control theory (Merton, 1938/1957) and has moved progressively away from rational choice assumptions. In his historically important variant of strain theory, Cohen (1955) introduced the reaction formation defense mechanism, making the delinquent's behavior nonutilitarian by definition and clearly overdetermined by the emotions of the situation. Cloward and Ohlin (1960) also described a "desperate" offender forced into crime by unwarranted discrimination.

Labeling theory has roots in symbolic interactionism, a tradition often seen as friendly to choice theory. However, no choice element appears in labeling theory as described by Colvin and Pauly. On the contrary, labeling theory too assumes an animal incapable of sustained violence or greed without social support.

At first glance, conflict theory also sounds as though it might be based on assumptions rather different from those thus far encountered. Again not so. The conflict that is crime is conflict between groups, all of whose members are so well socialized that they cannot even consider acts contrary to their values or to their group's interests. They can, however, recognize criminality in the behavior of those outside their group and can, apparently, choose to notice or ignore it. Such voluntarism is offensive to the authors of the article in question, to whose theory we now turn.

In the "structural-Marxist perspective" described by Colvin and Pauly, the structure of authority on the job is reproduced in the home, in the school, and in the peer group, where it has the same attitudinal and behavioral consequences. The alienated, hostile, and eventually criminal child is a result of the "coercive workplace control structure" experienced by his parents. So, once again, our good animal is made evil by evil institutions, and the solution to crime is to join in "the workplace struggle by subordinates for more equal and democratically controlled forms of production relations that shape their lives and the lives of their families" (Colvin and Pauly, 1983:545).

The integrated theory proposed by Elliott, Ageton, and Canter is the example of integrated theory discussed by Colvin and Pauly. As indicated earlier, this theory meets the test of the social animal model by acceding to those constituent theories based on such a model. As far as I can determine, the bulk of integration efforts in sociology accede to this model. How, then, do they deal with control theory, a theory based explicitly on the assumption that humans are self-seeking animals?

Colvin and Pauly simply reject the idea of quantitative variation in bonding in favor of the idea that bonding distinctions are qualitative. This is a direct and complete rejection of the basic assumption of control theory. It is a restatement of the position that people differ in the content of socialization rather than in the degree of socialization, from which it follows that all are well and equally socialized. Colvin and Pauly also reject the idea of a "society" or a "conventional order" to which people may be more or less bonded in favor of pluralist, conflict, or class images of the social order. This, too, is a restatement of the traditional position of cultural deviance theory to the effect that people must have different values (preferences?) because they occupy different structural positions and because they behave differently.

So, Colvin and Pauly reject the constituent assumptions of control theory on the grounds that they are "uncritical" or "untenable," and the mystery is why they bother to include control theory in their list in the first place. (One reason control theories are sometimes included in integrations proposed by sociologists is that such integrations are really multiple factor theory in disguise. Such integrations give researchers an excuse to look at everything and still allow them to appear to accede to modern demands for theoretical relevance. Given their frequent appearance in research proposals, integrated theories might well be called "grant" theories.)

In any event, we must conclude that little has changed in the hundred or so years since sociology came into being. Sociology rejected rationalistic, voluntaristic, and individualistic theories then, and it rejects them now. The reasons for rejection remain much the same: Adequate theories of crime must be positive. They must provide the motives for or the causes of criminal behavior. They cannot assume that crime will occur in the absence of restraint, because absence-of-restraint theories are nonscientific in two senses of the term: They are contrary to the scientific assumption that behavior is caused by antecedent events, and they are contrary to the scientific observation that people are naturally social and must therefore be propelled into antisocial behavior by forces over which they have no control.

Causation and Determinism

In my view, the causation issue is easily resolved. As I have argued in detail elsewhere (Hirschi, 1978), positivists often seem to misconstrue cause as synonymous with force or motive when, by their own definitions, causes are merely nonspurious correlates of the effect in question. As such, causes may as well be restraints as motives. Take, for example, IQ, a variable that probably qualifies as a cause of crime by the usual criteria: association, causal order, and nonspuriousness. Assuming that IQ is a cause of crime, we can ask how it is related to crime without being forced to give it to one theoretical scheme rather than another. The strain theorist could and probably would interpret the association between IQ and crime as resulting from cruelty or injustice in the social system. Low-IQ people commit crimes as a means of venting rage at a system that has unfairly oppressed them. As hypothesis, this is fair enough. Its truth is neither confirmed nor denied by the existence of a causal relation between IQ and crime. It certainly has no more a priori claim to accuracy than the hypothesis that low-IQ people are more likely than high-IQ people to commit crimes because they are less able to effect profitable exchange relations with conventional institutions. Being relatively unrewarded by conformity, low-IQ people are simply freer to commit criminal acts and will be more likely to do so should the opportunity arise.

Note that the rational choice explanation also asserts nothing contrary to or inconsistent with the initial conclusion that IQ is a cause of crime. Choice theory is therefore perfectly compatible with the idea that criminal behavior is caused, and choice theory therefore cannot be rejected on grounds of inconsistency with the idea of causation. In choice theories, causes of crime are factors consistently taken into account by the choice maker.

Determinism is harder than causation to deal with in the context of choice theory, if only because the word itself seems to deny choice. Because space is limited, let me quote my earlier conclusion on this question:

Some believe that accepting a probabilistic definition of cause implies retreat from the postulate of determinism. Actually, it does not. To assume that delinquent acts are caused by prior states or events is not to assume that they are determined by any single state or event, but only by some combination of all states and events present at the time they are committed.... Some of the [states and events present at the time delinquent acts are committed] are the calculations and desires of the actor himself. It is he who wants sex, money, or peace; it is he who decides they may be had by robbing a liquor store; it is he who concludes no policeman is near the scene.... If he is 'compelled' to commit the act, it is by forces common to us all.... (Hirschi, 1978:327–330)

Whatever the adequacy of my effort to show agreement between choice theorists and positivists on the question of determinism, the fact remains that the concept of causation does not commit us to a particular theory of crime. In particular, the concept of causation does not require preference for motivational theories over choice or restraint theories.

If there is nothing in the logic of positivism that would require rejection of rational choice theory, how do we deal with the positivistic *observation* that we are social animals and with the logical consequence of this observation that positive motivation is therefore necessary to explain our criminal acts? I am afraid I know no way to bring rational choice and sociological positivism together on this point. Man the social animal is of course not an observation at all. It is an image, a picture in the mind. Images are theories, and the image of man as a social animal is the core of sociological theories of crime, just as man the rational animal is the core of choice theories of crime. If sociologists will not accept the idea that some people are more social than others (which they apparently will not), we cannot hope to reconcile the social and the rational images, and those who claim to have done so have almost by definition rejected one image in favor of the other.

I come, by a long and circuitous path, to some conclusions: There is no hope for reconciliation of rational choice theory and those theories derived directly from sociological positivism. There is no hope for reconciliation of social control theory and the sociological theories in question. Rational choice theory and social control theory share the same image of man, an image rather different from the image of sociological positivism. Rational choice theory and social control theory are therefore the same theory reared in different disciplinary contexts. Given their distinct histories and circumstances, we would expect social control theory and rational choice theory to have developed models differing markedly in detail and emphasis. If our analysis is correct, however, it should be possible to account for these differences in a reasonably straightforward way. Let us look at some of the more apparent differences between the two theories with this thought in mind.

Crime and Criminality

An obvious difference between choice and social control theory is that one tends to focus on specific crimes—the decision to burgle or not to burgle, to kill or not to kill—whereas the other tends to ignore distinctions among crimes, treating them as being all of a piece. In other words, one theory concentrates on what Clarke and Cornish (1985) call events, and the other concentrates on what they call involvement. Michael Gottfredson and I (Hirschi and Gottfredson, 1986) have explored the same distinction using the words *crime* for events and *criminality* for involvement. (Criminality, by the way, we define as "relatively stable differences among individuals in their propensity to engage in criminal or equivalent acts.") Whatever the terms used, the distinction seems worth making. We do need theories of offenders and we also need theories of offenses, and in the best of all possible worlds these theories would be compatible. It turns out that we seem already to have arrived at this ideal state, for control theory is a theory of criminality, and choice theory is a theory of crime. If, then, the offender is a choice maker whose general situation is such that he or she is likely to depreciate the costs of crime and the benefits of noncrime, it is not difficult to imagine the offender weighing the difficulties in gaining access to a building, the risk of detection, and the probable gain against the desire for a little something extra for a night on the town. In other words, if the offender has been constructed by control theory, the choice theorist need not worry about predispositions or other tendencies of the actor inconsistent with a choice model. I might add that if the offense has been constructed by a choice theorist, the control theorist need not worry about the offender behaving at the scene of the crime in a way inconsistent with control theory—for example, acting as though compelled to commit crime by forces over which he or she has no control.

The distinction between crime and criminality and the division of labor between choice and control theories thus allows us to resolve the long-standing dispute between those who favor looking at specific offenses and those who would treat offenses as interchangeable. At the offender level, it is reasonably clear that offenses are interchangeable. Offenders may be studied without too great concern for the mix of offenses used to describe them. Their general tendency is toward short-term, immediate pleasure without undue concern for how such pleasure is obtained or for long-range consequences. Given this tendency, many criminal acts will suffice, and many noncriminal activities are the functional equivalents of crime (e.g., job quitting, drinking alcohol in the morning on a workday). As a result, offenders rarely specialize in particular crimes, and few have careers in crime in a meaningful or informative sense of the term *career*. (The idea of a career contradicts the idea of criminality, because one involves a capacity for long-term commitment denied by the other.)

At the same time, distinctions among offenses are worthwhile for all sorts of theoretical and practical purposes having little to do (at least directly) with the characteristics of offenders. Burglary can be usefully studied (from a choice or routine activities perspective) without concern for its connection to robbery or rape. It can, we assume, given our theory of the offender, be prevented without producing equivalent increases in robbery or rape. (Displacement effects are limited by the sloth of the offender.) Because the causes of crime are to some extent independent of the causes of criminality, the rate of burglary may change without a change in the number of potential burglars. So it is for all offenses sufficiently serious to warrant individual attention.

Our distinction also allows us to comment on the serious versus trivial crime issue often encountered in etiological research: It turns out that trivial offenses may be as good as—and in some respects, such as frequency of occurrence, better than—serious offenses in establishing levels of criminality. The assumption that serious crime scales are automatically better than trivial crime scales flows from failure to recall that in research on offenders the criminal event is used as an indicator of some underlying propensity. Seen in this light, it is evident that "more serious" is not identical to "more valid." In fact, the reverse may well be true, because serious crimes almost by definition have more of an eventlike character than trivial crimes. (Person crimes, involving inter-action between victim and offender, may be especially problematic as indicators of the criminality of the offender, however serious they or their consequences may be.)

Mindlessness and Intellectualism

In the revolt against the rational choice model, positivists often transformed the offender from a deliberating, intellectual animal to an organism reacting mindlessly to the forces in the environment. In some positivistic research on offenders, such as that of Sheldon and Eleanor Glueck (1950), there is reason to wonder whether the investigators bothered even to talk to their subjects, let alone concern themselves with their decision-making strategies. In the current counterrevolt there is a reverse tendency to see the offender as thoughtful and intellectually sophisticated. I think this tendency should be resisted. Accepting a choice model does not require that we assume planning or foresight beyond the bare minimum necessary for the act to occur. If greater levels of planning and foresight were required by a choice model, I believe the model would be in trouble.

Let me briefly mention some observations I think relevant to this question. The median age of persons arrested for burglary in the United States is about 17. Whatever their age, burglars on the whole are described as having limited skills at gaining entrance to buildings, as doing little in the way of scouting or planning, and as reaping at best modest profits for their efforts (Reppetto, 1974). Robbers tend to be older than burglars, but not because robbery requires more skill or planning than burglarly. According to the reports of robbers themselves, robbery is pursued at more advanced ages (here the median is about 22) because robbery is easier than other forms of instrumental crime. In a nutshell, the criminal career does not appear to be a career of increasing skill and sophistication but the reverse, a career that starts with little of either and goes downhill from there. (Material on robbers cited is from Petersilia et al., 1978).

If my facts are accurate, I see no problem in them for rational choice or control theory. The burglar who enters a house by smashing doors with a crowbar is as compatible with a rational choice model as the burglar who opens doors with counterfeit keys obtained through clever long-range planning. In fact, the crowbar burglar is more compatible with a choice model than the counterfeit-key burglar because it is easier to see burglary as a reasonable choice of occupation for one whose door-opening skills are limited to crowbars. In any event, if choice models are developed to guide crime prevention policy, accurate portrayal of the skills of the offender would seem to be an important ingredient of effective policy.

With its origins in the positivistic disciplines, control theory exhibits little tendency to romanticize offenders or to ascribe to them unusual awareness or foresight. In fact, control theory explicitly asserts that people often turn to crime because their prospects for gain through noncrime are limited. This "loser" image of the offender then carries over into his or her career in crime. Control theory therefore has no difficulty with the view that offenders on the whole are not very good at what they do.

The same kinds of considerations seem to apply in assessing the role of offender-talk in studies from a rational choice perspective. The perspective itself tells us that reason is a servant of the passions, that offenders will use their tongues to cover their tracks, to hide their purposes from themselves as well as from the researcher. So, if the rational choice perspective is open to listening to offenders, to hearing their assessment of the reasons for their actions, it is not committed to believing all it hears.

Correlates of Crime

The choice perspective typically pays little attention to correlates of crime beyond the certainty, celerity, and severity of legal punishment. (The fact that these deterrence variables have an impact on crime in choice theory reminds us that the idea that crime is caused by external events was around long before the positivists made such a fuss about it.) The general tendency is to treat other correlates as "root causes" or "background variables" about which little can be done and which are therefore largely irrelevant to a choice or policy perspective.

This tendency stems from the belief that choice analysis and causal analysis are incompatible. We have seen that this is not the case, that at least in some instances causes of crime may be interpreted as factors that reliably influence the decision to engage or not to engage in criminal acts. This leads to another distinction that has not heretofore been pursued to the extent it might be, namely, the distinction between correlates of crime and correlates of criminality. There is reason to believe that some individual-level properties affect the likelihood that people will commit crimes without affecting their relative propensities to commit crime—that is, without affecting their criminality. For example, age is strongly related to arrests, but differences across people in the likelihood of arrest remain reasonably stable over long periods of time. This suggests that age is in effect a situational rather than an offender variable and that as such it should be of special interest to choice theory. Other variables that may be related to crime and unrelated to criminality include body build, gang membership, and sex. In all these cases, those in the high-rate categories (males, gang members, those with muscular bodies) may be there because they are more likely to discount the risk of injury from victims or guardians (or the risk of legal penalty). If so, these, too, would be crime rather than criminality variables, variables with a direct impact on the likelihood of criminal events, variables that do not operate through the criminality of the actor.

If there is anything to these speculations, choice theory could benefit from close examination of those individual-level correlates of crime usually relegated to positivistic research. If there is anything to these speculations, the field as a whole could benefit from efforts to measure criminality independent of involvement in crime.

Conclusion

It appears from this brief examination of the history of sociological and choice theories of crime that the image behind a theory is more important than its disciplinary base in determining its compatibility with other theories. Thus, sociological control theories and rational choice theories have much in common, and neither is compatible with those sociological theories that may be traced to the positivistic origins of the discipline.

I continue to see little point in attempting to integrate theories whose basic assumptions are incompatible. In this case, each theory should face the data alone in open competition with alternative theories. At the same time, I see considerable merit in efforts to combine compatible theories that have developed independently of each other. A list of such theories would certainly include rational choice, social control, routine activities, socialization, and at least some varieties of social learning theory.

In this chapter I have mentioned possible contributions of social control theory to development of the rational choice perspective. I am confident that choice theorists could do much to sharpen the insights of control theory were they to accept the task. Certainly they could be more constructive than those who continue to reject control theory on grounds of incompatibility with some sacred image of man.

References

Clarke, Ronald V. and Derek B. Cornish
  1985 "Modelling offenders' decisions: a framework for research and policy."
        Pp. 147–85 in M. Tonry and N. Morris (eds.), Crime and Justice, Volume
        6. Chicago: University of Chicago Press.
Cloward, R. A. and L. Ohlin
  1960 Delinquency and Opportunity. New York: Free Press.
Cohen, A. K.
  1955 Delinquent Boys: The Culture of the Gang. New York: Free Press.
Colvin, M. and J. Pauly
  1983 "A critique of criminology: toward an integrated structural-Marxist
        theory of delinquency production." American Journal of Sociology
        89:513–51.
Elliott, D. S.
  1985 "The assumption that theories can be combined with increased explan-
        atory power: theoretical integrations." Pp. 123–49 in R. F. Meier (ed.),
        Theoretical Methods in Criminology. Beverly Hills, CA: Sage.
Elliott, D. S., S. S. Ageton and R. J. Canter
  1979 "An integrated theoretical perspective on delinquent behavior." Journal
        of Research in Crime and Delinquency 16:3–27.
Glueck, Sheldon, and Eleanor Glueck
  1950 Unraveling Juvenile Delinquency. Cambridge, MA: Harvard University
        Press.
Hirschi, T.
  1969 Causes of Delinquency. Berkeley, CA: University of California Press.
  1978 "Causes and prevention of juvenile delinquency," Pp. 322–41 in H. M.
        Johnson (ed.), Social System and Legal Process. San Francisco: Jossey-
        Bass.
  1979 "Separate and unequal is better." Journal of Research in Crime and
        Delinquency 16:34–8.
Hirschi, T. and M. Gottfredson
        "The distinction between crime and criminality." In T. F. Hartnagel and
        R. A. Silverman (eds.), Critique and Explanation: Essays in Honor of
        Gwynne Nettler. New Brunswick, NJ: Transaction (in press).
Kornhauser, R.
  1978 Social Sources of Delinquency. Chicago: University of Chicago Press.
Merton, Robert K.
  1957 Social Theory and Social Structure. New York: Free Press.
Petersilia, J., P. W. Greenwood and M. Lavin
  1978 Criminal Careers of Habitual Felons. Washington, DC: U. S. Govern-
        ment Printing Office.
Reppetto, T.
  1974 Residential Crime. Cambridge, MA: Ballinger.

8
Linking Criminal Choices, Routine Activities, Informal Control, and Criminal Outcomes

Marcus Felson

Editors' Note

> Marcus Felson's chapter is an ingenious attempt to link two currently influential theories in criminology: his own routine activity theory, which explains the supply of criminal opportunities but takes the supply of offenders as given, and Travis Hirschi's control theory, which does precisely the opposite. Felson's key linking concepts are those of the "handled offender," the individual susceptible to informal social control by virtue of his or her (perhaps idiosyncratic) bonds to society, and the "intimate handler," someone with sufficient knowledge of the potential offender to grasp the "handle" and exert control. The routine activities of everyday life set the scene for the web of interaction between these people and between the crime target and any guardians. Felson's chapter also attempts to link these two themes with a rational choice perspective, arguing that, together, routine activity theory and control theory provide the context within which choices are made. This aspect of his synthesis would seem to need further elaboration; at first glance it seems to us to neglect some of the social, psychological, and perhaps even constitutional influences on decision making. Nevertheless the chapter as a whole represents an important pioneering effort to provide a synthesis of theories.

People make choices, but they cannot choose the choices available to them. Nor can they be sure what chain of events will follow from their choices, including choices made by others. People blunder and fail, just as they often get what they want. This chapter seeks to place rational choice theories of crime into a broader context. This context considers how the larger structure of opportunities sets the stage for criminogenic choices as well as influences whether these choices result in successes or failures for those who make them. This approach takes into account regularities in how choices become available or remote to those with criminal inclinations or to those who might, by choice or happenstance, contribute to the informal social control of criminal behavior. The focus here is upon exploitative crimes in which a victim is clearly distinguished from an offender.

This chapter takes certain human inclinations as given. It is assumed that some people are inclined to break laws, that others are inclined to protect their own person and property, that others are inclined to keep their children out of trouble. These inclinations may vary, but that variation is not the topic of concern here. Rather, this chapter considers how the structure of social life makes it easy or difficult for people to carry out these inclinations.

The hallmark of this analysis is that, although people may have lots of desires and inclinations, they cannot always carry them out. The opportunity structure of society places a limit on human ability to act, including acting on inclinations to commit crimes, to avoid victimization, or to control one's offspring. Moreover, changes in community life can indeed produce more crime without requiring any change in motivations of the population of likely offenders.

Economists might call this a supply question, but most economic theory is based on markets, where supply is allocated to demand via price. I want to buy nails, you want to sell them, and the price is influenced by supply and demand.

Exploitative crime is fundamentally different. If bashing heads is your business, I do not want you to bash mine. We have no meeting of the minds in this matter, and hence no market. If you catch me, it is not by my choice but rather my misfortune. Your mother probably disapproves of your behavior, as well. To attack other people or their property, you usually need to gain direct physical access to them. You have to find or stumble upon them, or they may stumble upon you. This suggests a fundamental principle for understanding the rational order of exploitative crime: The criminal event is a systematic result of the convergence of people and things over space and time. It has a rational order in the sense that we can study it systematically, like the movements of electrons or the responsiveness of price to supply and demand. This does not mean, however, that every party to the event chooses or prefers it or knows the facts leading up to it. It is a convergence without a concurrence, a product of uncoordinated, asymmetric choices.

Indeed, each event requires that one party fail to get what it wants. If a crime occurs, the victim failed to get what he or she wanted. If a crime does not occur, the potential victim succeeded but not the offender. The rational order of how many of the one and how many of the other occur goes beyond the preferences of one actor. Moreover, its dependence upon the physical structure of social phenomena—where people are when and what they are doing—renders crime analysis a special case of the ecology of daily life. Routine activity patterns provide choices to individuals, including criminals, and set the stage for subsequent events determining the success of the offender in carrying out the crime, or of the potential victim in avoiding victimization, however unwittingly (see Felson, 1983). This boils down to a simple theory of crime production: Changes in the daily life of the community alter the amount of criminal opportunity in society, hence altering crime rates.

This chapter considers the rational structure of crime from the viewpoint of the analyst, not of the offender. The rational crime theory must explain not only the offender's successes but also the offender's failures, as well as the successes and failures of the potential victim.

Let us assume that criminals think and forget, plan and blunder, work and idle, choose and stumble, reason and react, all with some order and predictability. Let us assume also that most victims think or fail to think about their risks, are informed or misinformed, move about or stay put according to certain regularities. Furthermore, let us consider that parents interact predictably with their children, informally controlling them or failing to do so. Finally, let us assume that daily life systematically brings together or disperses offender and victim, parent and child, person and property, and so on.

The basic elements of crime and its control as suggested in this chapter include something old, something borrowed, and something new. To repeat (Cohen and Felson, 1979), a criminal act has three minimal elements: a likely offender, a suitable target, and the absence of capable guardians against crime. The capable guardian is seldom a policeman, more likely a housewife, brother, friend, or passerby. These three elements must converge in time and space for a direct-contact, predatory violation to occur.

Now, let us borrow from Travis Hirschi (1969) the fundamentals of control theory. Hirschi's four elements in the informal social control of delinquency are commitments, attachments, involvements, and beliefs. He reviews these in another chapter of this volume, but I am going to summarize them with one word: handle. Society gains a handle on individuals to prevent rulebreaking by forming the social bond. People have something to lose if others dislike their behavior, if their future is impaired, if their friends and families are upset with them, if they are occupied with conventional activities, or if their beliefs can be situationally invoked to make them feel bad every time they break a rule.

The handle is a necessary condition for informal social control to occur. Lacking commitment to the future, attachments to others, or conventional involvements and beliefs in the rules, an individual has no handle that can be grasped, and informal social control is impossible. The social bond is the handle. This chapter does not consider how handles are affixed as people grow up. Just assume that almost everyone has a handle, and consider how others may grasp that handle to impose informal social control.

In some cases, handles may be sufficiently graspable that they work without names. An older stranger scolds a child, who walks away shamed, informal sanctions having succeeded anonymously. A young adolescent is humiliated by being told that he will never amount to anything, and he does not stop to think that the humiliator does not know his name, address, or parents.

In time, children learn to go in groups, cheering one another up after scoldings by adults and inoculating one another against future scoldings. On reaching this stage, anonymous scolding loses its force, and handles cannot be grasped by just anyone.

Some youths scoff at parents and the future, but most seem to have specific handles, even if they are not readily controlled by sheer respect for adults in general. If Fred wants to hide his misbehavior from anybody at all, if he pursues any long-term goal, or if his mind contains any belief by which he can be shamed, then a handle remains. Such handles are personal and specific. To grasp the handle you have to know it. Information about Fred's actions last Friday may reach somebody who knows Fred's handle and can grasp it. This information makes Fred subject to informal social control, and its absence makes Fred immune from such control. Effective informal social control over Fred is possible, using his strong social bonds. Yet this potential informal control may be difficult to put into practice. This difficulty stems from poor channels of communication and interaction that prevent existing handles from being grasped by persons who might know how to keep Fred in line.

Combining the old and the borrowed, here is something slightly new. Figure 8.1 presents the "web of informal control" as it applies to exploitative offenses. Four minimal elements are considered: (1) a handled offender, that is, someone who can both offend and be handled; (2) an intimate handler, that is, someone close enough to grasp the handle; (3) a suitable target of crime; and (4) a capable guardian against such a violation. (In the special case where a potential offender is unhandled—that is, lacking in commitments, attachments, involvements, and beliefs—the intimate handler does not exist. In this case, the four

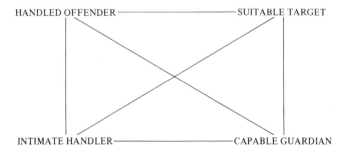

FIGURE 8.1. The web of informal crime control.

minimal elements are reduced to three: offender, target, and guardian.)

To assess the importance of the four elements and the web linking them, let us start with the situation of tightest informal social control and work toward the situation in which such control is most lax. Informal control is tightest when all four elements are in direct physical contact and when relevant people know one another very well. Imagine a duplex with a boy and his mother living on the left and a nice television set and its owner living on the right. The boy has some criminal inclination and is tempted by the TV set, but he is close to his mother, who would never allow him to steal it. She is also a significant mother in crime-control terms because she is at home, knows the neighbor, and recognizes the neighbor's TV set. (She may even function partly in the role of guardian for the neighbor's TV, but we will neglect this point to keep the discussion tidy.) In such a situation, theft is highly unlikely. Even if mother is out and her son can easily monitor the guardian next door, he may be reluctant to risk mom's return at an inopportune moment. Household items and scents may also serve to remind him of his social bonds and to discourage him from committing delinquent acts.

It is likely that this youth will look for or stumble upon criminal opportunities further from home, where he can escape his mother's watchful eye as well as reminders of her bond. However, if he goes a block away, he is endangered by an important intermediary omitted from Figure 8.1: the informant. Someone who knows him and his mother might tell her she saw him over there after dark. Someone who recognizes the television set might ask what he is doing with it. Someone else may function as a guardian.

A tight community—where people know people, property, and their linkages—offers little opportunity for common exploitative crime. The Israeli kibbutz, where crime rates are low because there is not much to steal and nowhere to go with it, is a case in point. (Bordua, David, personal communications, 1973, 1982). The dispersion of kinship and friendship over a wider metropolitan space and the automobilization of the population make more difficult the kind of informal control discussed earlier.

Nonetheless, carrying out an ordinary violation requires that minimal conditions be met, even in a modern metropolis. The handled offender must not have the intimate handler near and must get to a target with the guardian away. As daily activity patterns disperse people away from family and household situations (Felson and Gottfredson, 1984; Cohen and Felson, 1979), it is more likely that criminogenic conditions will apply. Not only will offenders find targets with guardians absent, but they will be able to get away from their handlers and be fairly sure that their handlers will not recognize the loot or compare notes with the guardians. It is not that urbanites lack friends or family ties, or that they are unhandled, but merely that their handlers are scattered and segregated from the suitable targets and capable guardians. Informants are less and less likely to link the handler to the evidence that Fred has been bad.

Even if Fred is apprehended in a theft situation, the guardian will not be able to invoke informal control easily, not knowing Fred's name or his family. The choices available are to invoke the law of the jungle or the criminal justice system, but not informal social control. It does not take Fred long to learn that "I'll call your mama" is an empty threat from a total stranger, who probably will not notice his lawbreaking anyway.

Some technological and genetic factors assist informal control. Telephones may allow informants to call around quickly and try to find out who the freckle-faced boy belongs to and which one is missing from school at the moment. Adults can compare notes and solve the puzzle. Genetic inheritance of appearance makes it so that, without knowing your name, I might be able to ask, "Is that red-haired kid one of the Johnson boys? He was hanging around when your TV was taken. Maybe I'll have a talk with his dad." The modern, multinucleated family, with stepparents and half-brothers, makes this genetic branding less dependable and reduces the clear link between the intimate handler and the handled delinquent.

The single-parent household gives the community only one parent to know and hence reduces the potential linkages that can be evoked for informal social control. Lower fertility has the same effect. In large families, there is a greater chance I will know one of the brothers and have a good guess that this is the O'Reilly kid. In smaller families, this is less likely, and knowing the particular Smith becomes necessary. High geographic mobility rates make it harder to maintain recognition of one family versus another and to piece together the relationships needed for evoking informal social control. The automobile makes it simpler for youths to evade the risk that this will happen in the first place.

In the event that informants do figure out who an offender is and talk to his or her parents, if they are complete strangers there is greater likelihood that the parents will dismiss the stranger's accusation rather than blame their own flesh and blood. In a tight community, however, where one parent knows another, they may accept the unpleasant truth that their freckled, angel-faced boy broke the law, and then impose informal social control.

Application of technology to personal appearance further clouds responsibilities for informal social control. If the Jones family all have curly, red hair and light complexions, identifying Jones Jr.'s transgressions is simpler. If each Jones selects a different wave and tint, informal social control is complicated. Adolescent adornment patterns may impair informal social control without the need of a subculture simply by impeding identification. Increases in within-family variance and decreases in between-family variance in appearance may be a long-term social trend detracting from informal social control. Similarly, mass production of goods makes them difficult to identify with a particular owner.

That conventional activities serve to control delinquency was well explained by Hirschi (1969). In his treatment of the issue, involvements in conventional activities can reduce delinquency by keeping youths occupied. Other possibilities can also be imagined. Conventional activities might reduce delinquency if they occur near handlers or their informants, or if they produce new handlers. Also, involvement in desirable activities provides handlers with something they can withdraw as a punishment for delinquency, and hence with an extra handle. When conventional activities have a routine time, place, and list of participants, informants have some facts to check if delinquency is suspected at nearby times and places or if someone is suspiciously absent from conventional activities. The location and timing of conventional activities can be important, for these can be proximate or distant from criminal opportunities. Conventional activities can tie down potential delinquents, but they can also hamstring potential handlers and guardians. Sometimes they bring offender and target together, assemble accomplices, or facilitate transgressions at proximate times and places, after the adults have gone home (see Klein, 1971). Clearly, conventional involvements are a mixed bag. Indeed, Cohen and Felson (1979) argued that increases in certain conventional activities fostered rising crime rates.

None of this discussion hinges on normlessness or changing standards. Indeed, crime can increase even when social bonds persist, parents care deeply, and offender motivation stands pat. All one needs for a crime wave is a decline in the ability of handlers to handle or guardians to guard. What varies is the pattern of daily life and the structure of households, work, school, and transport, as these make it more or less possible for conventional parents to carry out their inclinations and keep their kids out of trouble. Indeed, criminal opportunity can increase greatly if the changing physical structure of communities obstructs the watchful eye of parents. (see Felson and Gottfredson, 1984). When people choose to drive a car, to let their children drive the family car or have their own, to live several miles from work and relatives, to have smaller families, to divorce and remarry, to send their children away to college, to purchase lightweight durable goods, to enjoy alcoholic beverages, or to go out at night, these choices set the stage for criminal events. The latter occur as the result of combinations of choices by different actors, moving about but not consulting one another. They are happenstances resulting from prior decisions. Highly predictable on an actuarial basis, with systematic consequences for crime rates, they yet occur without a meeting of the minds. Handled offenders, intimate handlers, capable guardians, and victims converge and diverge without consultation.

Let me add one more triplet of simple concepts: space, time, and relationships. Here we have some basics of human ecology and social control. People and things stay put and move over space and time and are tied into relationships while doing so. Things belong to people who belong to each other, but these ties are not always reinforced by proximity. When those so tied move together, guardianship and handling are simple. When they diverge, guardianship and handling are impaired. One might envision daily life as an ebb and flow of routine activities, setting the stage for informal social control to succeed much of the time, but not always.

Social change alters the stage, alters the probability that a handled offender and a suitable target will converge without handler or guardian near. The technology of the automobile disperses people over space and time, away from their property, guardians, and handlers. The organization of daily life in the modern metropolis assembles or disperses people for work, school, shopping, and leisure in a fashion that invites crime. Modern metropolitan life disperses people away from family and household settings, drawing strangers together, assembling adolescents without parents or other adults who know them, and otherwise putting informal social control at a disadvantage. The rational order of modern metropolitan life is one in which likely offenders have a greater supply of choices and less room for blunder and are more likely to get what they want, whereas potential victims are less likely to get what they want with regard to evading crime. Moreover, freedom and prosperity, enticing people with social life or stereo components, systematically expose them to the risk of victimization.

Human choice enters at many steps in this process. The choice to move to a new neighborhood is as important as the choice to steal a car. The decision to buy a new car is, in the most basic sense, criminogenic. The decision to buy your son a car may be even more criminogenic. The decision to select a residence on a cul-de-sac or to move to the countryside may be criminocclusive. Different stages of choice affecting the genesis or occlusion of criminal opportunity have been considered by different scholars. Cusson (1983) considers strategic analysis from the offender's viewpoint, taking into account not only property gain but also power and excitement. Brantingham and Brantingham (1984) cataloged the spatial, temporal, and activity features of criminal choice. Rengert and Wasilchik (1980) explored geographic impingements on offender awareness and choice. Hindelang, Gottfredson, and Garafolo (1978) showed that decisions about life-styles greatly influence risk of victimization. Mayhew, Clarke, Sturman, and Hough (1976) demonstrated that public system planning has consequences for crime rates. Each of these studies have added an important piece to the puzzle, demonstrating that the rational structure of crime rates has more to it than an all-seeing, all-knowing offender. Indeed, the criminally inclined population, too, is subject to the irreducible and stubborn facts of the larger environment.

Criminal decision analysis must therefore consider many choices made by many actors at many stages in social and economic life, nor can these decisions be considered in isolation from the physical world. The convergences and divergences of people and things needed for normal crime to occur and the possibility that decisions will go sour make rational analysis of crime more complex. Let me specify another triplet: decisions, situations, and outcomes. To understand criminal opportunity, we need to know not only some of the decisions made by offenders, human targets, guardians, and handlers, but also the situations of their physical convergence as a result of these decisions, regardless of whether the decision makers know what we, as analysts, know. And we have to know the outcome. Was the offender wrong, missing a golden opportunity or committing a silly blunder? Did the getaway car stall or did the selected target trap him? Did the victim succeed by going through the day safe from crime, regardless of whether he or she thought about it? What choices on the part of a citizen produce an unplanned victimization and impair or assist guardianship of targets and handling of offenders? Indeed, a criminal situation is made possible by various decisions by those who set the stage for the convergence of the four minimal elements, however inadvertently. Any set of decisions that assembles a handled offender and a suitable target, in the absence of a capable guardian and intimate handler, will tend to be criminogenic. Conversely, any decision that prevents this convergence will impair criminal acts. Even though an offender may prefer to violate the law, his or her preference can be thwarted by the structure of decisions made by others, regardless of whether they know they are preventing a crime from occurring. In short, we cannot understand the rational structure of criminal behavior by considering the reasoning of only one actor in the system.

These ideas lead to practical advice for the crime researcher and theorist: Count television sets, monitor their portability, check their location. Examine travel patterns away from home; numbers of persons moving about with family, friends, or strangers; adolescent activities with peers and parents; automobilization of youth; shopping patterns, parking patterns, and so forth. Check household composition, housing types, and patterns of occupancy of buildings and of ties among occupants. Examine when crime fails and when it succeeds, as well as its control. Look at hourly patterns of activity and where people are on the map. Check parental position vis-à-vis their own children and patterns of recognition among neighbors. Like physics and physiology, criminogenesis derives from a movement of physically bounded and identifiable entities about the physical world—movements that can be tracked according to map, clock, and calendar, and that from time to time assemble or disperse the four minimal elements in the web of informal crime control.

A good start can be made by studying just three populations of entities: adolescents, parents, and television sets. Find out the size, location, movements, and convergence of these three populations of entities and you will go a long way in understanding crime rates and their variance over space and time.

Although any event may surprise, the larger population of events is systematized by daily life: the volume of people and goods, their location, and their movements over space and time (see Felson, 1980). To understand the rational order of crime, one must study the volume and composition of people and property, their relationships, and their movements according to map, clock, and calendar.

References

Brantingham, Paul and Patricia Brantingham
    1984   Patterns in Crime. New York: Macmillan.
Cohen, L.E. and Marcus Felson
    1979   "Social change and crime rate trends: a routine activity approach."
           American Sociological Review 44 (August): 588–608.
Cusson, Maurice
    1983   Why Delinquency? Toronto: University of Toronto Press.
Felson, Marcus
    1980   "Human chronography." Sociology and Social Research 65 (October):
           1–9.
    1983   "The ecology of crime." Pp. 665–70 in Encyclopedia of Crime and
           Justice. New York: Free Press-Macmillan.
Felson, Marcus and Michael Gottfredson
    1984   "Social indicators of adolescent activities near peers and parents."
           Journal of Marriage and the Family 46 (August): 709–14.
Hindelang, Michael, Michael Gottfredson and James Garafolo
    1978   Victims of Personal Crime: An Empirical Foundation for a Theory of
           Personal Victimization. Cambridge, MA: Ballinger.
Hirschi, Travis
    1969   Causes of Delinquency. Berkeley and Los Angeles: University of
           California Press.
Klein, Malcolm W.
    1971   Street Gangs and Street Workers. Englewood Cliffs, NJ: Prentice-Hall.
Mayhew, Pat, Ronald V. G. Clarke, A. Sturman and Michael Hough
    1976   Crime as Opportunity. Home Office Research Study No. 34. London:
           HMSO.
Rengert, George and J. Wasilchik
    1980   "Residential burglary. The awareness and use of extended space." Paper
           read at the American Society of Criminology Annual Meeting, San
           Francisco.

9
Models of Decision Making Under Uncertainty: The Criminal Choice

PAMELA LATTIMORE AND ANN WITTE

Editors' Note

Gary Becker's comment that a useful theory of criminal behavior could "...simply extend the economist's usual analysis of choice" (1968:170) marked the beginning of attempts to apply economic models of rational decision making, such as expected utility theory, to offending. Such models, in common with those of statistical decision theory, were essentially prescriptive rather than descriptive, although it was also assumed that real-life decision making would tend to accept and conform to their axioms. In the present chapter, Pamela Lattimore and Ann Witte review the theoretical and empirical shortcomings of a commonly used economic model, the expected utility model of decision making under uncertainty, and suggest that these seriously impair its adequacy as a descriptive or predictive theory of choice behavior. They then proceed to examine an alternative theory, namely, prospect theory, a descriptive model developed by Kahneman and Tversky, on the basis of empirical research into individual decision-making behavior, specifically to account for those observed deviations of actual choice behavior from ones predicted by expected utility or subjective expected utility theory. Prospect theory's emphasis on the ways in which risky alternatives (or 'prospects") are edited into simpler representations suggests just those sorts of information-processing activities that may well underlie aspects of the criminal decision-making activities described in part 1, where operations must be swift or deal with complex arrays of alternatives. Similarly, its discussion of the judgmental principles governing choice—notably the replacement of probabilities (objective or subjective) by decision weights, and of utilities by values assigned to changes in wealth rather than to final assets, and its treatment of attitude to risk—illustrate the potential value of increasing the responsiveness of normative economic models to questions of procedural rationality, and specifically to the results of empirical research on individual choice behaviors. Some examples of prospect theory's potential for coping with behavior not readily explicable in terms of expected utility models are given, and Lattimore and Witte end by operationalizing the two approaches, in preparation for a proposed empirical analysis. They draw attention to the practical importance of developing more adequate models of criminal decision making and exploring their implications for the formulation of criminal justice measures (such as deterrence) designed to influence criminal choices.

Theoretical models of decision making under uncertainty are applied to criminal choice in an effort to determine the variables that can be manipulated by criminal justice agencies to reduce criminal activity. For example, three policy alternatives come to mind for the expenditure of public funds: (1) increase funding for police services, thereby increasing the probability of apprehension and conviction; (2) establish longer sentences for crimes (which must necessarily be accompanied by increased funding for prisons), thereby increasing the cost or penalty associated with a criminal act; and (3) increase funding for rehabilitative programs, thereby reducing the proclivity of an individudal to commit crimes or, for vocational programs, increasing the opportunity costs (legal income foregone) to the criminal of engaging in illegal activities. As public funds are not unlimited, theoretical models can provide a basis for establishing the most efficient expenditure of available resources.

Since the pioneering article by Gary Becker (1968), economists have used the von Neumann–Morgenstern expected utility paradigm to model the criminal choice. (See Schmidt and Witte, 1984, and Roth and Witte, 1985, for surveys.) This approach assumes that the individual contemplating a criminal act will decide to commit the crime only if he or she expects that committing the crime will lead to a more satisfactory outcome than not doing so. This hardly seems controversial, although some would object to modeling the criminal choice as a rational decision.

Objections to the expected utility approach to criminal choice are both theoretical and empirical. From a theoretical perspective, the paradigm views the individual as carefully estimating the probability p that a criminal act will lead to punishment and the utility (satisfaction) that he or she would receive if the act (1) does or (2) does not lead to criminal sanctions. For example, an individual contemplating breaking into a warehouse will estimate the probability that he or she will be apprehended (e.g., as .25), the possible gains and punishments to be achieved, and the levels of satisfaction that will be gained from the break-in if he or she is not apprehended (e.g., the utility of gaining $500) or is apprehended (e.g., the utility of gaining $500 and receiving a $700 fine). Under this paradigm, the individual next calculates his or her expected utility by weighting the utility attached to the two possible states (punishment and no punishment) by the probability that each state will occur (p and $1 - p$, respectively). To continue our example, the individual would make the following calculation:

$$EU = .75u(x^0 + \$500) + .25u(x^0 + \$500 - \$700), \quad (9.1)$$

where u is a function that converts dollars into levels of satisfaction, and x^0 is the individual's initial wealth. The individual will commit the criminal act if his or her expected utility, as calculated above, is higher by doing so than by not doing so.

From an empirical perspective, the existing literature seeking to estimate the expected utility model of criminal choice calls the model into question. Most of this empirical research has used aggregate data (see Blumstein et al., 1978; Brier and Fienberg, 1980; Cook, 1980, for surveys). Such data can be used to estimate a model of individual choice such as the expected utility model only if very stringent assumptions are made. For example, in an early and now quite famous attempt to estimate the economic model of crime, Ehrlich (1973) justified using aggregate data to estimate this expected utility model by assuming that all individuals are identical. The data appropriate for testing the expected utility model, however, are individual, not aggregate data. There have now been a few studies that use data for individual offenders (see Witte and Long, 1984, for a survey). Whether aggregate or individual data are used, these studies provide only very weak support for the expected utility model.

A number of laboratory and survey studies (e.g., Claster, 1967; Carroll, 1978; Cimler and Beach, 1981) of criminal choice provide possible explanations of the poor predictive performance of expected utility models of criminal choice. These studies have found that probabilities used in decision making tend to be subjective rather than objective. Further, they suggest that individuals view aspects (gain, penalty, probabilities) of the criminal choice independently and not in the multiplicative form assumed by expected utility theory (Equation 9.1).

In this chapter, we carefully examine the expected utility model of decision making in risky situations, such as the criminal choice, and an alternative to this model that is based on prospect theory, suggested by Kahneman and Tversky (1979). More specifically, in the next two sections, we briefly review the expected utility model and examine the major criticisms that have been leveled against this model. In the section entitled "The Prospect Theory Model," we describe prospect theory, an alternative model of decision making under uncertainty; the section entitled "Expected Utility and Prospect Theory Models of Criminal Choice" develops an expected utility model and a prospect theory model of criminal choice and contrasts these two models. The final section contains our summary.

The Expected Utility Model

The expected utility model, which has been widely used by economists to model criminal choice, was originally developed by John von Neumann and Oskar Morgenstern (1944) as a general model of decision making in risky situations. This paradigm, as a formal mathematical model, assumes that the decision maker has a complete and transitive preference ordering of all outcomes that could result from a choice (see von Neumann and Morgenstern, 1944; Friedman and Savage, 1948; Hey, 1979).

To expand our example, suppose the criminal is faced with three possible outcomes from burglarizing a warehouse: (1) finding goods with a market value of $500, (2) finding $300 in cash, and (3) finding nothing. The individual would have a complete preference ordering if, for example, he or she could say that Outcome 1 was at least as desirable as Outcome 2, and Outcome 2 was at least as desirable as Outcome 3. The individual's ordering would be transitive, as required by the paradigm, if the individual who prefers Outcome 1 to Outcome 2 and Outcome 2 to Outcome 3 also prefers Outcome 1 to Outcome 3.

The expected utility model also requires that the individual know the probability with which each outcome may occur, that the sum of the probabilities of all possible outcomes is 1, and that he or she uses the standard rules of probability theory to determine the probability of compound events. For example, our criminal is assumed to know the probabilities with which Outcomes 1 through 3 will occur if he or she burglarizes the warehouse. Also, if we assume that our criminal is interested in cash and will therefore fence any stolen goods, then he or she is assumed to know the probabilities with which the $500 worth of goods can be converted to cash. Figure 9.1 illustrates the calculations expected of the criminal.

In addition to the restrictions on preferences and the requirements on the manipulation of probabilities, expected utility theory also possesses several other, more technical axioms. A complete listing of the axioms underlying expected utility theory is presented in Appendix I.

If all of the axioms are satisfied, then we can define expected utility as we have in Equation 9.1 or, more generally as follows:

$$EU(X) = p_1u(x_1) + p_2u(x_2) + \ldots + p_nu(x_n), \qquad (9.2)$$

where p_k is the probability that state $k = 1,2,\ldots,n$ will occur, and x_k is the outcome if state k occurs.

To understand fully the expected utility model, it is necessary to consider carefully the meaning of probability and of the utility function u as used in the model. The concept of probability as used in the expected utility model has been debated vigorously, with some authors contending that these probabilities are objective (e.g., the actual probability of being apprehended for some crime) and others that the probabilities are subjective (e.g., the criminal perceives a probability that may differ from the actual probability). (See Sinn, 1983:6–40, for an extended discussion

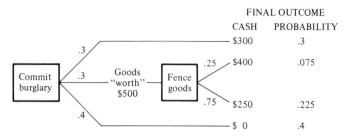

FIGURE 9.1. Possible outcomes (returns only) resulting from burglarizing a hypothetical warehouse. Decimal numbers represent the probabilities of the outcomes occurring.

and Schoemaker, 1980, 1982, for reviews.) Whether probabilities attached to the states of the world are objective (as assumed by von Neumann and Morgenstern) or subjective (as developed by Ramsey, 1931; de Finetti, 1937; Savage, 1954; and Pratt et al., 1964; and applied to expected utility theory by Edwards, 1955), it is necessary that the objective probability p_k or the subjective probability $f(p_k)$ conform to the rules of probability theory (for example, see Figure 9.1). In other words, "subjective probabilities are mathematically indistinguishable from other types of probabilities" (Schoemaker, 1982)—a finding that, Hey (1979:41) noted, "saves us from the difficult task of making the distinction."

Utility, as used in this model, is quite different from utility as used in traditional economic models such as models of consumer choice. In these models, there is no uncertainty and the consumer knows what level of satisfaction he or she will attain from a given choice. The utility function simply converts any level of consumption to a level of satisfaction (or utility). By way of contrast, the von Neumann–Morgenstern utility function measures both the value of the outcome under certainty (i.e., the strength of preference) and the decision maker's attitude toward risk. (See Hershey and Schoemaker, 1980, and Schoemaker, 1982, for an extended discussion of various concepts of utility.)

Attitudes toward risk are central to models of criminal choice. Thus, it behooves us to explain how attitudes toward risk are measured. These attitudes are discerned from the shape of the utility function. If the utility function is as in Figure 9.2(a), the individual is said to dislike risk (i.e., to be risk averse). If the individual's utility function is as in Figure 9.2(b), he or she is said to be indifferent to risk (i.e., to be risk neutral). Finally, if the utility function is as in Figure 9.2(c), the individual is said to like risk (i.e., to be risk preferring). Some authors (Arrow, 1974; Pratt, 1964) have suggested that the shape of the utility function is not adequate to explain attitudes toward risk; for details of these authors' proposals, see Appendix II.

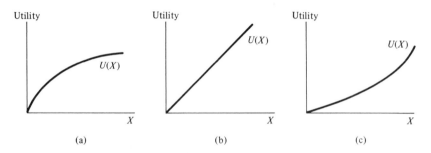

FIGURE 9.2. Examples of the individual utility function illustrating (a) risk aversion, (b) risk neutrality, and (c) risk preference.

Criticisms of the Expected Utility Model

The validity of the expected utility model as a descriptive or predictive model of decision making under uncertainty has been challenged by empirical studies. (Note that we make no distinction between risk and uncertainty in this chapter. See Knight, 1933, for a discussion of this issue.) Violations of the axioms underlying the model appear to be common. Also, in many cases the model fails to predict individual choices accurately. It has been suggested that the model's failures are due to such things as cognitive limitations (Simon, 1957), short-cut decision making, (Corbin, 1980) and processing heuristics (Kahneman and Tversky, 1979). A brief review of studies revealing violations of the expected utility assumptions regarding preferences, probabilities, and attitudes toward risk is presented below.

As previously noted, expected utility theory requires that people have definite preferences and that those preferences be transitive. Schoemaker (1982) cites early work by Frederich Mosteller and Philip Nogee (1951) that shows that subjects did not give consistent responses on repeated measures of preferences. More recently, experimental work by Sarah Lichtenstein and Paul Slovic (1971; Slovic and Lichtenstein, 1983) has revealed a phenomenon termed "preference reversal." Preference reversals occur when individuals prefer to play a gamble that features a high probability of winning a modest sum of money (e.g., an 80% chance to win $10) rather than a gamble that features a small probability of winning a large amount of money (e.g., a 1% chance to win $800) but, at the same time, attach a higher monetary value to the low probability/large return than to the high probability/small return bet. Such preferences represent reversals because the individual is simultaneously preferring one choice and placing a higher value on the other choice. David Grether and Charles Plott (1979) attempted to discredit the results of preference reversal experiments by conducting a series of experiments designed to accommodate 13 hypothesized causes of the phenomenon. The only theory they could not reject allows individual choice to depend upon the context in which the choices are made. As they noted, such a theory is not very pleasing from a modeling perspective. In responding to the Grether and Plott findings, Slovic and Lichtenstein (1983) pointed out that reversals can be seen not as an isolated phenomenon, but as one of a broad class of findings that demonstrate violations of preference models due to strong dependence of choice and preference upon information-processing considerations.

Differences in the expressed preferences of individuals have also been found in studies of alternative descriptions of mathematically identical choice problems. These "context effects" have been observed in experiments where subjects are presented with equivalent lotteries formatted as either gamble or insurance decisions (Hershey and Schoemaker, 1980). The effect of context on preferences and the interaction between the context effect and the levels of probability and loss cannot be explained by expected utility theory and, as Hershey and Schoemaker (1980) noted, requires deeper knowledge of the psychology of problem representation in general. They also suggested that it is likely that the context effect will be stronger yet in real-world situations where probabilities and outcomes are not known with certainty.

A final comment on violations of the expected utility assumptions on preferences derives from the work of Kahneman and Tversky (1979). In a series of experiments, they found that individuals tend to overweight certain outcomes, a clear violation of the predictions of the expected utility model. Additionally, they have found that people often employ a heuristic when predicting values of outcomes (Tversky and Kahneman, 1982d). This heuristic applies when people make estimates by starting from an initial value that is adjusted to yield the final answer. They report that research has shown that the adjustment is usually insufficient, with final answers being biased toward initial values.

Violations of the assumptions underlying the expected utility model have also been found in studies of the formation and use of probabilities. Expected utility theory requires (1) the identification of appropriate probabilities (either objective or subjective) for each possible state of the world, and (2) the reduction of compound lotteries to equivalent single lotteries. (See Figure 9.1 for an example and Appendix I for the axioms.) Tversky and Kahneman noted that people often rely on heuristic principles when assessing probabilities. Specifically, Tversky and Kahneman (1982d) hypothesized that in developing "probabilities" people rely (1) on how closely an object resembles a class or process and (2) on how easy it is to recall similar instances. Both of these heuristics, although useful, may lead to systematic errors in assessing the required probability. Additionally, Tversky and Kahneman suggested that people have misconceptions about chance such that they expect that a sequence of events generated by a random process will represent the essential characteristics of that process even when the sequence is short; they found these beliefs to persist even for "statistically sophisticated subjects." (See also Bar-Hillel, 1973, 1982; Kahneman and Tversky, 1982a, 1982b, 1982c; Ross and Sicoly, 1982; Taylor, 1982; Tversky and Kahneman, 1982a, 1982b, 1982c, 1983.)

Although it might seem reasonable to expect that individuals would learn through experience that their heuristic judgments are inadequate and take appropriate corrective action, experimental evidence does not support this supposition. Hillel Einhorn (1980, 1982; see also Einhorn and Hogarth, 1978) reported that because task structures are often unknown and people often act in ways that preclude learning, it is unlikely that appropriate adjustments are made.

Considerable evidence also exists that individuals underweight objective probabilities when forming subjective probabilities, unless the probabilities are "small," in which case they are overweighted (Hershey and Schoemaker, 1980; Ali, 1977). Additionally, the formation of subjective probabilities appears to be affected by whether a situation is strictly a gamble or one in which an individual feels capable of exerting control (Langer, 1982; Andriessen, 1971).

Thus, the ability of people to form "accurate" subjective probabilities seems to be very limited. What of the individual's ability to follow the rules of statistics? Is it reasonable to assume that the individual possesses statistical intuition that approximates the rules of mathematical probability? Extensive research by Tversky and Kahneman (1983) and Bar-Hillel (1973) indicates that the answer to this question is no.

These findings suggest that people's preferences and abilities to formulate and use probabilities do not conform to the axioms underlying the expected utility model. As Tversky and Kahneman noted,

A system of judgments that does not obey the conjunction rule [of probability] cannot be expected to obey more complicated principles that presuppose this rule, such as Bayesian updating, external calibration, and the maximization of expected utility. (1983: 313)

The final area of research to be considered here that casts doubt upon the validity of the expected utility paradigm is studies of the risk properties of the utility function. Individuals have generally been assumed to exhibit global risk preferences, usually risk aversion—that is, to have a utility function as pictured in Figure 9.2(a)—although this is not a formal axiom of expected utility theory. This assumption precludes rather common behavior such as the simultaneous purchase of insurance and participation in (actuarially unfair) gambles. The assumption of global risk attitudes has therefore been the subject of considerable theoretical and empirical investigation.

Friedman and Savage (1948) were among the first to address this problem. They suggested that the simplest utility function that could explain simultaneous purchasing of insurance and gambling is one that is first concave, as pictured in Figure 9.2(a), then convex, as in Figure 9.2(c), and then concave again. They also suggested that most individuals tend to have incomes that place them in one of the two concave segments of the utility function. Markowitz (1959) proposed a similar shape for the utility function but hypothesized that all individuals occupy an initial position on the curve such that the individual will be risk preferring for small and moderate gains (i.e., the utility function over this region is convex) and risk averse for small and moderate losses (i.e., the utility function over this range is concave). The Markowitz utility function therefore accommodates both the purchase of insurance and gambling. Recent studies support the existence of an inflection point in the utility function, but the prevailing view is that the individual is risk averse for gains and risk preferring for losses as shown in Figure 9.3 (cf. Fishburn and Kochenberger, 1979; Hershey and Schoemaker, 1980; Kahneman and Tversky, 1979).

The Prospect Theory Model

The findings described above have led to modifications of the expected utility model and to the development of alternative models of decision making under uncertainty. Examples of models that alter certain aspects of the expected utility model include the subjective expected utility model (Edwards, 1955), the certainty equivalent model (Handa, 1977), the subjectively weighted utility model (Karmarkar, 1978), the differentially

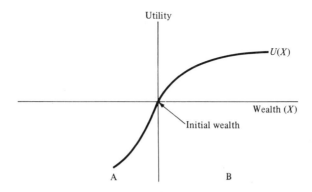

FIGURE 9.3. Example of a utility function for an individual who is risk seeking for losses (region A) and risk averse for gains (region B) relative to the initial wealth position.

weighted product-averaging model (Lynch and Cohen, 1978), the regret theory model (Bell, 1982), and the prospect theory model (Kahneman and Tversky, 1979). In this section, we describe prospect theory and contrast it with the expected utility model.

Kahneman and Tversky suggest that individuals choose between risky alternatives using a two-phase assessment process. In the first phase, alternatives are edited; in the second phase, "the edited prospects are evaluated and the prospect of highest value is chosen" (Kahneman and Tversky, 1979).

The Editing Phase

Kahneman and Tversky (1979) suggested that six operations are carried out during the editing phase. These operations are performed over the set of offered prospects and result in a simpler representation of these prospects:

Coding

Coding is the first editing operation that Kahneman and Tversky proposed. They postulated that potential outcomes from prospects are valued relative to some reference point (usually the current asset level) as gains or losses. The coding operation, with its underlying assumption of a reference point, differs from the usual von Neumann–Morgenstern utility assumption that the carrier of value is the final asset position rather than changes in assets (cf. von Neumann and Morgenstern, 1944; Friedman and Savage, 1948).

Combination

Combination, the second activity of the editing phase, is performed to simplify compound outcomes by combining probabilities associated with identical outcomes. For example, an individual breaking into a ware-house might perceive a 25% chance of finding $200 in cash and a 45% chance of finding goods that can be fenced for $200. The value of this prospect, which we will denote ($200, .25; $200, .45), will be reduced to the prospect ($200, .70). A similar combination operation is consistent with expected utility theory (see Appendix I, Axiom 5).

Segregation

Segregation is an editing operation that eliminates riskless components of prospects (i.e., amounts that will be obtained regardless of outcome) from risky components. For example, ($300, .80; $200, .20) will be reduced to ($200, 1; $100, .80).

CANCELLATION

Cancellation, the fourth activity in the editing phase, eliminates from consideration components that are shared by all prospects. The decision maker is assumed to focus only on those components that differ.

SIMPLIFICATION

Simplification is the fifth activity in the editing phase and entails rounding probabilities and outcomes. For example, .48 and .52 would both be considered .50, and $99 and $101 would both be considered $100. As Kahneman and Tversky (1979) pointed out, simplification can lead to apparent intransitivities of preference.

DETECTION OF DOMINANCE

Detection of dominance is the final editing operation proposed. Kahneman and Tversky (1979) noted that this operation is a particularly important form of simplification that involves the discarding of prospects clearly dominated by others. For example, the prospect of burglarizing an unguarded warehouse in a desolate area (with an attendant low probability of detection and capture) will dominate the prospect of burglarizing an equally well-stocked warehouse that is adjacent to a police station.

Kahneman and Tversky (1979) proposed that "because the editing operations facilitate the task of decision, it is assumed that they are performed whenever possible." As noted above, when it was indicated that simplification can lead to apparent intransitivities of preferences, the editing operations can lead to anomalies of preference and, in particular, "the preference order between prospects need not be invariant across contexts, because the same offered prospect could be edited in different ways depending on the context in which it appears" (Kahneman and Tversky, 1979:275). Once the editing operations are complete, the decision maker proceeds to the evaluation phase of the choice task.

The Evaluation Phase

Once the decision maker evaluates all prospects, he or she then chooses the prospect that offers the highest overall value, denoted V. V in prospect theory is calculated in a manner analogous to expected utility $EU(X)$ (see Equation 9.2). However, decision weights (ws) replace probabilities, and subjective value functions (vs) replace utility functions (us). Thus,

$$V = w_1v(x_1) + w_2v(x_2) + \ldots + w_nv(x_n). \qquad (9.3)$$

Kahneman and Tversky (1979) suggested that the decision weights (ws) are functions of the objective probability, for example, $w_1 = w(p_1)$, but not equal to them. They further hypothesized that the decision weights do not follow the rules of probability theory. For example, $w_1 + w_2 + \ldots + w_n < 1$.

Returning again to our criminal choice example, we can construct a V function for our burglar that would be analogous to Equation 9.1. The overall value for the prospect would be:

$$V = w(.75)v(\$500) + w(.25)v(\$500 - \$700). \qquad (9.4)$$

Although Equation 9.1 and Equation 9.4 (or, more generally, Equations 9.2 and 9.3) are similar in form, the components of the two models are quite different. In the following paragraphs, we will consider the nature of the value function v and the weighting function w and contrast these functions with the utility function u and probability p of the expected utility model.

The Value Function

The value function over outcomes v, as distinct from the value function over prospects V, is a function that is defined on deviations from the reference point, usually the initial asset position. Thus, the values x_k ($k = 1, 2, \ldots, n$) in Equation 9.3 represent only the changes in wealth or, more specifically, the differences in final wealth (x^*_k) and initial wealth (x^0), whereas in the utility function of Equation 9.2 the x_k values represent the final wealth positions. Kahneman and Tversky (1979) hypothesized that v is concave above the reference point and convex below the reference point (see Figure 9.4). In other words, the marginal value of both gains and losses generally decreases with their magnitude. Finally, they believe that the value function for losses is steeper than the value function for gains, implying that the loss of a specific sum of money is more painful than the gain of the same sum is satisfying.

These characteristics of the value function suggest, for example, that tax cheating may be more prevalent among those owing taxes at the end of the year (who are thus seeking to reduce a loss) than among those receiving a refund (and thus facing a gain). As underwitholding is more likely for individuals earning either low incomes or high incomes, prospect theory offers an explanation of why tax cheating is more common at the lower and upper ends of the spectrum. (For a more extensive discussion of tax cheating and prospect theory, see Johnson and Payne, this volume.)

Four differences between the v function of prospect theory and the von Neumann–Morgenstern utility function are readily apparent. The first is that v is defined over certain outcomes, as opposed to u which is defined over uncertain outcomes. Second, the v function does not reflect attitude toward risk, whereas by definition the u function incorporates attitude toward risk as well as preferences. Third, the value function is assessed

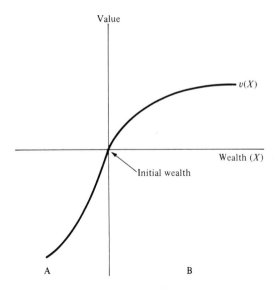

FIGURE 9.4. Example of the Kahneman–Tversky value function where the value function reflects the satisfaction to be derived from changes in wealth obtained with certainty. Region A indicates increasing marginal valuation of losses, and region B indicates decreasing marginal valuation of gains.

over changes in assets rather than over final asset levels as is the utility function. Fourth, the value function, as previously noted, includes both concave and convex sections, whereas, although not a formal requirement, the utility function has been generally assumed to be everywhere concave (compare Figures 9.2(a) and 9.4).

The Weighting Function

The weighting function $w(\cdot)$ proposed by Kahneman and Tversky is a radical departure from the probability weights attached to utilities in expected utility theory. For Kahneman and Tversky, decision weights measure the impact of events on the desirability of prospects and not merely the perceived likelihood of these events. Thus, decision weights are *not* probabilities: "They do not obey the probability axioms and they should not be interpreted as measures of degree or belief" (Kahneman and Tversky, 1979:280). Kahneman and Tversky did note, however, that if the expectation principle holds, then $w(p) = p$.

Kahneman and Tversky also proposed that the decision weights may be functions of factors other than the probabilities associated with the prospects. In particular, they suggested that "ambiguity" could influence the weight. The results of studies on the effect on risky choice of the perception of control (Langer, 1982) and of skill (Andriessen, 1971) suggest that perception of control or skill might also affect the decision weights.

Restricting their discussion to decision weights as a function only of objective probability—i.e., $w(p)$—Kahneman and Tversky proposed the following characteristics for the weighting function (Figure 9.5):

1. The weighting function is an increasing function of p.
2. The weighting function scale is anchored at 0 and 1; in other words, $w(0) = 0$ and $w(1) = 1$.
3. For small p (less than about .1), the weighting function is a subadditive function of p—i.e., $w(rp) > rw(p)$ for $0 < r < 1$—and $w(p) > p$. For example, if $p = .1$ and $r = .2$, then $w(.1 \times .2) > .2w(.1)$ or $w(.02) > .2w(.1)$. This characteristic implies the overweighting of small probabilities.
4. For all p, the weighting function exhibits subcertainty. In other words, $w(p) + w(1 - p) < 1$ for all $0 < p < 1$.
5. The weighting function w is regressive with respect to p. In other words, as p increases, $w(p)$ also increases, but not as much. This characteristic implies that individuals are less sensitive to changes in

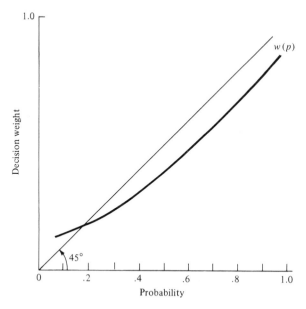

FIGURE 9.5. Example of a hypothetical decision-weighting function where the decision weight is a function of probability as proposed by Kahneman and Tversky. *Note*: Small probabilities are overweighted, and there are discontinuities near the endpoint. (The 45° line shows the value of the decision weight if the decision weight equals the probability; i.e., if $w(p) = p$.)

probability than the expectation principle would dictate, and, for our criminal, that he or she would be less sensitive to an increase in the probability of punishment than would be predicted by the expected utility model.

6. The ratio of weights is closer to 1 for small probabilities than for large ones. This property, which Kahneman and Tversky called subproportionality, constrains the shape of w and holds "if and only if log [w] is a convex function of log p" (Kahneman and Tversky, 1979:282).

7. Finally, Kahneman and Tversky hypothesized that w "is not well-behaved near the endpoints" (p. 283). This hypothesis is based on their supposition that people ignore highly unlikely events and do not differentiate between highly probable and certain events. To return to our example, this characteristic implies that a potential criminal may well ignore low probabilities of apprehension and see high probabilities of gain from breaking into a warehouse as a certain outcome.

Attitudes Toward Risk

Kahneman and Tversky (1979:285) claimed that attitudes toward risk are determined jointly by v and w in prospect theory. Relying on their hypotheses that the value function over gains is concave (Figure 9.4) and that $w(p) > p$ for small p (Figure 9.5), they proved that risk seeking over gains (i.e., gambling behavior) can be explained by their theory. Similarly, given a convex value function over losses and the overweighting of small probabilities, they showed that risk aversion over losses (i.e., insurance purchasing) can also be explained by their theory. Thus, prospect theory is able to explain simultaneous gambling and insurance purchasing, both of which are characterized by small probability/high gain (loss) outcomes.

Prospect theory (as presented and summarized by Figures 9.4 and 9.5) does not accommodate risk seeking over gains when the probability of realizing those gains is large—i.e., when $w(p) < p$. However, the discussion on shifts of reference provides some insight into how this behavior could be accommodated by prospect theory. Specifically, Kahneman and Tversky noted that there are situations in which gains and losses are coded relative to an expectation or aspiration level that differs from the status quo. As an example, they described a person who has recently lost $2,000 and is faced with a choice between a sure $1,000 ($1,000, 1) or an even chance to gain $2,000 or nothing ($2,000, .5; $0, .5). The large probability and the concavity of the value functions for gains would predict that the individual would choose ($1,000, 1) over the riskier choice ($2,000, .5; $0, .5); however, if the person codes the prospects as a choice between (−$2,000, .5; $0. .5) and (−$1,000, 1), prospect theory would predict that the individual would choose the riskier choice.

Additionally, as Johnson and Payne (this volume) point out, if an individual's aspiration level is wealth attainable from criminal activity, desistance from crime implies a loss. Thus, the individual may be willing to take greater risks in criminal activity to remain at the aspiration level than would be expected if the reference point were the status quo and returns to crime were viewed as gains.

Thus, risk attitude is determined by the value function to the extent that the reference point establishes the changes in marginal valuation of the outcomes (i.e., whether the outcome is a gain or loss and therefore whether value is determined in the concave or convex section of the value function). Thus, for our potential criminal a change in initial wealth (the reference level of wealth) would shift the value function rather than simply result in movement along the function as occurs along the utility function in expected utility theory.

Expected Utility and Prospect Theory Models of Criminal Choice

An expected utility model and a prospect theory model of criminal choice should yield different theoretical predictions of the way in which changes in criminal justice policy will affect the decisions of criminals. To compare the theoretical predictions of these alternative models, it is necessary to develop expected utility and prospect theory models that incorporate major factors affecting criminal choice similarly

An Expected Utility Model of Criminal Choice

Consider first an expected utility model. We assume that when deciding upon the amount of time to allocate to criminal activity, the individual attempts to maximize expected utility (in other words, that the potential criminal wants to be as well off as possible). The model presented below contains elements from one of Isaac Ehrlich's models (Ehrlich, 1973) of criminal activity (a fixed amount of time allocated to one activity) and one of the models developed by Schmidt and Witte (1984) (both leisure time and wealth enter the utility function). For our model, we assume that the criminal gains utility (U) from two items: the total wealth or income that he or she has available (W) and the amount of leisure time at his or her disposal (T). Specifically, we assume that

$$U = U(W, T),$$

where W is defined to be the sum of income from legal endeavors (w^0) and the returns on illegal activities, and T is defined to be the amount of nonwork (legal and illegal) or leisure time available.

The returns on illegal activities are assumed to depend upon the time spent in illegal activities (t_I) and other factors such as the community's stocks of durable goods and investment in protective devices such as safes. These other factors (denoted α) are assumed to shift the illegal gains function. We assume that all gains from illegal activity can be converted to monetary equivalents by a function that we denote X_1. To summarize,

$$W = w^0 + X_1(t_I, \alpha).$$

T is defined to be equal to the individual's total time available (T^0) minus a constant amount of time devoted to legal work (e.g., 40 hours per week, denote $\bar{t}_L$), a variable amount of time devoted to illegal activity (t_I), and an amount of time that may be required to satisfy sentences meted out by the court for illegal activity. The sentence is assumed to depend upon the amount of time that the individual allocates to illegal activity and other factors such as the current policy of the criminal justice system. These other factors (denoted β) are assumed to shift the penalty function. We assume that all penalties can be converted to an amount of time required to satisfy them by a function that we denote X_2. To summarize,

$$T = T^0 - \bar{t}_L - t_I - X_2(t_I; \beta).$$

Now, we assume that there are only two possible outcomes to the commission of a criminal act: State A if the individual is caught and punished (with the probability p) and State B if the individual is not caught. Then, we can write the individual's positions in the two states of the world as follows: For State A:

$$W^A = w^0 + X_1(t_I; \alpha) \tag{9.5}$$

$$T^A = T^0 - \bar{t}_L - t_I - X_2(t_I; \beta). \tag{9.6}$$

For State B:

$$W^B = w^0 + X_1(t_I; \alpha) \tag{9.7}$$

$$T^B = T^0 - \bar{t}_L - t_I. \tag{9.8}$$

Given the above structure, the individual's decision problem is to maximize expected utility, which is defined to be the sum of the individual's utility in the two states weighted by the probability that the individual will find himself or herself in that state. More formally, the individual seeks to maximize:

$$EU(W, T) = pU(W^A, T^A) + (1 - p)U(W^B, T^B), \tag{9.9}$$

with respect to the time devoted to illegal activity (t_I).

The (potential) offender is assumed to derive increased satisfaction from additional amounts of W and T but to value additions at an increasingly lower rate. In other words, the individual is assumed to have a utility function with respect to wealth (leisure time held constant) and a utility function with respect to time (wealth held constant) that take the shape shown in Figure 9.2(a). Technically, these assumptions imply the following restrictions on the utility function:

$$\partial U(W^i, T^i)/\partial W > 0,$$

$$\partial U(W^i, T^i)/\partial T > 0,$$

$$\partial^2 U(W^i, T^i)/\partial W^2 < 0,$$

$$\partial^2 U(W^i, T^i)/\partial T^2 < 0,$$

where i = State A or B.

There is little guidance for assumptions concerning the way in which the marginal utility of wealth changes with a change in leisure time. In other words,

$$\partial^2 U(W^i, T^i)/\partial W \partial T > = < 0, \qquad (9.10)$$

for states i = A, B (see Schmidt and Witte, 1984:191). If we assume multivariate risk aversion (see Richard, 1975), the individual will value increases in wealth less as the amount of leisure time increases, and Equation 9.10 will be negative. The implication of this assumption is that poor people value leisure more than rich people. There is no good basis for such an assumption (or for the opposite one), although one normally thinks of people as disliking risk. We make no a priori assumptions about the sign of Equation 9.10.

The returns on crime $X_1(t_I; \alpha)$ and the penalty for crime $X_2(t_I; \beta)$ schedules are assumed to be increasing functions of the time allocated to illegal activity t_I. This assumption simply means that the criminal gains more loot or is subject to greater penalties the greater his or her involvement in crime. However, it is also assumed that increases in gains and penalties occur at a decreasing rate as more and more time is devoted to criminal activities. Technically, these assumptions mean that the first partial derivatives of $X_1(t_I; \alpha)$ and $X_2(t_I; \beta)$ with respect to t_I are positive, and the second partial derivatives are negative.

To determine the implications of this theoretical model for criminal behavior, it is necessary to examine mathematically the way in which the amount of time allocated to crime changes as factors outside the criminal's control change. For example, we can use standard techniques from the classical calculus (i.e., the implicit function theorem and Cramer's rule) to discern the way in which the criminal will change the amount of time he or she allocates to crime as the gains to crime or possible penalties increase.

A Prospect Theory Model of Criminal Choice

We now develop a prospect theory model of criminal choice that is analogous to the expected utility model developed above. Under a prospect theory approach, the individual will evaluate a potential choice by considering the change in wealth ΔW as a gain and the change in leisure time ΔT as a loss that may result from the choice. (Recall that in the expected utility model the individual looked at final levels of wealth and leisure, not at changes in these variables.) Thus, prospect theory posits that the individual will code the outcomes in State A and State B (Equations 9.5 through 9.8) to arrive at an expression for these changes. The editing phase is therefore hypothesized to yield the following outcomes for the two states. For State A:

$$\Delta W^A = X_1(t_I; \alpha) \text{ and}$$

$$\Delta T^A = -t_I - X_2(t_I; b).$$

For State B:

$$\Delta W^B = X_1(t_I; \alpha) \text{ and}$$
$$\Delta T^B = -t_I.$$

As can be seen by comparing these equations with Equations 9.5 through 9.8, the outcomes upon which the individual is hypothesized to make valuations (or utility assessments) are quite different for the expected utility and prospect theory models.

The evaluation phase immediately follows the coding of gains and losses and requires the individual to value the criminal prospect by weighting the subjective value v of State A and State B by an individually determined decision weight w. Formally, the evaluation phase requires the individual to maximize

$$V(\Delta W, \Delta T) = w(p)v(\Delta W^A, \Delta T^A) + w(1 - p)v(\Delta W^B, \Delta T^B) \quad (9.11)$$

with respect to t_I.

Comparing Equation 9.11 with the comparable function for the expected utility model (Equation 9.9), we note two major differences: (1) The decision weights depend on the probability that each state will occur but are not identical to them, and (2) valuation depends on changes in and not levels of income and leisure. Further, the behavioral assumptions of prospect theory imply a more complex shape for the value function than the expected utility model assumes for the utility function (compare Figure 9.2(a) and Figure 9.4). More formally, the shape of the prospect theory value function places the following restrictions on the signs of the derivatives:

$$\partial v(\Delta W^i, \Delta T^i)/\partial W > 0,$$

$$\partial v(\Delta W^i, \Delta T^i)/\partial T > 0,$$

$$\partial^2 v(\Delta W^i, \Delta T^i)/\partial W^2 < 0,$$

$$\partial^2 v(\Delta W^i, \Delta T^i)/\partial T^2 > 0,$$

for outcomes i = A, B. Comparing these with the derivatives of the expected utility function, we note that expected utility theory sees the individual as treating gains and losses analogously, whereas prospect theory posits that they are treated quite differently. Gains are valued at a decreasing marginal rate as in the expected utility model, but losses are valued at an increasing marginal rate.

As was the case with the expected utility model, there is little theoretical guidance for discerning the effect of an increase in leisure on the marginal value of wealth. Thus,

$$\partial^2 v \, (\Delta W^i, \, \Delta T^i)/\partial T^i \partial W^i >=< 0,$$

for outcomes i = A, B.

The returns and penalty schedules (X_1 and X_2, respectively) are identical with those proposed for the expected utility model. Thus, the assumptions given in the previous section about the shapes of these two functions apply here as well.

As in the case of the expected utility model, it is necessary to discern the way in which changes in such things as gains and penalties affect the time allocated to criminal activity. Specifically, the effect of changes in the probability of apprehension and the penalty should be quite interesting and different from the analogous results for the expected utility model. Further, the effect of a change in initial wealth in the prospect theory model is quite different from that in the expected utility model. In the expected utility model, initial wealth is treated like any other exogenous (to the criminal) variable, whereas in the prospect theory model it serves to shift the reference point (Figure 9.6).

Summary

In the first section of this chapter, we described the expected utility model that has been the base for economic models of criminal behavior. This model has been widely used to study decision making in risky situations ranging from investment decisions to gambling and insurance. In recent years the model has come under increasing attack, as neither the model's predictions nor its behavioral axioms appear to closely reflect actual decision-making behavior in either the criminal or other decision-making realms. We summarized these criticisms in the second section of the chapter.

Criticisms of the expected utility model have led researchers to alter the model and seek alternative models. In our third section we described one such alternative, the prospect theory model.

In the fourth section we developed and compared analogous expected utility and prospect theory models of criminal choice. We suggested that these two models are likely to lead to quite different conclusions

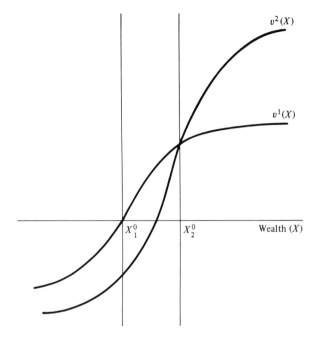

FIGURE 9.6. The effect of a change in initial wealth (X^0) on the value function. *Note*: $X^0_1(X^0_2)$ represents initial wealth in the first (second) instance, and $v^1(X)$ ($v^2(X)$) represents the value function associated with that level of initial wealth.

regarding the way in which changes in criminal justice policy (i.e., changes in the probability of apprehension and punishment and the severity of punishment) and changes in initial wealth affect criminal behavior.

Acknowledgment. We would like to thank the National Science Foundation (NSF) for funding which allowed part of the work contained in this chapter to be completed. NSF's support for this work does not imply its endorsement of the work or of its conclusions.

Appendix I

The von Neumann–Morgenstern expected utility model is derived from a set of axioms that place restrictions on the preference relations that exist among outcomes of various risky situations or lotteries and on the nature of the probability weights that are attached to the outcomes (see von Neumann and Morgenstern, 1944; Friedman and Savage, 1948; Luce and Raiffa, 1957; Hey, 1979). The von Neumann–Morgenstern expected utility axioms are as follows:

Axiom 1 (Complete Ordering of Alternatives). For basic (mutually exclusive) outcomes X_j and X_k, the decision maker either prefers X_j to X_k ($X_j > X_k$), or prefers X_k to X_j ($X_k > X_j$), or is indifferent between X_j and X_k ($X_j \sim X_k$), for all j, k.

Axiom 2 (Transitivity). If $X_j > X_k$ and $X_k > X_n$, then $X_j > X_n$.

Axiom 3 (Continuity). If X_1 is the best outcome and X_n is the worst outcome, then for every X_k ($k = 1, 2, \ldots, n$) there exists some p_k such that the decision maker is indifferent to receiving X_k with certainty or the gamble X_1 with probability p_k and X_n with the probability $(1 - p_k)$.

Axiom 4 (Substitutability). If $X_k \sim Y_k$, then Choice 1 is indifferent to Choice 2 ($C_1 \sim C_2$) where $C_1, = [(p_1, X_1), \ldots, (p_k, X_k), \ldots, (p_n, X_n)]$ and $C_2 = [(p_1, X_1), \ldots, (p_k, Y_k), \ldots, (p_n, X_n)]$. This axiom implies the "independence of irrelevant alternatives."

Axiom 5 (Reduction of Compound Lotteries). This axiom requires the decision maker to use the rules of probability theory to reduce compound lotteries to equivalent simple lotteries. Underlying this requirement are the implications that the decision maker knows the probabilities associated with each state, that these probabilities follow the ordinary rules of probabilities, and that probabilities are combined to produce simple lotteries from compound lotteries. This axiom also implies that the formulation of the lottery will not affect the resulting decision.

Axiom 6 (Monotonicity). The lottery $[(p, X_1), (1 - p, X_n)]$ is preferred to the lottery $[(q, X_1), (1 - q, X_n)]$ if and only if $p > q$ (where X_1 is the most preferred outcome and X_n is the least preferred outcome).

Appendix II

Some authors (e.g., Pratt, 1964) believe that neither the slope nor the curvature of the utility function is adequate to describe attitude toward risk. Pratt (1964) and Kenneth Arrow (1974) proposed using the (negative) ratio of the second derivative $[U''(X)]$ to the first derivative $[U'(X)]$ of the utility function as a measure of absolute risk aversion. This measure is thus,

$$R_A(X) = -U''(X)/U'(X) = -\partial \log U'(X)/\partial X,$$

where X is wealth. They also define a measure of local proportional (sometimes called relative) risk attitude as follows:

$$R_p(X) = -XU''(X)/U'(X) = XR(X).$$

Individuals are characterized as risk preferring, risk neutral, or risk avoiding as $R(X) <=> 0$. Arrow (1974) and Pratt (1964) further suggested that individuals are predominantly characterized as exhibiting decreasing absolute risk aversion; in other words, $R'(X) < 0$, which implies that the willingness to engage in small bets of fixed size increases with income. Both measures are local measures in that they are functions of the value of X.

References

Ali, M.M.
1977 "Probability and utility estimates for racetrack bettors." Journal of Political Economy 85(4):803-15.

Andriessen, J.H.
1971 "Comments on a new risk taking model." Acta Psychologica 35:173-87.

Arrow, K.J.
1974 "The theory of risk aversion." Pp. 90-120 in Essays in the Theory of Risk Aversion. Amsterdam: North-Holland.

Bar-Hillel, M.
1973 "On the subjective probability of compound events." Organizational Behavior and Human Performance 9:396-406.

Bar-Hillel, M.
1982 "Studies of representativeness." Pp. 69-83 in D. Kahneman, P. Slovic and A. Tversky (eds.), Judgment Under Uncertainty: Heuristics and Biases. New York: Cambridge University Press.

Becker, Gary S.
1968 "Crime and punishment: an economic approach." Journal of Political Economy 76(2):169-217.

Bell, D.E.
1982 "Regret in decision making under uncertainty." Operations Research 30(5):961-81.

Blumstein, A., J. Cohen and D. Nagin (eds.)
1978 Deterrence and Incapacitation: Estimating the Effects of Criminal Sanctions on Crime Rates. Washington, DC: National Academy of Sciences.

Brier, S.S. and S.E. Fienberg
1980 "Recent econometric modelling of crime and punishment: support for the deterrence hypothesis." Evaluation Review 4:147-91.

Carroll, J.S.
1978 "A psychological approach to deterrence: the evaluation of crime opportunities." Journal of Personality and Social Psychology 36(12):1512-20.

Cimler, E. and L.R. Beach
1981 "Factors involved in juveniles' decisions about crime." Criminal Justice and Behavior 8:275-86.

Claster, D.S.
1967 "Comparison of risk perceptions between delinquents and nondelinquents." Journal of Criminal Law, Criminology, and Police Science 58:80-6.

Cook, P.J.
  1980 "Research on criminal deterrence: laying the groundwork for the second
         decade." Pp. 211–68 in N. Morris and M. Tonry (eds.), Crime and Justice:
         An Annual Review of Research, Volume 2. Chicago: University of
         Chicago Press.
Corbin, R.M.
  1980 "Decisions that might not get made." Pp. 47–67 in T.S. Wallsten (ed.),
         Cognitive Processes in Choice and Decision Behavior. Hillsdale, NJ:
         Erlbaum.
de Finetti, B.
  1937 "La prévision: ses lois logiques, ses sources subjectives." Annales de
         l'Institut Poincaré 7:1–68.
Edwards, W.
  1955 "The prediction of decision among bets." Journal of Experimental
         Psychology 50:201–14.
Ehrlich, I.
  1973 "Participation in illegitimate activities: a theoretical and empirical
         investigation." Journal of Political Economy 81:521–65.
Einhorn, H.J.
  1980 "Learning from experience and suboptimal rules in decision making."
         Pp. 1–20 in T. S. Wallsten (ed.), Cognitive Processes in Choice and
         Decision Behavior. Hillsdale, NJ: Erlbaum.
Einhorn, H.J.
  1982 "Learning from experience and suboptimal rules in decision making."
         Pp. 268–83 in D. Kahneman, P. Slovic and A. Tversky (eds.), Judgment
         Under Uncertainty: Heuristics and Biases. New York: Cambridge
         University Press.
Einhorn, H.J. and R.M. Hogarth
  1978 "Confidence in judgment: persistence in the illusion of validity."
         Psychological Review 85:395–416.
Fishburn, P.C. and G.A. Kochenberger
  1979 "Two-piece von Neumann–Morgenstern utility functions." Decision
         Sciences 10:503–18.
Friedman, M. and L.J. Savage.
  1948 "The utility analysis of choices involving risk." Journal of Political
         Economy 56(4):279–304.
Grether, D.M. and C.R. Plott
  1979 "Economic theory of choice and the preference reversal phenomenon."
         American Economic Review 69(4):623–38.
Handa, J.
  1977 "Risk, probabilities, and a new theory of cardinal utility." Journal of
         Political Economy 85:97–122.
Hershey, J.C. and P.J.H. Schoemaker
  1980 "Risk taking and problem context in the domain of losses: an expected
         utility analysis." Journal of Risk and Insurance 47:111–32.
Hey, J.D.
  1979 Uncertainty in Microeconomics. New York: New York University
         Press.

Kahneman, D., P. Slovic and A. Tversky (eds.)
1982 Judgment Under Uncertainty: Heuristics and Biases. New York: Cambridge University Press.

Kahneman, D. and A. Tversky.
1979 "Prospect theory: an analysis of decision under risk." Econometrica 47(2):263-91.

Kahneman, D. and A. Tversky.
1982a "On the psychology of prediction." Pp. 48-68 in D. Kahneman, P. Slovic and A. Tversky (eds.), Judgment Under Uncertainty: Heuristics and Biases. New York: Cambridge University Press.

Kahneman, D. and A. Tversky.
1982b "Subjective probability: a judgment of representativeness." Pp. 32-47 in D. Kahneman, P. Slovic and A. Tversky (eds.), Judgment Under Uncertainty: Heuristics and Biases. New York: Cambridge University Press.

Kahneman, D. and A. Tversky
1982c "The simulation heuristic." Pp. 201-208 in D. Kahneman, P. Slovic and A. Tversky (eds.), Judgment Under Uncertainty: Heuristics and Biases. New York: Cambridge University Press.

Karmarkar, U.
1978 "Subjectively weighted utility: a descriptive extension of the expected utility model." Organizational Behavior and Human Performance 23:61-72.

Knight, F.H.
1933 Risk, Uncertainty, and Profit. Boston: Houghton-Mifflin.

Langer, E.J.
1982 "The illusion of control." Pp. 231-38 in D. Kahneman, P. Slovic and A. Tversky (eds.), Judgment Under Uncertainty: Heuristics and Biases. New York: Cambridge University Press.

Lichtenstein, S. and P. Slovic.
1971 "Reversals of preferences between bids and choices in gambling decisions." Journal of Experimental Psychology 89:46-55.

Luce, R.D. and H. Raiffa
1957 Games and Behavior. New York: Wiley.

Lynch, J. and J.L. Cohen
1978 "The use of subjective expected utility theory as an aid to understanding variables that influence helping behavior." Journal of Personality and Social Psychology 36:1138-51.

Markowitz, H.M.
1959 Portfolio Selection. New York: Wiley.

Mosteller, F. and P. Nogee.
1951 "An experimental assessment of utility." Journal of Political Economy 59(5):371-404.

Pratt, J.W.
1964 "Risk aversion in the small and large." Econometrica 32:122-36.

Pratt, J.W., H. Raiffa and R. Schlaiffer
1964 "The foundations of decisions under uncertainty: an elementary exposition." Journal of the American Statistical Association 59:353-75.

Ramsey, F.P.
   1931 "Truth and probability." Pp. 151–98 in Foundations of Mathematics and
         Other Logical Essays. London: Paul, Trench, Trubner.
Richard, S.F.
   1975 "Multivariate risk aversion, utility independence and separable utility
         functions." Management Science 22(1):12–21.
Ross, M. and F. Sicoly
   1982 "Egocentric biases in availability and attribution." Pp. 179–89 in D.
         Kahneman, P. Slovic and A. Tversky (eds.), Judgment Under Un-
         certainty: Heuristics and Biases. New York: Cambridge University
         Press.
Roth, J.A. and A.D. Witte
   1985 "Understanding taxpayer compliance: major factors and perspectives."
         Pp. 53–78 in Proceedings of the 1985 IRS Tax Conference. Washington,
         DC: U.S. Department of the Treasury.
Savage, L.J.
   1954 The Foundation of Statistics. New York: Wiley.
Schmidt, P. and A.D. Witte
   1984 An Economic Analysis of Crime and Justice. New York: Academic
         Press.
Schoemaker, P.J.H.
   1980 Experiments on Decisions Under Risk. Boston: Martinus Nijhoff.
Schoemaker, P.J.H.
   1982 "The expected utility model: its variants, purposes, evidence, and
         limitations." Journal of Economic Literature, 20:529–63.
Simon, H.A.
   1957 Models of Man. Social and Rational Mathematical Essays on Rational
         Human Behavior in a Social Setting. New York: Wiley.
Sinn, H.
   1983 Economic Decisions Under Uncertainty. Amsterdam: North-Holland.
Slovic, P. and S. Lichtenstein
   1983 "Preference reversals: a broader perspective." American Economic
         Review, 73:596–605.
Taylor, S.E.
   1982 "The availability bias in social perception and interaction." Pp. 190–200
         in D. Kahneman, P. Slovic and A. Tversky (eds.), Judgment Under
         Uncertainty: Heuristics and Biases. New York: Cambridge University
         Press.
Tversky, A. and D. Kahneman
   1982a "Availability: a heuristic for judging frequency and probability." Pp.
         163–78 in D. Kahneman, P. Slovic and A. Tversky (eds.), Judgment
         Under Uncertainty: Heuristics and Biases. New York: Cambridge
         University Press.
Tversky, A. and D. Kahneman
   1982b "Belief in the law of small numbers." Pp. 23–31 in D. Kahneman, P.
         Slovic and A. Tversky (eds.), Judgment Under Uncertainty: Heuristics
         and Biases. New York: Cambridge University Press.
Tversky, A. and D. Kahneman
   1982c "Judgment of and by representativeness." Pp. 84–98 in D. Kahneman, P.

Slovic and A. Tversky (eds.), Judgment Under Uncertainty: Heuristics and Biases. New York: Cambridge University Press.

Tversky, A. and D. Kahneman
1982d "Judgment under uncertainty: heuristics and biases." Pp. 3–20 in D. Kahneman, P. Slovic and A. Tversky (eds.), Judgment Under Uncertainty: Heuristics and Biases. New York: Cambridge University Press.

Tversky, A. and D. Kahneman
1983 "Extensional versus intuitive reasoning: the conjunction fallacy in probability judgment." Psychological Review 90(4):293–315.

von Neumann, J. and O. Morgenstern
1944 Theory of Games and Economic Behavior. Princeton, NJ: Princeton University Press.

Witte, A.D. and S.K. Long
1984 "The effect of criminal justice system actions and macroeconomic conditions on criminality: eclectic and longitudinal research." Grant proposal to the National Science Foundation.

10
The Theory of Reasoned Action: A Decision Theory of Crime

MARY TUCK AND DAVID RILEY

Editors' Note

The rational choice perspective as outlined in the Introduction to this volume is concerned mainly with presenting in a general way the advantages of treating criminal behavior as a broadly rational activity. It therefore has little directly to say about the specific nature of the decision-making processes used in making criminal choices. Despite the criticisms of expected utility theories met with elsewhere in this volume, there is no doubt that subjective expected utility (SEU)-derived expectancy-value theories have proved successful at predicting some aspects of choice behavior in certain areas of application. In the present chapter Mary Tuck and David Riley provide a succinct outline of one such approach. Fishbein's theory of reasoned action (TORA), a sophisticated social psychological theory whose origins lie in attitude theory and measurement research. TORA is intended both to explain and to predict human behaviors by means of a small number of concepts—beliefs, attitudes, and intentions—located within a single theoretical framework. As Tuck and Riley argue, given the likely importance of social and familial norms to the decision to offend (and, hence, to questions of deterrence), the fact that TORA was specifically developed to take such variables into account is a significant argument in its favor. The theory is seen as applicable to all criminal decision making, whether related to events or involvement, whatever the time-scale, whatever the level of generality or specificity under current consideration (e.g., from traveling on public transport without a ticket to "delinquency"), and whatever the forms of information processing involved. Given its range of applications to date, however (for example, career intentions, family-planning behaviors, voting behavior, consumer choice) and its continued reliance on certain aspects of the SEU paradigm, the theory may initially prove more useful in exploring the determinants and processes of choice behavior in relation to criminal involvement, continuance, and desistance than in relation to criminal events. Within the former spheres, TORA's emphasis upon (and methods for) exploring the influence of salient behavioral and normative beliefs on the formation of an intention to commit a crime offers an important and potentially policy-relevant new perspective on deterrence issues.

Human beings like things to be simple, and never more so than when discussing crime. We know that criminal behavior is widely various, yet this does not stop us from looking for the single "best" strategy to reduce delinquency and for the "most important factors" that affect crime. The fault may be more one of policymakers and the public rather than of criminologists, but much of criminological discourse itself is taken up with debate which pits one general theory of crime against another, searching for the best strategies and the best explanations. Recently, for instance, there has been a debate as to whether organizational factors or individual factors are more important for understanding juvenile delinquency (Farrington, 1985). Again, situational theories of crime have sometimes been seen as polar opposites of treatment models, so that proponents of one feel they should reject the other. Currently in the United Kingdom there is a debate between those who believe the best strategies for reducing crime are those of situational crime prevention (target hardening, opportunity reduction, physical methods of changing the environment) and those who believe there is much to be said for softer "hearts and minds" methods such as improving the quality of life on derelict estates by better housing management, propaganda, teaching, and social work strategies.

Nowhere are these arguments and polarities more acute than on the subject of deterrence. The public is divided between the tough and the tender, between those who see the answer to crime as swifter and more severe punishment and those who doubt the effectiveness of punishment and look rather to a general improvement in the welfare of the deprived and to a more gentle and careful treatment of, at least, the early offender. It is the contention of this chapter that these polarities can best be reconciled in terms of a cognitive or decision-making approach.

Deterrence Research

As an example of how such a perspective can shed new light on old arguments, we would quote the recent history of deterrence research. In the mid-1970s the criminological consensus (as exemplified in two important reviews: Zimring and Hawkins, 1973, in the United States and Beyleveld, 1980, in the United Kingdom) was that the evidence for deterrence was somewhat doubtful. The well-attested finding of similar rates of recidivism from dissimilar disposals of offenders had shed doubt on the efficiency of individual deterrence, that is, the ability of the criminal justice system to deter practicing offenders. General deterrence, or the ability of the system to deter the public at large from crime, looked in equally bad shape.

This picture began to change in the late 1970s and 1980s, and it changed because criminologists began at last to measure individual cognitive processes more carefully. The well-known paper by Grasmick and Green (1980) is a convenient landmark. This paper built on earlier work (in particular Jensen et al. 1978, and Erickson and Gibbs, 1978), but it marked a new stage in the debate. Grasmick and Green argued that much of the earlier deterrence work had failed because of measurement deficiencies. Most crucially, they stressed that it was a person's own perception of his or her own risks of detection and punishment that could best predict personal behaviors, rather than the person's general views as to the likelihood of others getting caught and punished. Drawing on subjective expected utility (SEU) theory, Grasmick and Green proposed a much improved and more personal measure of sanction strength: the multiplication of a scaled measure of the perceived certainty of punishment with an evalutaive measure on a similar scale of its perceived severity. They also saw that this measure should be related not to past behavior but to intended future behavior. They further widened the question from the effects of purely legal punishments to consider the effects of social disapproval and of a variable they called "moral commitment." It would be possible to quarrel over the details of the measures they proposed, but nonetheless they found that these two normative variables (as we can perhaps call them) added considerably to the prediction of intended future offending.

However, Grasmick and Green's work was still open to the objection that it could conceivably be measuring only paper-and-pencil corre- lations present at one moment in time. Silberman (1976) had already recognized the causal order problem, but it was left to Paternoster et al. (1982) and Bishop (1984) to introduce two-wave studies into this field, enabling them to test the effects of cognitions at Time 1 not only on behavioral intentions at Time 1 but also on reported past behavior between Time 1 and a subsequent wave of the study at Time 2. Using this improved criterion measure, Bishop tested the effect of measures of legal sanctions, social threat, and internalized norms on criminal behavior. Unfortunately, Bishop's measure of the effects of legal sanctions was a very general one, lacking the greater precision of Grasmick and Green's multiplicative SEU personal measure. She simply gave respondents a generalized Likert scale including items such as, "Most people who do things that are only minor violations of the law never get caught." She herself admitted, "It makes intuitive sense to suggest that stronger relationships should emerge when perceptual measures having a self- referent are used" (p. 410), but for some reason she did not use them. Nonetheless, Bishop's results show a clear relationship between this generalized sanction measure and subsequent criminal behavior. She also included in her study measures of "internalised normative con- straint" and of the perceived risk of informal sanctioning, and once again found that these, too, were related to subsequent criminal behavior at significant levels. Although all three independent variables were inter-correlated, they each separately added to prediction. The measure she christened internalised normative constraint (essentially a Likert scale made up of items similar to those used by Hirschi, 1969, to tap belief in the moral validity of the law) was the strongest predictor of behavior, but perceptions of both formal and informal sanctions had predictive power over and above that of this measure alone. What can we make of these results from the point of view of cognitive or decision theory approaches to crime? Neither study (Grasmick and Green or Bishop) accounts for anything like the major proportion of the variance in reported offending. Taken together, however, they provide strong evidence that some at least of this variance is due to such cognitive factors as the perception of legal sanctions, the perceptions of social threat, and the mysterious and powerful variable called moral commitment. Any decision theory of criminal behavior must be able to deal with such variables.

Wider Criminological Theories

These findings are not, of course, unexpected from the point of view of wider criminological theory. For example, both Elliott (Elliott et al., 1979) and Akers (Akers et al., 1979) have stressed the role of social influences in producing delinquent behavior. Their work was in its turn preceded by Hirschi (1969). Indeed the tradition of recognizing the importance of social and familial norms can be traced back to Durkheim and beyond and is in any case a pretty common intuition. However, there is another whole set of findings that must be taken into account in any theory of criminal action. The well-evidenced situational and opportunity theories such as those of Clarke and Mayhew (1980), Cohen and Felson (1979), and Felson and Cohen (1980) remind us that immediate environmental factors are also important in producing criminal behavior. Any full cognitive modeling of crime must cover not only the role of legal sanctions, informal sanctions, and normative or moral perceptions, but also that of the rewards and losses contingent on the immediate environment of any criminal act. Further, for any decision model of crime to be effective it must be both inclusive and flexible. Insofar as any decision model can be shown to fail to deal with the factors we already know from earlier work to affect criminal behavior, it will be prima facie inadequate. We know, for example, that decisions concerning criminal acts vary over time and over the course of a criminal career. Offending rates peak in the early teens and decline sharply thereafter (the so-called "aging out" phenomenon). The implications of this pattern of decision making require us to pay attention to the developmental correlates of age. Changes in social status and in social networks (e.g., from dependent to adult, from school to work, from peer group to family orientation) and in the use of leisure time (from street corner to tavern, from public to personal transport, from public space to private space) are likely to prove powerful determinants of the decision-making process (see, for example, Richards et al., 1979, and Sviridoff and McElroy, 1984). There is a danger that studying decision making as a "snapshot" may fail to give sufficient weight to these time-dependent processes (cf. Hirschi and Gottfredson, 1983). Any adequate model of criminal decision making needs to be able to take account of them.

It is also clear that criminal acts are not the result solely of decisions made by the potential offender himself or herself. Ideally, one would like a model that would take account of crime-relevant choices made by others, too. These would include the decisions of commercial organizations, local and central government, police, potential victims, and so on (see, for example, Taub et al., 1984). This might more clearly indicate the full range of policy options when it comes to identifying ways in which crime levels may be reduced. A policy perspective should also encourage consideration of decision making at other points in the sequence of events which link the offense and its final outcome in the courts. Criminologists have begun to study some of these postoffense decision points, beginning, for example, with decisions about whether to report crimes, through police decisions about which crimes to investigate first and about how to deal with offenders, to the decision to prosecute and to how benches and juries decide on guilt and sentence.

It may be felt that the argument has widened too much. It has been suggested that normative expected utility theory has been shown (not least through deterrence research) to be inadequate to model criminal decisions. Nor is classic SEU theory in itself sufficient—a fact again evidenced by deterrence research. Any adequate model of criminal decision making should be capable of covering those situational, social learning, and normative factors we know to be related to criminal behavior. It must also be capable of dealing with and illuminating shifts in the character of decisions over time, and ultimately it would also be applicable to all those other decisions relevant to criminal choice that are not those of the actor himself or herself.

A Theory Expounded

The theory of reasoned action (TORA; Fishbein, 1963, 1973; Fishbein and Ajzen, 1975) was developed in the context of social psychological studies of behavior and attitudes and has attained wide currency in applied studies in fields as varied as family planning behavior, voting behavior, and studies of nuclear risk and of consumer behavior (e.g., Fishbein and Coombs, 1974; Tuck, 1976). It is one of a family of expectancy value theories that emerged in social psychology during the

1960s and 1970s, building on SEU theory. Its peculiar strengths for dealing with criminal decision making are (a) that it gives a central and formal role to those processes of social norm formation that we know to be crucial in our field and (b) that it can deal with differences in the levels of specificity of decisions; that is, it can deal with general decisions at an intermediate level (e.g., "I will do some burgling") as well as decisions at a particular level (e.g., "I will burgle this house now") without proposing different formal models.

The theory applies to all intentional human acts. It takes as its starting point a variable called "behavioral intention," which is the intention to engage in a given behavior and which, it is held, precedes—at least fractionally—such behavior. Behavioral intentions can occur at any level of specificity and at different points in time. In different cognitive frameworks, decisions of different levels of specificity will be present to potential actors, but, according to TORA, all these different behavioral intentions arise in the same way, from two, and only two, variables. The first variable is a person's attitude to an act. Does the person perceive the act in a positive or a negative light? The second variable is the person's "norms" about the act. Does the person perceive it as something that others who are important to him think he should or should not do?

At this level of description, the theory may appear banal. All it is saying is that whether a person intends to do something or not depends on whether that person likes (or dislikes) the idea of his doing it (the attitude to the act) and whether he thinks he should do it (the subjective norm). The power of the theory arises from the precise measurement methods proposed for these two variables and from its capacity to "unpack" each particular variable in terms of the underlying beliefs. Thus, attitudes are held to be dependent on beliefs about outcomes (both what the actor expects will happen and how he or she evaluates these possibilities), and norms are seen to be dependent on the expectations of salient others.

More formally, behavior (B, any conscious action) is preceded by a behavioral intention, and this behavioral intention (BI) is itself a result of two and only two measurable variables: the attitude to the behavior (A_{act}) involved (not the attitude to the object with which the behavior is concerned but the attitude to the act or behavior itself) and the individual's subjective norm (SN) concerning the act. The term *subjective norm* refers to perceptions that most important others think the person should or should not engage in the act. The weighting of subjective norms and attitudes in the formation of behavioral intentions is held to vary both across individuals and across acts in ways that can be determined empirically. This theory is expressed in the regression equation:

$$B \ (- \ BI) \ = \ A_{act} \ + \ SN.$$

There is a large literature in which this equation has been applied and found to hold (see Ajzen and Fishbein, 1980). With appropriate measurement the equation is robust. The behavioral theory is supplemented by a theory of attitudes based on beliefs and evaluations that can be stated formally in the equation:

$$A_{act} = \Sigma b_i e_i$$

where b is the belief held about the act—that is, the probability that it will lead to the consequence or outcome, i; and e is the individual's evaluation of the outcome, i.

Note that the theory is uncompromisingly cognitive. It holds that the effect of any other variables on actions, including criminal actions (be these variables situational or personal, measuring learning history or moral commitment), will be filtered through two and only two variables which are held to affect behavioral intention: the subject's attitude to the act concerned and his or her subjective norm concerning the act. Because beliefs (and subjective norms) are responsive to factors external to the individual, this superficially simple model of the form of the decision process is capable of dealing with the subtleties of crime choices and avoids the deterministic problems associated with dispositional approaches. But can such a theory meet our specifications for a cognitive model of crime?

TORA and Situational Theory

TORA can deal easily with the variables held by situation and opportunity theorists to affect the incidence of crime. These would come into the equations of TORA as salient beliefs contributing to the attitudinal (and normative) sides of the equation. Maguire (1982) and Bennett and Wright (1983) have taught us that characteristic salient beliefs of burglars about burgling and about a potential target house will include judgments as to whether it is secluded, has burglar alarms, appears occupied, or looks prosperous. Different burglars of differing degrees of experience considering different targets may well have different salient beliefs, but Maguire's and Bennett's work suggests that the characteristic sets of situational beliefs for different kinds of burglars attacking different kinds of targets can be empirically identified. The same is true for other crimes such as shoplifting or vandalism, as shown by other contributors to this volume. Indeed, from the point of view of TORA, process-tracing techniques (see, for instance, Carroll, 1982) are essentially tools for identifying salient beliefs about particular actions. As other contributors have argued, it is necessary to pay attention to how choices are framed or represented by the potential actor, and in terms of TORA this means identifying the actor's salient belief set about the action concerned. The empirical work reported elsewhere in this book by Walsh and others shows that salient belief sets concerning potential criminal acts characteristically include those descriptive beliefs about the immediate environment on which the situational theory of crime has correctly laid stress.

TORA, however, holds that it is not sufficient simply to identify the potential actor's salient beliefs about the expected outcomes of different choices. It is also necessary to measure, in the SEU mode, how strongly each belief is held and the evaluation of the outcome connected to the act. Thus, a Type-A burglar and a Type-B burglar might both allow into their salient belief sets the fact that a house had or did not have a burglar alarm fitted, but each might attach to this belief different evaluations. The Type-A burglar might be experienced and know that he could short-circuit the alarm easily; the fact that it existed could then signal for him a positively evaluated outcome: The house probably contains property worth protecting. The Type-B burglar on the other hand might be more naive: He does not know how to short-circuit the alarm. For him its existence is attached to a negatively evaluated outcome: detection. Unless these different possibilities and others like them are allowed for in empirical research and measured, misleading results might follow. Thus, TORA can contain within one model the insights of process tracing and of SEU theory. This may be one reason why, in the field in which it has been applied (for a summary, see Ajzen and Fishbein, 1980), it can account for a far larger proportion of observed behavioral variance than is common in criminological studies.

Not all salient beliefs concerning specific criminal acts will necessarily be connected with the immediate environment. For the practical criminal out on a job they may well be, but for the novice, or for an individual coming close for whatever reason to retirement from a criminal career, beliefs as to ·the likelihood of detection or the possible severity of punishment may be equally salient. In particular circumstances, beliefs about sanctions may also be salient for the habitual burglar in midcareer. Bennett and Wright have shown that, throughout their careers, burglars said they would not choose to burgle a house next to a police station.

The Normative Measure

It is the normative side of the TORA behavioral decision-making model that is of particular importance to criminology, however. As attitude to an act is dependent on salient beliefs about the outcome of that act, so, it is held, subjective norms reflect the summation of the perceived views of salient others as to what the individual should do. It has been shown in the empirical work on TORA that the generalized measure, "Most others important to me think I should/should not do X" (the usual measure of subjective norm), correlates well with an additive measure of the perceived expectations of salient others. It may perhaps be easily acceptable that this measure will cover the variance of such different measures as "threat of social disapproval" prominent in the deterrence and related literature. However, the subjective norm measure may well be affected not only by the threat of social disapproval but also by legal sanctions. The naming of a given act as a crime has some effect on its incidence. More people wear seat belts when there is a law about it. It is generally held that laws about racial or sexual discrimination have some declaratory effect. It seems plausible that the declaratory effect of the law would work through subjective norms. Aware that respected others now have certain expectations, the individual modifies his or her behavior accordingly.

The Moral Commitment Variable

One variable identified by previous criminological research as important in predicting criminal behavior does not at first sight seem to enter very clearly into the TORA model. This is the important variable of moral commitment, called by Bishop (1984) "internalised normative constraint." The criminological literature distinguishes this variable sharply from the "perceived risk of informal sanctioning," which we have argued is subsumed by the TORA subjective norms variable. Only empirical work could give an answer as to whether the moral commitment variable would add to prediction over and above the attitude and subjective norm variables in the case of criminal acts. Our own hypothesis is that it would not. It seems on the face of it unlikely that criminal or delinquent acts in all their wide variety would be different from those other acts with a moral dimension (as, for instance, the use of birth control) that have already been studied in terms of the TORA model. It seems possible that the SN measure itself includes some of the variance christened by criminologists as moral commitment. Only empirical work will show.

There is one further clue as to how moral commitment might enter into the model in the existing work on TORA. It has been shown that people with identifiably different cognitive styles tend systematically to put variant weights on the attitudinal and normative sides of the TORA equation in combining them to form behavioral intentions. Thus, those with consistently high scores on the Californian F scale measure of authoritarianism tend, over a range of behaviors, to weight more than average on the normative side of the behavior equation. It is possible that the same dimension as the criminologists' moral commitment might be tapped by a habitual tendency to weight more one or the other side of the equation. Only the socialized, those who *have* salient normative others, can form strong subjective norms. In the absence of subjective norm weightings, the more utilitarian attitudinal side of the equation could pick up most of the variance in behavioral intention. This can be no more than speculation, but it offers the interesting possibility of bringing in the convincing but superficially discrepant findings of Yochelson and Samenow (1976) into the proposed cognitive model. Yochelson and Samenow, on the basis of detailed clinical interviews, thought they had identified a specific cognitive style among career criminals. This cognitive style was marked by its self-seeking and compartmentalized nature, little weight being given to the views, attitudes, or interests of others. It would seem an interesting hypothesis for further work that serious career criminals would show a habitual tendency to weight the attitudinal rather than the normative side of the TORA equation—that is, to tend to disregard the normative views or values of others into decisions and to act solely in terms of personal, hedonistic utilities.

Crime and Secrecy

A further point should be made in this connection. One of the best established results of earlier deterrence research is that criminal behavior varies more with the certainty than with the severity of punishment. Irrespective of the level of expected punishment, most offenders do what they can to minimize their detection risks, and they do their best to commit their crimes unobserved. Why? It does not seem solely a question of fearing legal sanctions. It seems reasonable to propose that one way changes in detection risks influence behavior is by increasing the weighting of negative social forces. The offender may know perfectly well that salient others do not approve of his or her potential criminal behavior, but the offender may be prepared to ignore this. After all, those others may never know the offender has shoplifted this article, forged this check, or stolen this object. The fact that criminal behavior is so often and routinely private and secretive is perhaps another pointer to the importance of variant weightings given to attitudes and norms in predicting criminal behavior.

TORA and Judgmental Heuristics

So far it has been argued that TORA's simple but robust equations can deal with those variables identified by traditional criminology as important in affecting offending. However, a word should be said as to the relationship of this theory to the work on judgmental heuristics of Tversky and Kahneman and others. The importance of this work has been rightly emphasized by other contributors, one of whom (see, for instance, Payne, 1976) has also been influential in the development of a multistage or contingent-processing view of decision making. It is true that Simon (1977) has suggested that there were difficulties in reconciling the well-evidenced use of heuristics in problem solving with the use of additive models in decision making, such as those of Fishbein and Ajzen. The conflict, however, may be more apparent than real, as is suggested by the work of Tversky and Kahneman (1974) themselves. The key to the reconciliation of the two bodies of research lies in the concept of salience. TORA is content to use a purely operational definition of salience. Salient beliefs are, according to the theory, those elicited in a free-response situation by asking the subject to list the characteristics, qualities, or attributes of an object or the consequences of performing a behavior. The closer in time the beliefs are elicited to the execution of the act under consideration, the better they predict the act. TORA, certainly as used in applied work, has little to say about the *grounds* of salience. Why in contemplating this act, this gamble, or this risky choice have these specific beliefs come to be salient? It is this last question to which much of the work of the judgmental heuristics school has been applied.

We do not wish to minimize the importance of this latter question in suggesting to practising criminologists that there could be, perhaps for the moment, more immediate applied value in simply observing and naming salient belief sets, and in exploring with the help of the TORA models how attitudes to an act (based on such observed salient belief sets) interact with norms. The great value of the TORA model is that it forces us to treat seriously those normative beliefs that the work of Hirschi and others has shown to be crucial in our field. It can stop us from producing models of rational criminal decision making that deal only, even if in a multistage and contingent way, with the trade-offs of perceived utilities. Criminology is going to need (as others have argued in this volume) studies that illumine by what judgmental heuristics or by what inferential processes certain beliefs about delinquent acts come into salience. In our view, however, there is a prior and more urgent need to *identify* the modal salient belief sets concerning criminal acts of different sections of the community and to understand how they interact with those personal normative beliefs we know to be crucial in our area of discourse.

Levels of Specificity

It may be felt by some that the high level of specificity of the TORA model as presented in this chapter minimizes its usefulness for general or applied studies, which must inevitably hope to produce findings applicable to a range of behaviors. It must be stressed, however, that the TORA model is held to apply to behavioral intentions at widely variant levels of specificity. The theory holds that intentions involve four different elements: the behavior, the target object at which the behavior is directed, the situation in which the behavior is to be performed, and the time at which the behavior is to be performed. Each of these elements varies along a dimension of specificity. At the most specific level, a person intends to perform a particular act with respect to a given object in a specified situation at a given point in time. For example, a man may intend to burgle a particular house in a particular street at 3 p.m. on a particular afternoon. At the most general level the person may intend simply to make some money by some criminal act, or he may have formed a general intention to be a burglar. The theory can deal with behavioral intentions at any level of specificity. Once, however, the intentional criterion has been selected, it is important that the measures of the attitudinal and normative components are calibrated at the same levels of specificity, as must be the measures of underlying beliefs.

It has been suggested (Clarke and Cornish, 1985) that separate models will be needed for the onset, continuance, and desistance of different types of crime. TORA proposes that the same formal model will operate in each situation, although, of course, in each case there will be different salient beliefs and relevant referents, different attitudes and different subjective norms, all to be empirically determined. This concept seems preferable to that of two-stage models (i.e., a prior decision to be a burglar and a subsequent decision to burgle this particular house). Two-stage models (i.e., a prior decision to vote and a subsequent decision to vote for candidate X) have not been very successful in the parallel field of voting behavior (see Fishbein et al., 1985).

Conclusion: The Need for Empirical Work

This chapter has presented a purely analytic and abstract argument for why we believe additive expectancy-value models in general and the Fishbein and Ajzen theory of reasoned action in particular have much to offer criminology. Only empirical work will show if we are right. We had hoped to present some empirical results with this discussion, but our work is not far enough advanced to do so. The present chapter must stand merely as a contribution to theoretical debate.

Criminology has need of theories that can deal with the wide variety of criminal behavior alluded to at the opening of this chapter. It has need too of theories that will free us from the somewhat sterile either/or debates, the search for some single magic key, some single policy that can reduce crime. Criminal behavior is complex: Only cognitive and decision models have the power to deal with its wide variety.

References

Ajzen, I. and M. Fishbein
   1980   Understanding Attitudes and Predicting Social Behavior. Englewood Cliffs, NJ: Prentice-Hall.

Akers, R.L., M.D. Krohn, L. Lanza-Kaduce and M. Radosevich
  1979 "Social learning and deviant behavior: a specific test of a general
        theory." American Sociological Review 44:636–55.
Bennett, T.H. and R. Wright
  1983 Constraints and Inducements to Crime: The Property Offender's Per-
        spective. Cambridge, England: University of Cambridge, Institute of
        Criminology (mimeographed).
Beyleveld, D.
  1980 A Bibliography on General Deterrence Research. Farnborough,
        England: Saxon House.
Bishop, D.M.
  1984 "Legal and extralegal barriers to delinquency." Criminology 22: 403–
        19.
Carroll, J.S.
  1982 "Committing a crime: the offender's decision." Pp. 49–68 in V. Konecni
        and E. Ebbesen (eds.), The Criminal Justice System: A Social-Psycho-
        logical Analysis of Legal Processes. Oxford: Freeman.
Clarke, R.V.G. and P. Mayhew
  1980 Designing Out Crime. London: HMSO.
Cohen, L.E. and M. Felson
  1979 "Social change and crime rate trends: a routine activity approach."
        American Sociological Review 44:588–608.
Elliott, D.S., S.S. Ageton and R.J. Canter
  1979 "An integrated theoretical perspective on delinquent behavior." Journal
        of Research in Crime and Delinquency 16:3–28.
Erickson, M.L. and J.P. Gibbs
  1978 "Objective and perceptual properties of legal punishment and the
        deterrence doctrine." Social Problems 25:253–64.
Farrington, D.P.
  1985 "Delinquency prevention in the 1980s." Journal of Adolescence 8: 3–
        16.
Felson, M. and L.E. Cohen
  1980 "Human ecology and crime: a routine activity approach." Human
        Ecology 8:389–406.
Fishbein, M.
  1963 "An investigation of the relationships between beliefs about an ob-
        ject and the attitude toward that object." Human Relations 16:
        233–40.
Fishbein, M.
  1973 "The prediction of behavior from attitudinal variables." Pp. 3–31 in C.D.
        Mortenson and K.K. Sereno (eds.), Advances in Communication
        Research. New York: Harper and Row.
Fishbein, M. and I. Ajzen
  1975 Belief, Attitude, Intention and Behavior. Reading, MA: Addison-
        Wesley.
Fishbein, M. and F.S. Coombs
  1974 "Basis for decision: an attitudinal analysis of voting behavior." Journal
        of Applied Social Psychology 4:95–124.
Fishbein, M., S.E. Middlestadt and J. Chung
  1985 "Predicting participation and choice among first time voters in U.S.

partisan elections." Pp. 65–82 in S. Kraus and R. Perloff (eds.), Mass Media and Political Thought. New York: Sage.

Grasmick, H.G. and D.E. Green
1980 "Legal punishment, social disapproval and internalization as inhibitors of illegal behavior." Journal of Criminal Law and Criminology 71:325–35.

Hirschi, T.
1969 Causes of Delinquency. Berkeley: University of California Press.

Hirschi, T. and M.R. Gottfredson
1983 "Age and the explanation of crime." American Journal of Sociology 89: 552–84.

Jensen, G.F., M.L. Erickson and J.P. Gibbs
1978 "Perceived risk of punishment and self-reported delinquency." Social Forces 57:57–78.

Maguire, M.
1982 Burglary in a Dwelling. London: Heinemann.

Paternoster, R., L.E. Saltzman, T.G. Chiricos and G.P. Waldo
1982 "Perceived risk and deterrence: methodological artifacts in perceptual deterrence research." Journal of Criminal Law and Criminology 73: 1238–58.

Payne, J.W.
1976 "Task complexity and contingent processing in decision making; an information search and protocol analysis." Organizational Behavior and Human Performance 16:366–87.

Richards, P., R.A. Berk and B. Forster
1979 Crime as Play: Delinquency in a Middle Class Suburb. Cambridge, MA: Ballinger.

Silberman, M.
1976 "Towards a theory of criminal deterrence." American Sociological Review 41:442–61.

Simon, H.A.
1977 The New Science of Management Decision. Englewood Cliffs, NJ: Prentice-Hall.

Sviridoff, M. and J. McElroy
1984 Employment and Crime: A Summary Report. Report to the National Institute of Justice, Grant No. 81-IJ-CX-0024.

Taub, R.P., D.G. Taylor and J.D. Dunham
1984 Paths of Neighborhood Change: Race and Crime in Urban America. Chicago: University of Chicago Press.

Tuck, M.
1976 How Do We Choose: A Study in Consumer Behavior. London: Methuen.

Tversky, A. and D. Kahneman
1974 "Judgment under uncertainty: heuristics and biases." Science 185: 1124–31.

Yochelson, S. and S.E. Samenow
1976 The Criminal Personality, Volumes 1 and 2. New York: Jason Aronson.

Zimring, F.E. and G.J. Hawkins
1973 Deterrence. Chicago: University of Chicago Press.

11
The Decision to Commit a Crime: An Information-Processing Analysis

ERIC JOHNSON AND JOHN PAYNE

Editors' Note

Eric Johnson and John Payne's chapter provides a valuable overview of recent concepts and findings from behavioral decision theory and of their applicability to an understanding of criminal decision making. Taking as their starting point the expected utility model of decision making, they, like others in this volume, stress its inadequacies as a descriptive model of human decision making. Instead they suggest that, given the human cognitive system's limited information-processing capabilities, choice behavior is more realistically characterized in terms of its bounded rationality. They organize their discussion around two important themes: The first, which concerns the construction by the decision maker of internal representations of crucial aspects of the decision problem, leads them to assess the implications of prospect theory both for the "framing" of choices by the potential offender (tax cheating is their major example) and for the potential of criminal justice policies to bring about their "reframing." The second theme is concerned with the decision processes that operate upon these representations. As Johnson and Payne comment, the picture emerges of a limited information processor, often working under pressure of time, who uses many different strategies to simplify the task of evaluating choice alternatives in the complex environment of everyday life. In general, these strategies are distinguished by their noncompensatory nature, by a screening phase that ensures the early elimination of the most unsatisfactory alternatives, by the sequential scrutiny of alternatives according to "satisficing" rather than optimizing principles, and by the adoption of noncompensatory rules on the part of expert decision makers (examples were noted in some of the empirical studies: cf. Carroll and Weaver; Walsh). The authors go on to provide an illuminating discussion of the likely implications of their analysis for criminal decision making and for policies seeking to deter crime. As one of their conclusions, they suggest that the contingency of decisions upon task situations may argue in favor both of a crime-specific focus and of the separate modeling of event and involvement decisions.

Decision Making and Criminality

The decision to commit a crime is the first behavior of direct relevance to the functioning of the criminal justice system (Carroll, 1982). As noted by Carroll, decisions by the police, prosecutors, judges, juries, and parole boards all follow the offender's choice of which crime to commit, the choice of target, and the choice of the method and moment of committing the crime. Furthermore, it has been argued that a better knowledge of the offender's decision processes may have important implications for crime-control policies (Clarke and Cornish, 1985). Deterrence theories, for example, rest on the idea that the decision to commit a crime is the result of a rational consideration of the costs and benefits of a criminal act. Consequently, there is a growing concern with understanding the psychological processes leading to the decision to commit a crime. This chapter explores a few of the recent concepts and findings from a field of research called behavioral decision theory that may aid the under-standing of criminal behavior.

The Expected Utility Model

Since World War II, the predominant model of human decision making has been expected utility maximization. According to this model, people are assumed to assign probabilities and values to all the outcomes of an action, to multiply the probability and value of each outcome, and to sum the products over all outcomes into an overall evaluation of the action. This process is repeated for every action and ends with the selection of the action with the largest expected utility. The expected utility model has been used to predict and explain decisions in a wide variety of domains ranging from decisions about births to national security policies. For almost 20 years, it has been argued that criminal behavior could usefully be conceptualized in terms of the expected utility model (Becker, 1968). The idea is that people calculate the expected utilities of criminal and noncriminal actions and choose the one with the greatest expected utility.

Adoption of the expected utility model for offender decisions has a number of important implications for the criminal justice system. For instance, the idea that a criminal act is the result of a rational cost/benefit calculation suggests that everyone, not just "criminal types," may choose to commit a crime under the right circumstances. As noted earlier, the expected utility model also suggests a very precise form of deterrence theory, advocating the increase of either the probability of punishment or the severity of punishment as a crime-control policy.

Obviously, the assumption of a reasoned decision process does not apply to every crime. It is easy to think of crimes of passion or pathological acts where the assumption of rationality seems doubtful. Nonetheless, a considered decision process may underlie many criminal acts. This is particularly true if you allow for a current, apparently impulsive criminal act, such as shoplifting, to be the result of a prior decision to consider shoplifting in certain circumstances.

Bounded Rationality

Although widely used, the expected utility model has not gone unchallenged. One challenge is that the information-processing demands of an expected utility strategy are inconsistent with our knowledge of the human cognitive system. Research in cognitive psychology has shown that the active processing of information is a serial process that occurs in a memory of limited capacity, duration, and ability to place information in more permanent storage. As a consequence, people are forced to utilize heuristics to keep the information-processing demands of complex problem-solving tasks within the bounds of their limited capacity. A heuristic allows for efficient problem solving at the cost of some possibility of making a mistake. For example, one heuristic process a criminal might use to judge the probability of conviction for a type of crime is to try to recall the names of people who were convicted of that crime. The easier it is to recall such people, the higher the judged probability. Although roughly accurate, this use of the *availability heuristic* can be biased by factors that influence the memorability of events but not their probability. One such influence would be the amount of newspaper coverage. These factors will lead to judgments that are biased in predictable ways when compared to the actual statistics calculated using a much more effortful, but normatively correct, enumeration of all convictions.

The idea that human information-processing limitations place constraints on decision processes is referred to as the concept of bounded rationality (Simon, 1957). The bounded rationality hypothesis states that behavior is reasoned within constraints, but not necessarily rational in the strict expected utility maximization sense. The hypothesis of bounded rationality has led to many studies testing the adequacy of expected utility as a description of decision behavior. The result has been accumulating evidence that the expected utility model is at times inadequate. This evidence, provided by psychologists and increasingly by economists, has caused one recent reviewer in the economics literature to conclude "that at the individual level EU maximization is more the exception than the rule" (Schoemaker, 1982).

These deviations from the expected utility model are not just simply random error. The model fails in ways that are both systematic and well described by alternative theories, which outline some of the heuristics that may be used by decision makers. The central thesis of this chapter is that such deviations are not only interesting but of substantial potential benefit for understanding the criminal's choices. If we can better describe critical decisions made by a potential criminal, we might more effectively design deterrents or otherwise discourage criminal acts.

We now turn to a review of the behavioral decision literature. We concentrate on two broad and interrelated aspects of decisions: The first is the construction of a representation of the decision problem. This section concerns how criminals perceive potential criminal opportunities, what information they notice, and what they ignore. It suggests that understanding the decision maker's representation of the decision problem is crucial to predicting the choices that are made. The second area we will examine is the evaluation of alternatives. Here we are concerned with the actual decision process used to select crime opportunities, how decision makers compare committing a crime to the alternative of not committing a crime, and how those processes are affected by situational factors, such as time pressure or the number of alternatives. Although the line between these two activities may often blur in real-world tasks, it serves as a helpful organizational tool.

Constructing Representations

A central tenet of information-processing theory is that the internal representations constructed by the decision maker drive behaviors such as choice and problem solving. Choices are determined, therefore, not necessarily by the objective properties of the alternatives, but rather by how they are perceived by the decision maker. Because decision makers have a limited capacity to process information, these representations will often only contain part of the information that is potentially relevant to the decision, particularly in complex situations. Whereas an expected utility approach would suggest that all crimes and possible outcomes are considered for any criminal decision, a bounded rationality view suggests that only a few aspects of a few alternatives may be considered, and the rest ignored. For example, according to the bounded rationality view, a burglar might only consider houses near easy escape routes and only examine the probable take in choosing a target, ignoring other information. Evidence of such simplification is provided by Carroll (1982), who showed that criminals ignored certain aspects of possible crimes in judging their attractiveness.

Internal representations, in addition to being incomplete, are often influenced by seemingly inconsequential changes in the way decision alternatives are presented. Probably no set of findings is more dramatic than the "framing" results of Kahneman and Tversky (1979) and Tversky and Kahneman (1981) among others, who demonstrated that two formally identical choice problems, stated in slightly different fashion, can evoke very different preferences. This dependence of choice upon the external presentation of information is not only disturbing but also suggests important theoretical and pragmatic implications for understanding and influencing criminal behavior. Making penalties for speeding more salient by erecting large roadside signs would be an example of such a presentational factor. In describing these effects, we will make use of Kahneman and Tversky's descriptive model of decision under uncertainty, called prospect theory.

Let us recall that decisions are characterized by three components: (1) a set of actions or alternatives, for example a set of possible crimes or potential homes to burglarize; (2) a set of outcomes or payoffs, for example being apprehended or departing undetected; and (3) the probability of the occurrence of each outcome, for example the probability of being apprehended.

We turn first to representing the outcomes associated with alternatives; for example, how would prospect theory represent the acquisition of $1,000 in a robbery or a jail sentence or fine? To represent the values associated with outcomes, prospect theory proposes a value function that differs from the classical utility function in three ways:

First, outcomes are judged relative to some target or reference point. Outcomes below that reference point are viewed as losses, and those above it as gains. This is perhaps the most important modification to the standard utility analysis, because it allows a decision maker's expectations to influence the attractiveness of options. In the expected utility model, a criminal would integrate a $1,000 gain or a $500 loss (say from fines or legal fees) with his or her total wealth. If the criminal's total wealth had been $1,000, then expected utility would see these two outcomes of the robbery as wealth positions of $2,000 and $500. Prospect theory, in contrast, would identify the current wealth as the reference point and see the outcomes as a gain of $1,000 or a loss of $500. In other words, prospect theory suggests that decision makers are much more sensitive to changes in their current wealth, and less sensitive to the level of their current wealth than would be expected in an expected utility analysis.

Second, the value function is concave for outcomes above the reference point and convex below it, implying that decision makers will be risk averse for gains and risk seeking for losses. This suggests that a criminal would tend to avoid risk when it is associated with acquiring gains, but seek risk to avoid losses. Thus, although a criminal might reject an opportunity to commit a crime for a gain, he or she might accept it to prevent a loss, for example avoiding capture or a jail sentence. In contrast, the usual utility analysis assumes that decision makers tend to avoid risk in all cases.

Finally, the value function is sloped more steeply for losses than for gains. As a result, losses have more impact upon choices than equivalent-sized gains. Corroborating evidence on the importance of losses is provided by some early work examining choice among gambles (Slovic and Lichtenstein, 1968; Payne and Braunstein, 1971).

A typical value function is illustrated by Figure 9.4 in Chapter 9. The origin represents the reference point, usually the status quo, and the top right represents the mapping of gains, along the horizontal axis, into value, along the vertical axis. Note that the additional value of an amount of money decreases as the amount increases. Although $2,000 is valued more than $1,000, it is not valued twice as highly. Similarly, a loss of $2,000 is less than twice as bothersome as a $1,000 loss.

Because of these differences, the value function suggests that the perception of outcomes can radically alter preferences. Shifts in the reference point can cause the same outcomes to be perceived as either a gain or a loss. Although in many cases the status quo may serve as a natural reference point, reference points are open to manipulation (Tversky and Kahneman, 1981; Payne et al., 1980).

This is best illustrated by an example: Consider an individual contemplating underreporting his or her taxable income. Obviously, paying taxes can be seen as a loss, because it removes money from total income. Here, the reference point is one's total salary, and an appealing goal the reduction of total tax liability. However, an alternate reference point involves the amount already withheld from salary. Because this money has never been available to the decision maker, it may not be perceived as income, and the reference point might be one's salary after withholding. In this case a tax refund is perceived as a gain rather than a reduction in the loss. This view of the situation suggests that it is very attractive to reduce one's tax liability so that the amount owed is zero, and much less important to find further reductions. In terms of Figure 9.4, the impact of gaining $1,000 is much less than the impact of reducing a loss by $1,000.

Thus, according to prospect theory, tax cheating would seem most attractive to reduce losses rather than increase gains. If decisions about tax compliance are made based upon salary after withholding, cheating might seem less attractive when one is simply increasing a refund rather than decreasing one's tax bill. As a result, we would tend to see less compliance with the tax laws in those that have had less of their income withheld, relative to individuals with identical liabilities. To increase compliance, a taxing authority might want to ensure that withholding is, on average, at least equivalent to tax liabilities, and concentrate scrutiny upon those who owe money at the end of the year.

The perception of aspiration levels or reference points might well have a more general influence as well. The increased standard of living provided by criminal activities might well become a new reference point, making the option of continuing to commit a given crime more attractive than its first commission. Clarke and Cornish report that residential burglary is an often-repeated crime, with individual incidents caused by a need of money on the part of the burglar. Similarly, a sudden decrease in the economic standard of a population might well make criminal opportunities more attractive, because they represent a means of mitigating losses and returning to the former status quo.

The impact of probabilities upon decisions depends upon their representation as well. It would seem that in most cases it is subjective probabilities that influence a potential criminal's decisions. Behavioral decision research suggests that these subjective probabilities may have several interesting characteristics. First, subjective probabilities can be quite different from available objective estimates. Subjective judgments of the probabilities of events are estimated using heuristic rules, which, although often accurate, sometimes result in biased estimates.

Judgments of probability, for example, are often made using the availability heuristic: Frequency is judged by the ease with which events come to mind. More memorable events are judged as more probable than equally likely but less memorable events. An estimate of the probability of winning a lottery, for example, could be made by dividing the number of winners by the total number of tickets sold. Because these numbers are not easily available to potential customers, they may instead estimate probability by thinking about how many winners come to mind. Although the result of this calculation may be roughly correct, it is subject to other influences, such as the amount of publicity surrounding winners. Similarly, to increase the perceived probability of winning in a casino, operators often publicize large wins, making them more available (Cornish, 1978). By analogy, if information about the consequences of criminal acts is made more vivid and memorable, the perceived likelihood of being apprehended and suffering consequences might increase, even with no change in the actual probability. Finally, research in subjective probability suggests that vivid information about a single case may be much more effective in raising the perceived likelihood of capture and punishment than statistically diagnostic information (Tversky and Kahneman, 1974; Nisbett and Ross, 1980). Recent programs in the United States graphically illustrating the tragedies caused by driving while intoxicated are consistent with this approach.

There are many similar effects in which subjective probabilities may be distorted or biased. These include the mood or affect state of the decision maker (Johnson and Tversky, 1983) and the ability of decision makers to imagine various outcomes (Tversky and Kahneman, 1982). Although these various mechanisms may well offer opportunities for under-standing and influencing criminal behavior (see Kahneman et al., 1982, for a review), a complete review lies beyond the scope of this chapter.

Even if subjective probabilities were accurate, the impact of objective probabilities is not simply a function of their magnitude. Prospect theory, for example, posits a weighting function, which is a subjective measure of the impact of probabilities just as the value function is a subjective measure of the impact of outcomes. This function (See Figure 9.5 Chapter 9) suggests that moderate and high probabilities are underweighted and that the function is relatively flat within this range. Fairly small probabilities are, in contrast, overweighted, although this effect is less pronounced than the underweighting. Finally, the function is discontinuous at the extremes, with probabilities of 0 and 1.0 receiving their appropriate weight. These discontinuities serve to emphasize the distinct role of certainty: Probabilities of 1.0 have much more than twice the impact of a probability of .5, and very small probabilities will be perceived as being equivalent to 0. This first characteristic of the weighting function has been labeled the *certainty effect* by Kahneman and Tversky, indicating that sure outcomes are overweighted relative to their probabilistic equivalents. For example, a potential criminal might be more dissuaded by a deterrent that would be applied with certainty when compared to a more severe outcome that would be applied with a probability less than 1.0.

Taken together, the value and decision weight functions have some interesting implications for the design of deterrents. Deterrence theory, as proposed in an expected utility framework, suggests that decision makers evaluate the possible outcomes of the criminal act, each outcome weighted by the probability of occurrence. A prospect theory analysis would take a similar direction but replace probabilities with decision weights and utilities with value. What would such an analysis look like?

The weighting function has two relevant properties. First, penalties would be most effective if they could be assured for all offenders with certainty, and least effective if the probability of suffering some penalty is very small, and seen as zero. Work on the objective probability of arrest (Hindelang et al., 1977) suggests that the clearance rate, that is, the probability of being arrested for a reported crime, ranges between .15 for auto theft to .27 for robbery. Because crimes are underreported, or attempted without detection, the actual probabilities are probably significantly lower. Since about one third of all arrests end in release, and half of all convictions end in probation rather than prison terms (Hindelang et al., 1977), the actual probability of serious punishment for any one instance of this class of crime may appear to be relatively small, if not "practically zero."

How might we increase this perceived probability? One might consider reframing the probabilities in terms of a longer time period. For example, for any one commission of tax evasion or shoplifting, the probability of being apprehended and punished may be quite small, but the probability for a career of committing such a crime might be within the appropriate range; for example authorities might claim that 90% of all burglars eventually spend time in jail. Reframing contingencies has been a successful tactic in another applied setting. Slovic et al. (1982) presented accident and fatality rates to individuals either using a per-trip basis or aggregated over a lifetime of driving. The lifetime statistic seemed much more persuasive because the probability no longer was seen as "practically zero" but instead in the range of overweighted probabilities. The result was a more favorable attitude toward passenger restraints such as seat belts.

Another tactic involves the framing of contingencies. Whereas the probability of punishment for a criminal act may be low, the conditional probability of punishment, given arrest or conviction, might be quite high. For example, the probability of being convicted for a single burglary may be practically zero; however, publicizing the fact that all convicted burglars receive prison sentences might be quite persuasive. This basic effect was termed the *pseudocertainty effect* by Tversky and Kahneman, because it exploits the increased impact of certainty at one stage to increase the impact of an outcome. Together, these two tactics can increase the impact of potential punishment. Compare, for example, the following two hypothetical but equivalent facts: (1) For every instance of serious tax evasion, 1 in 500 people spend some time in jail. (2) Over the average lifetime (50 years) of paying taxes, someone who continues to seriously evade taxation faces a 1-in-10 chance of being caught and convicted, and, when convicted, is certain to spend time in jail.

In many cases, limited resources require a trade-off between the number of offenders punished and the severity of the punishment. Unfortunately, prospect theory is not at this time well enough specified to provide much help with this trade-off. Yet it clearly states that the probability of punishment should not be very small, and that doubling the probability from a small (say .2) to a moderate (.4) value will result in much less than twice the deterrent effect.

Contrast this to expected utility theory, which suggests that the effects of probability are linear. An economic analysis of deterrence might suggest that one should double the probability of punishment, even if it means halving its severity. In expected utility terms, this would increase, on average, the deterrent effect. Note that in prospect theory such a change in policy could be seen as significantly less effective if it merely shifted the probability within the moderate range, say from .3 to .6.

Any approach that posits strictly calculated rationality in criminal decisions suggests that criminals know the potential penalties for their actions, yet there is abundant evidence that criminals often do not know the penalties associated with the crimes they commit. Henshel and Carey (1975), for example, cite one study in which more than one quarter of respondents could not even guess the maximum legal penalty for a given crime. Thus it would appear that criminals may be influenced by an awareness of possible punishment, but not possess knowledge of the exact levels. Clearly the design of deterrents should involve understanding the perception, among criminals, of both the negative consequences of crime as well as the perceived probabilities of those outcomes.

Although prospect theory and related work give us much insight into the possible encoding of decision problems, it also is less powerful than we might like. Kahneman and Tversky's framing demonstrations are dramatic and convincing; unfortunately, it is less clear how to identify, a priori, which frame an individual might adopt. Secondly, there is some evidence that knowledge of the frame is not sufficient to predict choice at the individual level (Fischhoff, 1983). Measuring frames is difficult, and using such measures to predict choices at the individual level has been disappointing. The results at the group level, however, are much more encouraging, and success at the individual level has recently been reported by Puto (1985), who has used a refined set of measures in a marketing context. However, although no direct comparison of prospect theory and expected utility theories currently exists in a criminal decision context, the problems in operationalizing the theories seem equivalent, requiring a judicious set of assumptions which lie outside the theories themselves. Finally, although Kahneman and Tversky suggest several other operations that can be used to simplify choice problems, these mechanisms are not well explored empirically, and the extension of prospect theory to more complex decision problems involving multiple attributes does not seem to be particularly easy. To better understand criminal behavior we must understand the strategies used in evaluating these alternatives in more complex environments.

Evaluating Alternatives

Real decisions about crime occur in situations that are significantly more complex than those we have examined so far. They contain dynamic elements (when to commit) and a large number of complex alternatives (potential neighborhoods, houses within neighborhoods, etc.). Real-world alternatives are not necessarily presented to decision makers; instead they identify the set of possible options. The decision maker may need to decide when to terminate the decision process. Unlike the simple problems we have discussed so far, there may be a surplus of possible alternatives, and the decision maker must decide when the costs of more search would not yield sufficient benefit. Finally, such decisions must be made under time pressure. For example, a burglar would want to make sure that the crime is committed before the residents return.

Much of our knowledge about more complex, realistic decisions comes from research that is concerned with the time course of the cognitive processes underlying choice and judgment. This research observes people while they are making a decision, using techniques such as asking decision makers to think aloud as they decide, or observing the information they acquire while making a choice.

The picture that emerges from this research is clear. The human decision maker is a limited information processor who has many different simplifying strategies for making choices. The adoption of one strategy or another seems to be largely dependent upon characteristics of the task and upon characteristics of the particular decision at hand (Payne, 1982). For example, decision problems vary in complexity. A more complicated decision can contain either more alternatives or more attributes or outcomes. As this happens, it is clear that decision makers attempt to simplify the problem through a number of different methods, most notably by eliminating alternatives without completely examining their attributes. A particularly common choice rule seems to be to use one or two attributes to screen the alternatives, reducing the set under consideration to two or three members, and then to proceed with a more careful consideration of these alternatives.

These two phases of the choice process indicate a common distinction used in describing choice strategies, that between *compensatory strategies*, which look at all the relevant information for each alternative and allow trade-offs between the good and bad qualities of the alternatives, and *noncompensatory strategies*, which will evaluate an alternative on just a few attributes, choosing or rejecting it based upon those attributes alone. Consider a potential burglar. A compensatory model, such as that implied by the expected utility model, would suggest that he or she examines all the alternatives and evaluates them individually, combining their good and bad points into an overall evaluation. Thus a fairly visible house might be selected because the perceived benefits of the burglary are high. In contrast, a noncompensatory model might simply eliminate that alternative because it was too visible, ignoring all other factors, such as the potential take.

In general, noncompensatory strategies are less demanding of our cognitive resources (Russo and Dosher, 1983; Johnson and Payne, 1985) and should therefore be more frequently used when information processing demands are high. Thus it is no surprise that the use of noncompensatory rules becomes more common as choice problems become more complex (Payne, 1976). A related finding is that people shift in their use of information under conditions of time pressure (Wright, 1974). Under time pressure people consider less information and focus more on negative attributes. Finally, there is evidence (Johnson and Russo, 1984; Johnson, forthcoming) that the more expert decision makers are with a topic, the more likely they are to use noncompensatory rules. Thus there are several reasons why noncompensatory rules may be often adopted by criminals, who are often specialists in one general type of crime (Clarke and Cornish, 1985), face a large number of potential targets, and make decisions under time pressure.

In fact, criminals who are specialists may have advantages over generalists or those who are less experienced. For example, Weaver and Carroll (forthcoming) showed that shoplifters quickly screen opportunities on one or two attributes and that the more experienced shoplifters were more efficient, concentrating on the presence or absence of a small set of deterrents. Similarly, Johnson showed that experts concentrated upon a subset of cues that they thought were better predictors for the judgment tasks. Expert stock analysts, for example, looked at half as many cues as did novices, yet were significantly better at predicting stock prices. Expert decision makers possess another skill that may be a great advantage to the criminal: They make decisions more quickly than novices. Johnson (forthcoming), for example, showed that both physicians and stock analysts were almost twice as fast as untrained novices in judgment tasks within their expertise. Such quick decisions have obvious advantages for covert activity.

Given their possible importance, it is probably worthwhile to examine some general characteristics associated with noncompensatory rules and how they might be applied to understanding criminals' choices. First, recall that decision makers often screen complex environments by using one or two attributes. If a screening phase is utilized by a criminal searching for a crime opportunity, it would be useful to understand how screening occurs. By understanding the features of the situation that are used for screening, we might better predict which targets are most likely to be selected.

For example, although a large proportion of car thieves may indeed be able to steal a locked car, locked cars are stolen much less frequently. Why? Perhaps because a locked car is quickly screened out of the experienced car thief's choice set, as long as unlocked alternatives remain available. Thus, simply locking an automobile might be an effective deterrent, even though it does not render the commission of the crime impossible. Similar observations about screening alternatives seem to be made by Carroll and Weaver, and by Clarke and Cornish in their discussions of models for burglary.

However, it should also be noted that these screening rules may be flexible and subject to adaptive change. Clarke and Cornish (1985) described the introduction of steering column locks in Great Britain. Such locks did not immediately lower the car theft rate, but rather shifted it to slightly older cars which lacked locking devices. Apparently the screening rules used by car thieves had changed in a small way that would be very important for policymakers.

A second major characteristic of many heuristic choice rules is that they "*satisfice*" (Simon, 1957) rather than optimize. Often they involve the selection of the first alternative to pass a set of criteria. Another way of putting this is that choice will be determined, in part at least, by the order in which alternatives are presented to the decision maker. All other things being equal, the decision maker will be more likely to choose from the first alternatives presented. This has two implications: First, variables that may seem relatively meaningless from an expected utility perspective, for example distance from the perpetrator's residence, have more meaning within a noncompensatory model.

Our analysis raises several issues that might be of interest to researchers in criminal decision making. First, if decisions are highly contingent upon task considerations, more success may come from attempts to model specific decisions rather than to build a general model. As Clarke and Cornish argue, such models will probably be somewhat specific to the crime and be limited to a particular aspect of the decision to commit, such as the involvement decision, the decision about each criminal event, or the decision to discontinue participation in this particular activity.

Second, because decisions are highly contingent, we think models of decisions based upon mathematical models may fail to capture important aspects of the decision process. Although a compensatory mathematical model may do an acceptable job of predicting the choices made by a noncompensatory process (Dawes and Corrigan, 1974; Johnson and Meyer, 1984), they tend to average over a number of interesting differences. Whereas a mathematical model might assign a weight to a given attribute, process-tracing data might tell us that this cue is examined only if another cue has a high level. One might consider the level of punishment for a crime only when the probability of capture is high. When models are estimated, they tend to gloss over such contingent rules (Einhorn et al., 1979), and although these models do predict well, they do badly at explaining the behavior they predict.

Finally, the very nature of contingent choice suggests that there are several different points at which public policy might influence criminals' choices. As Carroll and Weaver suggest, deterrents can be constructed at several points where critical decisions concerning crime are made. Policy can influence decisions about initial involvement, the individual criminal event, and continuance of criminal behavior. However, it is necessary to have a fairly detailed understanding of such decisions to implement such policies, and this understanding is unlikely to develop from mathematical models based on aggregate data. Understanding these decisions in sufficient detail probably requires a process orientation and the development of appropriate techniques for gathering and analyzing such data.

We should note finally some of the limitations of both process models and techniques. Process tracing is hard work; the chapter by Carroll and Weaver in this volume suggests both some of the difficulties and some of the payoffs. Furthermore, the lesson that decision processes are contingent upon the decision environment makes it incumbent upon the researcher to make sure that studies of decision process are conducted in environments that are as close as possible to the actual settings. Thus a lesson to be learned from this research is that studies that attempt to study decision at a process level must be sensitive to issues of realism; in particular, studies of information usage must be sensitive to the format and availability of information in laboratory studies.

Conclusion

Our review has illustrated several aspects of behavioral decision theory that we believe to be of use in understanding criminal behavior. We have emphasized the contrast between such findings and those of the standard utility maximization analysis. The view of decisions that emerges is one that, at the individual level, differs radically from that proposed by utility maximization. We suggest that decision makers use highly flexible, contingent heuristics, and that resultant choices will depend upon a number of task and problem characteristics such as the manner in which information is presented.

Although we advocate a process orientation, we also face the reality that currently our tools for process research are best suited for individual-level studies of a small number of decisions. Carroll and Weaver have made several steps in using these techniques, and we look forward to the development of better methods for process research.

Acknowledgments. Preparation of this chapter was supported in part by the Engineering Psychology Program at the Office of Naval Research. We thank Derek Cornish and Ron Clarke for helpful comments on an earlier draft.

References

Becker, G.
   1968   "Crime and punishment: an economic approach." Journal of Political Economy 76:169-217.
Carroll, J.S.
   1982   "Committing a crime: the offender's decision." Pp. 49-67 in V.J. Konecni and E.B. Ebbesen (eds.), Social-Psychological Analysis of Legal Processes. New York: Freeman.
Clarke, R.V. and D.B. Cornish
   1985   "Modelling offenders' decisions: a framework for research and policy." Pp. 147-85 in M. Tonry and N. Morris (eds.), Crime and Justice, Volume, 6. Chicago: University of Chicago Press.
Cornish, D.B.
   1978   Gambling: A Review of the Literature and Its Implications for

Policy and Research. Home Office Research Studies No. 42.
London: HMSO.

Dawes, R.M. and B. Corrigan
1974   "Linear models in decision making." Psychological Bulletin
81:95–106.

Einhorn, H.J., D.N. Kleinmuntz and B. Kleinmuntz
1979   "Linear regression and process tracing models of judgment."
Psychological Review 86:465–85.

Fischhoff, B.
1983   "Predicting frames." Journal of Experimental Psychology:
Learning, Memory and Cognition 9:103–16.

Henshel, R.L. and S.H. Carey
1975   "Deviance, deterrence and knowledge of sanctions." Pp. 54–73
in R.L. Henshel and R.A. Silverman (eds.), Perception in
Criminology. New York: Columbia University Press.

Hindelang, M.J., M.R. Gottfredson, C.S. Dunn and N. Parisi
1977   Sourcebook of Criminal Justice Statistics—1976. Washington,
D.C.: U.S. Government Printing Office.

Johnson, E.J.
forthcoming   "Judgment under uncertainty: process and performance." In M.
Chi, R. Glaser and M. Farr (eds). The Nature of Expertise.
Hillsdale, NJ: Erlbaum.

Johnson, E.J. and R.J. Meyer
1984   "Compensatory representations of non-compensatory choice
processes: the effect of varying context. Journal of Consumer
Research 11:551–63.

Johnson, E.J. and J.W. Payne
1985   "Effort and accuracy in choice." Management Science 31:395–
414

Johnson, E.J. and J.E. Russo
1984   "Product familiarity and learning new information." Journal of
Consumer Research 11:542–50.

Johnson, E.J. and A. Tversky
1984   "Representations of perceptions of risk." Journal of Experimental Psychology: General 113:55–70.

Kahneman, D., P. Slovic and A. Tversky
1982   Judgment Under Uncertainty: Heuristics and Biases. Cambridge, England: Cambridge University Press.

Kahneman, D. and A. Tversky
1979   "Prospect theory: an analysis of decisions under risk." Econometrica 47:263–91.

Nisbett, R. and L. Ross
1980   Human Inference: Strategies and Shortcomings of Social
Judgment. Englewood Cliffs, NJ: Prentice-Hall.

Payne, J.W.
1976   "Task complexity and contingent processing in decision making: an information search and protocol analysis." Organizational Behavior and Human Performance 16:366–87.

Payne, J.W.
1982   "Contingent decision behavior." Psychological Bulletin 92:382–402.

Payne, J.W. and M.L. Braunstein
1971   "Preferences among gambles with equal underlying distributions." Journal of Experimental Psychology 87 (1):13–18.

Payne, J.W., D.J. Laughlann and R. Crum
1980   "Translation of gambles and aspiration level effects in risky choice behavior." Management Science 26:1039–60.

Puto, Christopher
1985   The Framing of Industrial Buying Decisions. Unpublished doctoral dissertation, Duke University, Durham, NC.

Russo, J.E. and B.A. Dosher
1983   "Strategies for multiattribute binary choice." Journal of Experimental Psychology: Learning, Memory and Cognition 9:676–96.

Schoemaker, P.J.H.
1982   "The expected utility model: its variants, purposes, evidence and limitations." Journal of Economic Literature 20:529–63.

Simon, H.A.
1957   Models of Man: Social and Rational. New York: Wiley.

Slovic, P., B. Fischhoff and S. Lichtenstein
1982   "Facts versus fears: understanding perceived risk." Pp. 463–92 in D. Kahneman, P. Slovic and A. Tversky (eds.), Judgment Under Uncertainty: Heuristics and Biases. Cambridge, England: Cambridge University Press.

Slovic, P. and S. Lichtenstein
1968   "Relative importance of probabilities and payoffs in risk taking." Journal of Experimental Psychology Monographs 78 (3 part 2).

Tversky, A. and D. Kahneman
1974   "Judgment under uncertainty: heuristics and biases." Science 185:1124–31.

Tversky, A. and D. Kahneman
1981   "The framing of decisions and the psychology of choice." Science 211:281–99.

Weaver, F.M. and J.S. Carroll
forthcoming   "Crime perceptions in a natural setting by expert and novice shoplifters." Social Psychology Quarterly.

Wright, P.
1974   "The harassed decision maker: time pressures, distractions and the use of evidence." Journal of Applied Psychology 59:551–61.

12
Offense Specialization:
Does It Exist?

KIMBERLY KEMPF

Editors' Note

As explained in the Introduction to this volume, the requirement that rational choice models of crime be specific to rather closely defined types of offense makes no assumptions about the degree of specialization or generalization in offenders' careers. Thus, even if an offender were a "generalist," the factors influencing decisions about some of the offenses he or she committed (residential burglary, for example) might be quite different from those factors influencing others of his or her offenses (shoplifting, for example). This being so, crime-specific modeling is needed if effective ways of preventing or controlling crime are to be developed. The virtues of rational choice approaches would be easier to communicate, however, the greater the degree of specialization that could be demonstrated. For this reason Kimberly Kempf's findings, using unrivalled data from the second Philadelphia birth cohort, of a greater degree of specialization in offending careers than has been shown before are helpful. As she points out, however, the issue is by no means settled. In particular, it would be interesting to see if greater specialization would be found if more complete information were available about the nature of offenses committed, if much finer subclassifications of offense types were used, and if offenders' careers were subdivided into more discrete periods. It is conceivable, for example, that a juvenile offender might for a few months (or even a year or two) have a small repertoire of offenses, including, let us say, shoplifting from local stores and smoking marijuana. Subsequently he or she might graduate to burglaries of local residences, and later still to mugging. Looked at over an entire career span of several years, this pattern of offending might well be characterized as generalist in nature. Considering, however, the complete range of crime types in which the offender *could* have become involved and contrasting this with the limited number of types actually committed at particular points in the offender's career, one could equally well make the case for a form of "serial specialization." The issues are definitional as well as empirical.

Clarke and Cornish's (1985) recent theory of offender decision making stipulates that four separate decision processes need to be modeled: the first relating to the criminal event and the other three to the career stages of offender involvement, namely, initial involvement, continuation, and desistance. Their theory further requires that crime-specific models, such as those they provide for burglary in a middle-class suburb, be developed for each decision process, because rational choices are likely to differ according to offense type. Thus, their continuance model is premised on the notion that a particular type of crime is repeated. This seems to imply a degree of crime specialization in the offender career, which is somewhat perverse in light of the literature, which has rather consistently argued that offense generalization rather than specialization is the norm. However, closer examination of previous research concerned with crime specialization reveals that the issue has not yet been investigated thoroughly and is by no means resolved. Following a brief review of the literature, this chapter will use data from the 1958 Philadelphia birth cohort to improve upon previous efforts to examine specialization in the delinquency career and discern contrasts among juveniles that could assist in the identification of adult offenders.

Previous Research

Despite the importance of the issue, research efforts concentrating on specialization have been few and limited in their success. The early work of Healy and Bronner (1926, 1936) was among the first systematic investigations of aggregate career patterns of individuals who experienced police, court, and correctional stages. With reference to specialization, they reported that continued offending or desistance from crime rarely had any relation to the type of offense committed (1926:177). Although the methodology of the study lacked sophistication and the offense categories examined were broad, the absence of specialization reported by Healy and Bronner was generally accepted and the issue was not carefully investigated again for several decades.

Conceptual efforts to establish offender typologies able to characterize different career patterns and specialties (Clinard and Quinney, 1973; Cloward and Ohlin, 1960; Gibbons, 1965), as well as numerous offender subtypes (Conklin, 1972; Guttmacher, 1960; McCaghy, 1967; Neustatter, 1957) and classification schemes for institutionalized offenders (Roebuck, 1966; Schrag, 1944, 1961; Sykes, 1958), were each designed to overcome the behavioral exceptions found in an individual, all-encompassing theory and to provide for differential treatment according to offender and offense type. Following his comprehensive review of offender typologies, Don Gibbons (1975) conceded that these classification schemes generally have been deficient in clarity and objectivity, have often failed to develop mutually exclusive and comprehensive categories, and seldom have been examined empirically. He further concluded, "After two decades of work in this tradition, relatively little progress in typological directions can be discerned" (p. 153).

By using stochastic (probability) techniques with longitudinal data to age 18 for a large (N = 9,945) cohort population, the 1945 Philadelphia Birth Cohort Study (Wolfgang et al., 1972) was better able than its predecessors to address the issue of specialization. In an analysis unmatched in 1972, the delinquency careers of the cohort were followed to the ninth offense in this study. The results showed that regardless of previous offense type an offender was most likely to have subsequent involvement in a nonindex event. If a nonindex event did not occur next, the state of desistance was likely. Among the index crimes, each category was more likely to follow itself than to change. Although these conditional probabilities of like-offense transitions for the index categories were taken as some indication of specialization, the estimates failed to achieve the probability of .5 for like-offense repeats (Wolfgang et al., 1972: 166–88).

The lack of juvenile specialization in the 1945 Philadelphia Birth Cohort Study was cited by Klein (1979:169) in his critique of deinstitutionalization and diversion programs for juvenile offenders as the explanation for failed programs established for status offenders and, more recently, in Petersilia's (1980:353) challenge to specially designated career-criminal prosecution units. Although the cohort study offered many advantages because of the quality of the data and the level of sophistication achieved in the analyses, some inherent limitations to the study require that the reported results be viewed cautiously. First, the crime categories in the Philadelphia study were designed for measurement of severity (Wolfgang et al., 1972:46; Sellin and Wolfgang, 1964) and were not ideally suited for measuring specialization. The requirement of mutually exclusive categories was not satisfied by this typology because the separate classification of nonindex crimes and events involving combinations from other categories allowed similar types of behavior to be contained in different crime groups. Second, less-active youth with delinquency careers that ended prior to the ninth offense who might have been less likely to develop patterns of specialization were included in the same analyses as the very active delinquents and were likely to confound the results. Finally, although specialization was traced to the ninth offense before cell frequencies became too small for analyses, and no other study progressed to this career stage, the total careers of many delinquents were not captured within this data-imposed boundary.

Five more recent studies, three of which were conducted by the Rand Corporation and were based on self-report data, have examined the issue of crime specialization (Bursik, 1980; Chaiken and Chaiken, 1982;

Petersilia et al., 1977; Peterson et al., 1981; Rojek and Erickson, 1982), and all have reported that the specialist career pattern is uncommon. Although it is plausible that a self-report study of offenders could reveal patterns of undetected, or "successful" criminal careers, the reliance on institutionalized inmates in the Rand surveys (Chaiken and Chaiken, 1982; Petersilia et al., 1977; Peterson et al., 1981) limited their findings to unique convicted offenders who were less likely to have been truly representative of the criminal population; consequently, the potential benefit of self-reported data was less fruitful in these investigations. A further limitation is that the 3-year recall stipulation unduly confined the length of careers to be studied. Using officially based data on juveniles, Bursik (1980) and Rojek and Erickson (1982) followed static probability procedures (similar to that used in the 1945 Philadelphia Cohort Study) to examine specialization among juvenile delinquents; however, data limitations prevented their examination of more than five offense transitions in each study.

To conclude this brief review, the analytical needs of an investigation of continued crime involvement within specific offense categories require longitudinal data capable of examining multiple crime categories and lengthy criminal careers for a large population. No previous results can be considered conclusive, because one or more of the data requirements were not satisfied in each of the investigations.

Data

This study utilized data from the 1958 Philadelphia Birth Cohort Study. These data comprise a population and, as such, are not vulnerable to the threats of validity posed by sampling procedures. These data include officially based information to age 26 on 27,160 males and females born in 1958 who resided in Philadelphia from the ages of 10 through 18. The cohort includes 13,160 males (6,216 white and 6,944 nonwhite) and 14,000 females (6,637 white and 7,363 nonwhite). The requirement of Philadelphia residence between ages 10 and 18 for defining the cohort provides a uniform time frame and setting within which cohort members are at risk of offending. Mortality is not problematic in this longitudinal investigation because the retrospective data collection involved unobtrusive archival examination of records maintained routinely by the Philadelphia Police Department, courts, and area schools.

Cohort members were identified and their demographic characteristics accessed from school records obtained from all public and private schools in Philadelphia. Rap sheets and police investigation reports, provided by the Juvenile Aid Division of the Philadelphia Police Department, were used to characterize all police encounters (including official arrests and police contacts with juveniles that resulted in remedial, or informal, handling of the youth by an officer whereby the youth was generally remanded to the custody of his or her parents) experienced by the cohort before age 18. The Municipal and Common Pleas Courts of Philadelphia served as data sources for offenses committed by the cohort after reaching the legislatively imposed adult status (age 18) through December 31, 1984, the date on which this data collection effort concluded. Further description of these data can be found in Tracy et al. (1984).

With information up to age 26 for these 27,160 individuals, these data are superior to those on which previous research was based and bountiful in their capability to support determination of whether offense specialization is a significant delinquency career pattern and, if so, whether juvenile specialists are more likely than other delinquents to commit adult crime.

Variables

Juvenile delinquency is defined as an official police contact before age 18. This comprehensive delinquency measure includes both criminal and status offenses. This variable is also less vulnerable to selection bias on the part of individual arresting officers because, in addition to official arrest forms, records of police encounters that resulted in informal remedial actions by the officer contribute to the delinquency measure. Traffic violations are excluded from consideration. The length of the delinquency career is characterized through the total number of police encounters experienced by each cohort member during the statutory juvenile period.

The typology adopted for examination of delinquency career specialization includes five mutually exclusive offense categories: personal offenses in which the potential for inflicting injury is apparent (such as murder, rape, and assault), robbery, property offenses (including burglary, theft, and vandalism), status offenses (such as truancy, incorrigibility, and curfew violation), and "other" offenses (primary crimes of vice such as drug violations, gambling, and prostitution, but also a catchall including loitering, perjury, and failure to disperse). This classification scheme provides offense divisions that are conceptually unique, yet inclusive of all activities for which there were police contacts.

Adult offender status is operationalized as a dichotomous (yes/no) criterion based on the presence of one or more charges recorded by the Philadelphia courts between 1976 and 1984. This study is limited to early adulthood offending, because the cohort is now only in its 27th year and the data capture adult records through 1984. Offenses committed outside the Philadelphia jurisdiction are not identified. The use of predisposition court data to define crime is also subject to concerns of internal validity because guilt has not been established at this stage. This measure of adult crime, however, is comparable to the police-based indicator of delinquency and therefore advantageous in its ability to identify similar levels of crime.

Methods

The nature of the research issue and the potential for confounding effects due to race and gender attributes of the subjects required that analyses be completed within particular subgroups. The following relationships are addressed in this research in order to separate early and late delinquency career stages and adult crime: First, do more adult offenders come from former delinquents? Second, do juveniles begin to specialize, especially later in their delinquency careers? Third, if the first two relationships hold, do more adult offenders come from juvenile specialists? In this study, event transition matrices were used to identify juvenile offending patterns for the entire careers of all delinquents and, discretely, for the early (first through fourth offense transitions) and late (fifth through ninth offense transitions) career stages for those identified as chronic delinquents with five or more offenses. To determine whether patterns of delinquency occur among categories of youth differentially by race, this study examined career transitions separately by race, although the classification was necessarily only dichotomous (white/nonwhite, the nonwhites being primarily blacks) because school and police files did not provide the identification of ethnicity for multiple categories. Analyses were also done independently for males and females to control for unique differences according to gender. To pursue the final research question of whether adult offenders were juvenile specialists, all analyses of offense transitions were completed for the aforementioned subgroups within the individual categories of delinquents who became adult offenders by age 27 and those who did not.

Overall transition matrices were computed for all transitions, and separately for early and late career stages for chronic delinquents. These matrices show the conditional probability that a juvenile committed offense j (indicative of either personal, robbery, property, other, or status offenses) on arrest k, given that offense i was committed on arrest $k - 1$. These matrices, identified as P_{ij}, assume constancy across all transitions and that the behavior is not contingent upon the number of the offense. (For more information on this simple Markov chain analysis see Figlio, 1981; Kemeny and Snell, 1960; McFarland, 1970). Conditional probabilities observed along the matrix diagonal, which reveal the proportion of like-offense transitions, are reported.

Results

It was necessary to verify the conditional relationship set forth in the research question that adult offenders are more likely to have experienced delinquency, before proceeding with analyses of juvenile specialization. The preliminary findings supported this assumption and served to substantiate the large number of research subjects required for this study. (An overview of the 1958 Philadelphia birth cohort is provided in the Appendix.) Only 3,195 (11.8%) of the total 27,160-member cohort were identified as adult offenders by age 27. The majority 1,843 (57.7%) of these offenders had been juvenile delinquents, including 1,640 (89.0%) males and 203 females. Of the male delinquents, 1,162 (70.9%) were nonwhite. Of the adult offenders, 620 (19.4%), including 583 males and 37 females, had five or more police contacts as juveniles. More than half, but by no means all, of the adult offenders had therefore been delinquents. The problem of inadequate cell size is expected in analyses of infrequent phenomena such as crime but is no doubt acute in criminal-career studies, as is forewarned by this early reduction of the data.

Twenty-four summary transition matrices were computed in this study. These several matrices make interpretation of the findings unwieldy; in an effort to be less cumbersome, probabilities observed along the main diagonals, where like-offense transitions appear and specialization would be found, were extracted from the original matrices and are shown in Tables 12.1 through 12.4. In every matrix, the cell chi-squares along the main diagonals were much larger than those in any other cells and are also included in the tables.

Table 12.1 shows the diagonals of the overall transition matrices for the total careers of all 4,315 male delinquents. Property crimes were committed more often than any other crime, and the probability of movement from one property offense to another was the most likely pattern shown for all male delinquents. The probabilities of specialization in all crime categories were greater for the 1,640 delinquents who became adult offenders than for the 2,675 delinquents who did not, and this relationship held for each category of race. The number of offense transitions differed little between adult offenders and nonoffenders; therefore the level of delinquency was greater for offenders. Over 79% of all transitions in each adult group involved nonwhites, who represented 71% of the adult nonoffenders and 65% of the offenders. In addition to more overall activity than whites, nonwhites were more likely to make transitions within the same crime category in all except the property and "other" crime categories.

The analyses of all transitions captured all movement by delinquents, which necessarily included the state of crime desistance. The transition from crime to juvenile desistance was the highest probability in every $k - 1$ crime category for each subgroup of the adult nonoffenders (tables

TABLE 12.1. Diagonals of the Summary Transition Matrices: All Offense Transitions for All Males During the Delinquency Career (N)

Category	No. of Subjects	N	$k - 1/k$	n	Cell χ^2	Probability
Adult nonoffenders	2,675	7,023	Personal	129	34.3	.1440
			Robbery	89	98.1	.1660
			Property	637	38.5	.2715
			Other	334	18.9	.1901
			Status	328	122.5	.2204
White adult nonoffenders	934	1,936	Personal	28	15.8	.1346
			Robbery	2	5.9	.0588
			Property	170	31.7	.2720
			Other	154	2.0	.2112
			Status	65	36.4	.1912
Nonwhite adult nonoffenders	1,741	5,087	Personal	101	19.7	.1468
			Robbery	87	56.5	.1733
			Property	467	15.8	.2714
			Other	180	12.1	.1751
			Status	263	82.7	.2291
Adult offenders	1,640	7,563	Personal	182	34.5	.1745
			Robbery	179	191.0	.2374
			Property	984	79.7	.3698
			Other	450	43.1	.2521
			Status	338	198.5	.2561
White adult offenders	478	1,788	Personal	19	0.5	.0979
			Robbery	4	8.2	.0870
			Property	270	31.7	.4036
			Other	173	4.6	.2869
			Status	53	21.7	.1920
Nonwhite adult offenders	1,162	5,775	Personal	163	33.3	.1920
			Robbery	175	126.3	.2472
			Property	714	49.3	.3584
			Other	277	32.0	.2343
			Status	285	175.5	.2730

not shown). Following desistance from delinquency, the second highest probability was that of specialization for property, other, and status categories, and that of property followed by specialization for personal and robbery. Among all adult offenders, the probability of desistance ranked first before specialization for personal and other crime, second following specialization for robbery and property, and third following property and specialization for status offenses. The probability of desistance was highest for personal crimes only; followed second to specialization for robbery, property, and other; and ranked fourth for status offenses among nonwhites. White offenders were likely first to desist from personal, robbery, and other offenses; second to desist after a status offense; and third to desist after property crime.

To avoid plausible confounding effects due to youths who had short delinquency careers, analyses were then restricted to juveniles with five or more delinquencies. Table 12.2 shows the results of the first four transitions (Offenses 1 through 5), during which desistance did not occur, for these chronic delinquents. The most frequently occurring event was property crime. The largest difference was the greater probability for nonwhite adult offenders (.2563) than nonoffenders (.1942) to commit personal crimes. The probabilities, overall, were higher than those shown in Table 12.1; the highest probability (.5178) was that of committing a property crime when the immediately previous offense also involved property. The likelihood of specialization during the first four transitions

TABLE 12.2. Diagonals of the Summary Transition Matrices: Offense Transitions 1 Through 4 for Males With Chronic Delinquency During the Delinquency Career (N)

Category	No. of Subjects	N	$k - 1/k$	n	Cell χ^2	Probability
Adult nonoffenders	399	1,488	Personal	37	10.7	.2114
			Robbery	16	2.5	.1280
			Property	209	8.9	.4172
			Other	80	12.1	.2985
			Status	154	24.8	.3675
White adult nonoffenders	84	312	Personal	10	8.8	.2778
			Robbery	1	2.2	.1000
			Property	48	3.5	.4486
			Other	34	2.2	.4048
			Status	27	8.8	.3600
Nonwhite adult nonoffenders	315	1,176	Personal	27	4.8	.1942
			Robbery	15	0.8	.1304
			Property	161	5.7	.4086
			Other	46	6.2	.2500
			Status	127	16.6	.3692
Adult offenders	583	2,228	Personal	67	18.1	.2318
			Robbery	39	38.5	.2407
			Property	341	13.0	.4200
			Other	116	12.6	.2843
			Status	209	62.5	.3752
White adult offenders	125	464	Personal	6	0.1	.1176
			Robbery	0	0.1	.0000
			Property	102	4.7	.5178
			Other	50	6.0	.4167
			Status	26	7.5	.2857
Nonwhite adult offenders	458	1,764	Personal	61	18.9	.2563
			Robbery	39	25.6	.2484
			Property	239	7.3	.3886
			Other	66	3.7	.2292
			Status	183	52.0	.3927

was highest in the property category for all offenders, followed by status offenses for nonwhite chronic offenders and both adult categories for race-combined results, and by other crimes for white chronic offenders. The proportion of transitions found within each summary race matrix does not suggest greater levels of activity by either subgroup of chronic delinquents; 79% of both adult offenders and nonoffenders were nonwhite, and 79% of the offense transitions in both groups involved nonwhite chronic offenders. The probability of specialization was greater for adult offenders than for chronic delinquents with no adult crime in all categories except other crime and was especially high for robbery.

Table 12.3 shows the diagonals of the matrices for the fifth through

TABLE 12.3. Diagonals of the Summary Transition Matrices: Offense Transitions 5 Through 9 for Males With Chronic Delinquency During the Delinquency Career (N)

Category	No. of Subjects	N	k − 1/k	n	Cell χ^2	Probability
Adult nonoffenders	399	1,163	Personal	33	9.7	.2000
			Robbery	26	40.2	.2476
			Property	172	17.8	.3991
			Other	70	9.6	.2545
			Status	43	21.8	.2299
White adult nonoffenders	84	250	Personal	4	1.8	.1481
			Robbery	0	0.0	.0000
			Property	42	4.2	.4330
			Other	35	4.2	.3846
			Status	6	2.4	.1875
Nonwhite adult nonoffenders	315	913	Personal	29	7.2	.2101
			Robbery	26	28.0	.2549
			Property	130	13.4	.3892
			Other	35	2.0	.1902
			Status	37	19.0	.2387
Adult offenders	583	1,902	Personal	60	10.7	.1974
			Robbery	47	17.0	.1950
			Property	308	30.1	.4356
			Other	100	14.3	.2427
			Status	50	41.1	.2101
White adult offenders	125	376	Personal	7	0.7	.1373
			Robbery	3	7.4	.2143
			Property	68	5.8	.4444
			Other	29	4.8	.2788
			Status	11	4.1	.2037
Nonwhite adult offenders	458	1,526	Personal	53	9.7	.2095
			Robbery	44	9.6	.1938
			Property	240	24.2	.4332
			Other	71	9.0	.2305
			Status	39	38.7	.2120

ninth transitions (Offenses 6 through 10) made by chronic delinquents. The probability of property crime repeats was high in every matrix. The probabilities of like-offense transitions again generally exceeded those found for all transitions made by all male delinquents. For chronic delinquents who were nonwhite, the probabilities were greater during the later career stage than during the early career in both adult groups for robbery-robbery transition and for property-property movement in the adult offender group. The likelihood of other same-category transitions, especially the status-status sequence, was less during movement between the fifth and tenth offenses for chronic delinquents. The transition from status offenses to property crime ranked first in all matrices, a relationship conceivably able to account for the diminished status-status probability among later careers for chronics and the virtual equivalence of the findings to those for total careers of all male delinquents. The activity level by race in each adult group remained comparable to the racial distribution of chronic delinquents: 20% to 22% of the transitions involved whites and 78% to 80% involved nonwhites.

Perhaps one explanation for the diminished probability of specialization in several categories is the inclusion of the opportunity to desist from crime in the later career summary matrices. The transition of specialization was more likely to occur first, before desistance, in property categories in all matrices; in the category of other crime for all white chronics; and in robbery for nonwhite adult offenders. The probability of desistance followed by either specialization, property, or other crime ranked first in all matrices when the immediately preceding state was personal crime, robbery in the individual and race-combined adult offenders matrices, and other crime for nonwhite adult non-offenders.

The results of the diagonals found in the overall transition matrices for all female delinquents are shown in Table 12.4; only 147 females achieved chronic delinquency, and so analyses of females were restricted to total delinquents. Females committed status offenses more often than any other crime. The career movement of white and nonwhite females was similar to their respective distributions in the population; for example, 70% of the transitions made by those without adult crime were made by the 68% of the female nonoffenders who were nonwhite, and 77% of the transitions for the offenders were made by the 78% of the offenders who were nonwhite. The highest probabilities were those with transitions from crime to desistance for all categories and all female delinquent sub-groups, except for adult offenders with $k - 1$ status offenses; these individuals were more likely, first, to commit another status offense and, second, to desist. The most common like-offense transition for all female delinquent groups was that of status offenses, followed by property-property for nonwhites and other-other for whites. Female delinquents made very few personal-personal and robbery-robbery transitions.

TABLE 12.4. Diagonals of the Summary Transition Matrices: All Offense Transitions for All Females During the Delinquency Career (N)

Category	No. of Subjects	N	$k - 1/k$	n	Cell χ^2	Probability
Adult nonoffenders	1,769	3,228	Personal	25	16.5	.0828
			Robbery	1	3.0	.0294
			Property	57	11.2	.1082
			Other	69	3.3	.1009
			Status	609	53.3	.3623
White adult nonoffenders	565	969	Personal	4	2.7	.0571
			Robbery	0	0.0	.0000
			Property	15	5.2	.1071
			Other	33	0.6	.1236
			Status	157	14.9	.3211
Nonwhite adult nonoffenders	1,204	2,259	Personal	21	12.6	.0905
			Robbery	1	2.5	.0323
			Property	42	6.3	.1085
			Other	36	1.7	.0863
			Status	452	37.9	.3792
Adult offenders	203	570	Personal	7	4.3	.1167
			Robbery	0	0.1	.0000
			Property	31	6.4	.2366
			Other	23	0.5	.1797
			Status	97	13.3	.4008
White adult offenders	45	129	Personal	0	0.2	.0000
			Robbery	0	0.0	.0000
			Property	5	2.5	.2174
			Other	11	0.3	.2619
			Status	21	1.8	.3621
Nonwhite adult offenders	158	441	Personal	7	4.4	.1273
			Robbery	0	0.1	.0000
			Property	26	4.0	.2407
			Other	12	0.0	.1395
			Status	76	11.9	.4130

Finally, the probability of movement within one crime category (shown along the matrix diagonal) was greater for both white and nonwhite females who became adult offenders than for those whose offending did not continue into early adulthood.

Summary of Results

The results of these analyses show that the majority of persons who committed at least one offense during early adulthood also experienced contact with the police during their youth. Moreover, although the tendency to specialize within one crime category was indicated throughout, the probabilities of like-offense transitions were greater among adult offenders overall and in separate analyses by race and gender. The inclination toward offense specialization, more marked among adult offenders, was augmented for males with lengthy juvenile careers during both their early and later stages of encounters with police. A few unique patterns were shown, such as a concentration among females in status-status transitions, among males for property-property transitions, and among nonwhite males for robbery-robbery transitions. Although it sometimes appeared second to desistance from crime and occasionally followed the probability of property crime, the propensity for juvenile specialization was shown and was greater among persons with subsequent crime involvement as adults.

Conclusion

This study examined juvenile specialization among 27,160 persons and followed their criminal behavior to age 27. The research findings indicated that patterns of specialization do exist and remain even when race, gender, unique juvenile career stages, and adult offender status are separately controlled. These findings suggest that notions such as Klein's (1979: 169) espousal of "cafeteria style delinquency" are premature in their dismissal of offense specialization and lend support to the emphasis on crime-specific explanations by Clarke and Cornish (1985). Although the magnitude of the 1958 Philadelphia birth cohort data afforded this study advantages unavailable in previous investigations, the results cannot be taken as conclusive evidence of crime specialization because not all data limitations were overcome. First, only criminal behavior that was brought to the attention of law enforcement officials was identified, and it is likely that crime types have a differential chance of arrest. It is also plausible that especially skillful offenders, perhaps specialists, are better able to avoid police contact. Second, the limitation to five categories in the analyses was perhaps unable to discern unique behavior patterns hidden within the crime classification. Third, the analyses also failed to provide for all potential controls, such as socioeconomic status, court disposition, and unique age-period involvement, because of limited cell frequencies even with a population of this size. Fourth, the restriction to immediately adjacent offenses for identification of specialization was stringent and excluded offenders without like-offense transitions whose careers were located primarily within one crime type. The solution to these measurement problems must be found in future research, possibly incorporating new techniques, before definitive statements on crime specialization can be made.

Evidence of offense specialization has important implications for policy because it could facilitate the estimation of risk to society for offender specialists and serve as a foundation from which policymakers could develop differential policing strategies and court and correctional treatment models directed at crime specialists.

Acknowledgments. Information presented in this chapter is elaborated from doctoral dissertation work in progress that is supported by a grant from the National Institute of Justice. I would like to acknowledge my dissertation advisors, Drs. M. Wolfgang, P. Tracy, and R. Figlio, in appreciation of their encouragement.

Appendix

Overview of the 1958 Philadelphia birth cohort

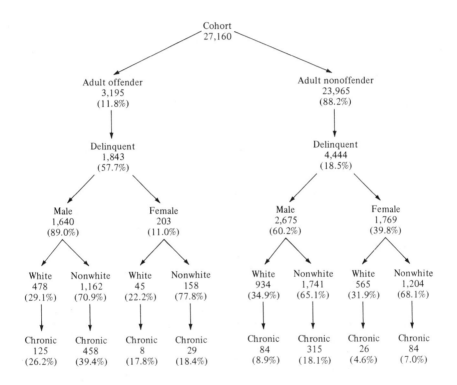

References

Bursik, R.
    1980   "The dynamics of specialization in juvenile offenses." Social Forces
            58(3):851–64.
Chaiken, J. and M. Chaiken
    1982   Varieties of Criminal Behavior. Santa Monica, CA: Rand.

Clarke, R. and D. Cornish
  1985 "Modeling offenders' decisions: a framework for research and policy." Pp. 147-85 in Crime and Justice: An Annual Review of Research, Volume 6. M. Tonry and N. Morris (eds.), Chicago: University of Chicago Press.
Clinard, M. and R. Quinney
  1973 Criminal Behavior Systems: A Typology. New York: Holt, Rinehart and Winston.
Cloward, R. and L. Ohlin
  1960 Delinquency and Opportunity: A Theory of Delinquency Gangs. Glencoe, IL: Free Press.
Conklin, J.
  1972 Robbery and the Criminal Justice System. Philadelphia: J.B. Lippincott.
Figlio, R.
  1981 "Delinquency careers as a simple Markov process." Pp. 25-37 in J. Fox (ed.), Models in Quantitative Criminology. New York: Academic Press.
Gibbons, D.
  1965 Changing the Lawbreaker. Englewood Cliffs, NJ: Prentice-Hall.
Gibbons, D.
  1975 "Offender typologies—two decades later." British Journal of Criminology, 15(2):140-56.
Guttmacher, M.
  1960 The Mind of the Murderer. New York: Farrar, Straus and Giroux.
Healy, W. and A. Bronner
  1926 Delinquents and Criminals: Their Making and Unmaking. New York: McMillan. (Reprinted by Patterson Smith, Montclair, NJ, 1969.)
Healy, W. and A. Bronner
  1936 New Light on Juvenile Delinquency. New Haven: Yale University Press.
Kemeny, J. and J. Snell
  1960 Finite Markov Chains. New York: Van Nostrand Reinhold.
Klein, M.
  1979 "Deinstitutionalization and diversion of juvenile offenders: a litany of impediments." Pp. 145-201 in Crime and Justice: An Annual Review of Research, Volume 1. N. Morris and M. Tonry (eds.), Chicago: University of Chicago Press.
McCaghy, C.
  1967 "Child molesters: a study of their careers as deviants." Pp. 75-88 in M. Clinard and R. Quinney (eds.), Criminal Behavior Systems: A Typology. New York: Holt, Rinehart and Winston.
McFarland, D.
  1970 "Intragenerational social mobility as a Markov process." American Sociological Review 35:463-76.
Neustatter, W.
  1957 The Mind of the Murderer. New York: Philosophical Library.
Petersilia, J., P. Greenwood and M. Lavin
  1977 Criminal Careers of Habitual Felons. Santa Monica, CA: Rand.

Petersilia, J.
   1980   "Criminal career research: a review of recent evidence." Pp.321–79 in, N. Morris and M. Tonry (eds.), Crime and Justice: An Annual Review of Research, Volume 2. Chicago: University of Chicago Press.
Peterson, M., H. Braiker and S. Polich
   1981   Who Commits Crimes: A Survey of Prison Inmates. Cambridge, MA: Oelgeschlager, Gunn and Hain.
Roebuck, J.
   1966   Criminal Typologies. Springfield, IL: Charles C Thomas.
Rojek, D. and M. Erickson
   1982   "Delinquent careers." Criminology 20(1): 5–28.
Schrag, C.
   1944   Social Types in a Prison Community. Unpublished master's thesis, University of Washington, Seattle.
Schrag, C.
   1961   "A preliminary criminal typology." Pacific Sociological Review (Spring): 11–16.
Sellin, T. and M. Wolfgang
   1964   The Measurement of Delinquency. New York: Wiley.
Sykes, G.
   1958   The Society of Captives. Princeton, NJ: Princeton University Press.
Tracy, P., M. Wolfgang and R. Figlio
   1984   Delinquency in a Birth Cohort II: A Comparison of the 1945 and 1958 Philadelphia Birth Cohorts. Washington, DC: National Institute of Juvenile Justice and Delinquency Prevention. (Final Report 83-JN-AX-0006.)
Wolfgang, M., R. Figlio and T. Sellin
   1972   Delinquency in a Birth Cohort. Chicago: University of Chicago Press.

13
Criminal Incapacitation Effects Considered in an Adaptive Choice Framework

PHILIP J. COOK

Editors' Note

Philip Cook's analysis of the possible adaptations made by offenders to policies of incapacitation constitutes a valuable example of the policy applications of a rational choice perspective. Taking as his starting point the assumption that people adapt their behavior in the light of information about the costs and benefits of alternative courses of action, Cook draws on the "danger compensation" thesis current in the road safety field to argue that such adaptations may sometimes act to partially negate the effects of policy. He shows clearly that selective incapacitation measures may, depending on the extent to which different classes of offender adapt their behaviors in the knowledge of the changing costs and benefits involved, very well lead to an increase rather than a decrease in overall levels of crime. His is a hypothetical example and needs to be fleshed out with interview and behavioral data, but it illustrates how important it may be for policymakers to obtain a clearer understanding of the way in which crime-control policies—whether incapacitative, deterrent, rehabilitative, or preventive—are perceived, evaluated, and reacted to by their intended objects. Neglect of the offender's perspective probably underlies the catastrophic failure of rehabilitation, and a similar neglect may well lead to the failure of many of the new deterrent policies. The situation can only be remedied by a large investment in research into offender perceptions.

One incontrovertibly effective method of preventing someone from committing crimes is to eliminate his or her opportunities for crime by means of physical restraint. Execution and solitary confinement are totally effective in this respect. Partial methods such as exile, maiming, and imprisonment may also be highly effective methods of incapacitation. In a period of intense concern about criminal activity, it is not surprising that such a plausibly effective mechanism for reducing crime has great appeal. The public's interest in reducing crime by incapacitating active criminals has created a receptive audience for the empirical and analytical research on the subject. Indeed, research on incapacitation effects may be the most successful research program in criminology during the last decade, in terms of interest among both scholars and practitioners in the field.

Unfortunately, the incapacitation research program has been guided by a conceptual framework that is simplistic and yields misleading predictions. This conceptual framework views individual criminals as automatons, insensitive to changing incentive structures and programmed to play out predetermined criminal careers subject only to possible interruptions due to incarceration. These assumptions are certainly open to challenge. A richer conceptual framework that incorporates the possibility of adaptive behavior to changing incentives may be more appropriate to analyzing the effects of incarceration on crime rates. This chapter presents such a framework and argues that assumptions undergirding incapacitation research represent a rather dubious special case that does not deserve any special standing in making policy prescriptions.

The chapter is organized as follows: The section entitled "Research on Incapacitation" reviews the incapacitation model and the policy research findings that have been generated by the application of this model to various sorts of empirical evidence. The subsequent section develops an alternative model that stresses the possibility of adaptive behavior of criminals and others. The conflict between the two models is elucidated by reference to the so-called "danger compensation" literature, which has most commonly been applied to evaluating regulations designed to promote highway safety. The third section then presents the results of a simulation study, demonstrating that a selective incapacitation sentencing policy may, under quite reasonable assumptions concerning adaptive behavior, be inferior from a crime-control perspective to a uniform sentencing strategy. The final section then considers the possibility that potential victims also exhibit adaptive behavior in protecting themselves. If so, the impact of implementing more effective crime-control measures could be undermined by compensating actions by the public.

This chapter does not explore the cognitive process underlying adaptive behavior. It is enough for my purposes simply to stipulate that one adaptation to a change in the severity of punishment for a crime may be a reduction in the rate of commission of that crime by some active criminals. My focus is on the aggregate consequences of adaptive behavior of this sort; a detailed consideration of the nature of the decision-making process by criminals would divert attention from this focus. Nonetheless, more complete exploration of deterrence and incapacitation effects requires some analysis of individual perception and decision-making processes (cf. Cook, 1980). Developing these cognitive aspects of adaptive behavior is left to other chapters in this volume.

Research on Incapacitation

The demography of criminal activity is characterized by heterogeneity and persistence (Petersilia, 1980). For any one year the bulk of all serious crime is committed by relatively few high-rate offenders. Those who are actively involved in crime in any one year are much more likely than others to be active in the following year. These characteristics together suggest that criminal offenders constitute a distinct subpopulation, and motivate the inquiry into the underlying differences between this group and the relatively law-abiding majority. Some of the most important readily observable correlates of criminal involvement, at least for common crimes of theft and violence, are sex, age, race, socioeconomic status, and population density of city of residence. A number of other, more subtle attributes have also been identified (Greenwood and Zimring, 1984). Presented with detailed descriptive information on a cohort of 10-year-old children, a criminologist could predict which would become high-rate offenders and be confident that these predictions, although not precisely accurate, would be far better than chance (Farrington, 1979). Many criminologists believe that such predictions could be improved markedly by additional collection and analysis of longitudinal data on individuals.

These observations regarding the marked and predictable inter-personal differences in criminal involvement support the assertion that incapacitating some people (the high-rate offenders) will prevent more crimes than incapacitating others, and that the high-rate offenders can be identified (albeit imprecisely) given sufficient information concerning their past behavior and other characteristics. The "science" of incapacitation is concerned with a number of related technical issues (Cohen, 1983), including (1) improving the accuracy with which high-rate offenders can be identified, using data that are typically available to criminal justice system (CJS) officials; (2) predicting the effects on crime rates of increasing or reducing the number of prisoners; and (3) evaluating alternative sentencing policies (i.e., alternative allocations of prison capacity) to identify the policy that would reduce crime the most given the current prison capacity. This last issue, called selective incapacitation, has been of particular interest because it seems to offer something for nothing: a reduction in crime engendered by employing existing CJS resources more efficiently.

There has been considerable controversy over the ethics and efficacy of selective incapacitation. One basic question is whether it is just to allow predictions of future criminal activity to guide prosecution and sentencing of individual defendants (Von Hirsch, 1976; Moore et al., 1984). If this future-oriented approach is deemed acceptable, there remains the related issue of whether employment history, marital status, and other such information should be used to help identify (predict) the high-rate offenders, or whether such predictions should be based solely on defendants' criminal records. There is also intense controversy over technical matters related to the precision of statistical prediction methods for identifying high-rate offenders (Cohen, 1983): The accuracy with which high-rate offenders can be identified influences the estimated payoff (in terms of reduced crime) of adopting a more selective allocation of prison capacity.

Notice that none of these three controversial aspects of a selective incapacitation policy challenges the basic factual assertion underlying this policy, namely, that the impact of imprisonment on the crime rate could be maximized (given a fixed prison capacity) by reserving prison for those convicts who would be the most active criminals if released. The assumptions that support this assertion constitute a rather simplistic conceptual framework for understanding crime. In essence, this framework postulates that each individual can be characterized by his or her personal crime rate, which is not influenced by the availability of attractive crime opportunities, the activities of the CJS (other than through the incapacitation effect), or other features of the individual's environment (Shinnar and Shinnar, 1975; Cohen, 1983). Thus, individuals are viewed as playing out their predetermined criminal careers completely insensitive to changes in the costs and benefits of criminal activity. In particular, the only mechanism by which prosecution and sentencing policies influence the crime rate is incapacitation.

These assumptions have the virtue of being sufficiently simple to generate clear implications, but they may be misleading as a guide to evaluating policy options. People adapt their behavior in response to the opportunities available to them. Criminals are not automatons, and neither are potential victims. Incorporating the possibility of adaptive behavior into the theoretical framework for evaluating incapacitation effects yields fundamentally different predictions. The next section develops the justification for assuming that criminals and others exhibit adaptive behavior.

Adaptive Behavior

There can be no doubt that people tend to adapt their behavior to environmental signals concerning the personal costs and benefits of alternative courses of action. The "signals" that are particularly relevant in evaluating incapacitation effects are generated by the activities of the CJS, especially prosecution and sentencing. Suppose that CJS authorities institute a selective incapacitation program that includes a career-criminals prosecution unit and a policy of sentencing on the basis of predicted future crime involvement. This new program would result in a change in the allocation of prison capacity, but it would also signal offenders that the structure of CJS threats had changed, with greater emphasis on some types of crimes and criminals and less emphasis on others. This message might be transmitted via publicity given to the new program, but probably more importantly the transmission would occur via word of mouth and personal experience. Active criminals tend to be better informed than the public at large about such matters, for obvious reasons (Cook, 1980; Erickson and Gibbs, 1979). Offenders faced with an increased threat of severe punishment could adapt in a variety of ways: by employing greater caution in choosing their accomplices, their modus operandi, and their crime targets; by investing more in their legal defense if arrested; and by committing fewer crimes. (Indeed, some may go into early retirement as a result of the increased threat.) Other, low-rate offenders, faced with a reduced threat of imprisonment as a result of the same program, may adapt along the same dimensions but in the opposite direction.

Why have incapacitation theorists not allowed for these possible changes in behavior? Both Greenwood (1982:4) and Cohen (1983:10) justify their exclusion of deterrence effects in part by reference to the conclusions of a special panel of the National Academy of Sciences (Blumstein et al., 1978). This panel critiqued various studies that used econometric methods to measure deterrence effects and concluded that these studies were so seriously flawed that their findings (which were supportive of a general deterrent effect) should be ignored:

The major challenge for future research is to estimate the magnitude of the effects of different sanctions on various crime types, an issue on which none of the evidence available thus far provides very useful guidance (Blumstein et al., 1978:7)

Greenwood (1982) asserted that the appropriate response to our ignorance concerning the magnitude of deterrence effects is to ignore them in setting sentencing policy:

The lack of evidence on the effects of either rehabilitation or deterrence leaves incapacitation as the only utilitarian basis for rationalizing differences in sentence severity for different types of offenders. (Greenwood, 1982:5)

This assertion deserves scrutiny. First, although Greenwood lumps rehabilitation and deterrence together as both lacking evidence on effectiveness, in fact the literature on these two mechanisms is not at all similar. There is considerable evidence on the effectiveness of a wide array of rehabilitation programs; this evidence strongly indicates that most of these programs have little or no effect (Martinson, 1974; Sechrest et al., 1979). On the other hand, quasi-experimental studies of a number of deterrence-oriented interventions have demonstrated that a wide range of crimes and types of offenders are responsive in the expected way to a change in the threat level (Zimring and Hawkins, 1973; Cook, 1977; Zimring, 1978; Cook, 1980). Although Greenwood is correct that criminologists cannot generate precise predictions about the deterrent effect resulting from a proposed change in CJS policy, the existence and potential importance of the general deterrent effect cannot be reasonably denied. Thus, Greenwood's assertion amounts to saying that it is appropriate to ignore the deterrence mechanism in setting a utilitarian sentencing policy, not because it is unimportant, but rather because we do not know just how important it will be in any particular instance. As a rule, limiting the analysis of a policy issue to those aspects for which good information is available, and ignoring other aspects, yields unreliable conclusions. In this instance, ignoring the deterrence mechanism may yield highly misleading results, as shown in the simulation presented in the following section. First, however, it is useful to note that my argument concerning the incapacitation effect has an exact parallel in the literature on highway safety.

Orr (1982) introduced his article "Incentives and Efficiency in Automobile Safety Regulation" with this statement:

> ... there is a strong theoretical presumption, and substantial empirical evidence, that driver response to mandated safety devices will offset at least a portion of their technical effectiveness .... the concept of danger compensation discussed here has application to other areas of social policy: especially the subset from the health and safety area where the nature of risk is well known and substantially controlled by the individual. (Orr, 1982:43)

The theory underlying the "danger compensation" thesis assumes that people do not respond passively to the hazards of their environment, but rather choose their desired level of safety and adapt their behavior accordingly. The environment in the case of highway travel includes road conditions, safety features built into vehicles, traffic patterns, and so forth. This environment does not determine the actual risk facing a driver, but rather in effect provides the driver with a set of opportunities relating the risks of serious accident to behavioral choices (when, where, what, and how to drive). The actual risk is then determined by the combined effect of environment and choices of behavioral response.

This perspective has important policy implications. The most notable example is with respect to federal auto safety standards. Predictions of the expected number of lives saved from a proposed requirement such as equipping all new autos with passive-restraint devices have generally been made on the basis of technical considerations, without admitting the possibility that drivers may choose to drive less safely in response to this new form of protection (Huelke and O'Day, 1981; Blomquist and Pelzman, 1981). Yet from the driver's perspective, the addition of a passive restraint device may be seen as lowering the "cost" (in terms of injury risk) of pursuing other objectives, such as reducing travel time (Pelzman, 1975). The decision to drive faster or more intensely is a decision to "spend" some of the increased protection offered by the restraint on the "purchase" of a reduction in travel time. If drivers do adapt their behavior in this fashion, then the predictions based on technical considerations will prove erroneous, exaggerating the number of lives that are ultimately saved by the safety requirement.

The nature and extent of compensating behavior will depend on the precise circumstances (Slovic and Fischhoff, 1982) and cannot be predicted given the current state of knowledge. Even after new safety measures have been implemented, it is difficult to determine their net effect on injury rates (cf. McKenna's, 1985, response to Wilde, 1982). The debate over the effectiveness of auto safety standards is a notable case in point (Pelzman, 1975; Graham and Garber, 1984), but there can be no question that danger compensation occurs in a variety of circumstances. We walk more cautiously when barefoot than when shod, and we drive more carefully (or stay home) when roads are icy. If these facts were ignored, an evaluation of proposals to ban walking barefoot or to place heating coils in roads would exaggerate their potential effects on injury rates.

There are two obvious applications of the danger compensation thesis to crime. As criminals become aware of a change in the likelihood or severity of punishment for criminal activity, they may change their behavior in various ways, as discussed above. Potential victims of crime may also engage in danger compensation: an increase in a neighborhood's crime rate may result in residents taking greater precautions. The implications of these adaptations are developed below.

The Effects of a Selective Incapacitation Policy: A Numerical Example

The example presented here explores the consequences of modifying an incapacitation model to allow for adaptive behavior on the part of criminals. For the sake of concreteness and realism, the example uses some of the parameter values estimated by Greenwood (1982) in connection with his study of the effect of imprisonment policy on robbery in California. He divided the population of imprisoned robbery convicts into three groups on the basis of a seven-factor predictive scale which included characterizations of prior criminal record, drug use, and employment. On the basis of interview data with these prisoners, he estimated an annual offense rate of 2.0 for the low-rate group, 10.1 for the medium-rate group, and 30.8 for the high-rate group (Greenwood, 1982:66). In my example, these rates are rounded off to 2, 10, and 30, respectively. On the basis of Greenwood's estimates, corrected by Cohen (1983), there were in the mid-1970s about 50,000 low-rate, 12,000 medium-rate, and 9,000 high-rate robbers in California. The probability of imprisonment for a given commission of a robbery was .0258. These numbers are used in my example.

The example compares a uniform sentencing policy, in which all prison sentences are 24 months, with a selective imprisonment policy. The selective policy is intended to make more efficient use of the same prison capacity by giving high-rate offenders a longer term and low-rate offenders a shorter term. I set the longest term (for high-rate robbers) at 60 months, and the shortest (for low-rate robbers) at 12 months. The prison term for medium-rate robbers was then set at 29.2 months, a number calculated to yield the same total prison population under the selective sentencing regime as occurs under the uniform sentencing regime assuming that individual crime rates are not affected by the change in sentencing policy. Given these parameter values, we can calculate the reduction in the crime rate resulting from allocating the given prison capacity selectively rather than uniformly among robbery convicts.

Here is how the simulation works. Each of the three types of robbers is assumed to commit offenses at a uniform rate (2, 10, or 30 offenses per year). Each offense exposes them to a .0258 probability of (immediate) imprisonment. This process eventually converges to a steady-state crime rate and prison population for each of the three groups. The steady-state equilibria for uniform sentencing and selective sentencing have the same number of robbers in prison, but the offense rate is 19% lower when sentencing is selective. This pure gain in efficiency of imprisonment is achieved by increasing the percentage of high- and medium-rate offenders who are in prison at any one time, while reducing the percentage of low-rate offenders who are imprisoned. These results illustrate the case for a selective incapacitation strategy, as developed by Greenwood and others.

Now suppose that the offenders change their behavior in response to the change from uniform to selective sentencing. Those classified under the selective system as low-rate offenders perceive that the threatened prison sentence for their robberies has been reduced from 24 months to 12 months, and hence increase their rate of offending. The high-rate group members perceive an increase in the threatened prison sentence from 24 months to 60 months, and hence reduce their rate of offending. The medium-group members also face a somewhat higher price for their crimes and adapt their behavior accordingly. The basic assumption, then, is that the change from uniform to selective sentencing has deterrent effects as well as incapacitation effects.

Further assumptions are needed to explore the implications of this adaptive behavior by criminals. For each of the three groups (low, medium, and high), I assume that the offense rate per year C_i for a free individual is given by this expression:

$$C_i = k_i \, T_i^E \text{ (for } i = \text{low, medium, high)},$$

where T_i is the discounted present value of the prison term (assuming an annual rate of time discount of 25%), E is the elasticity of the crime rate with respect to changes in sentence length, and k_i is a constant calculated to generate the original offense rates (2, 10, and 30) when sentences are uniform at 24 months. (Note that k_i depends on the value assumed for E.)

Table 13.1 reports crime rates for free individuals under selective sentencing. The first row is calculated on the basis of the usual assumption of incapacitation models: that offenders do not change their offending in response to changes in sentencing policy. The second row assumes a small deterrent effect ($E = -0.3$), and the third row a larger effect ($E = -1.0$). Notice that even under this last assumption, the high-rate offenders remain highest even when faced with a much stiffer punishment than the others. The deterrence effect does not change the rank order of offense rates among the different groups, but it does change the relative magnitudes.

Table 13.2 reports results of the simulation for each group of offenders and for all offenders combined. The relevant comparisons in each case are between selective sentencing and uniform sentencing regimes. In the last column of the bottom section of Table 13.2 we see that the annual offense rate falls 19% if $E = 0$, but falls only 14% if $E = -0.3$. If $E = -1.0$, then the offense rate actually increases when selective sentencing replaces uniform sentencing. Note that these differences are not the result of changes in the prison population, which surprisingly changes very little for different assumptions about elasticity. Rather, the total offense rate increases (when $E = -1.0$) as a result of moving from uniform to selective sentencing because the increase in offending by the low-rate group outweighs the reduction in offending by the other groups.

Another interesting set of results from this example can be generated by disaggregating the net change in crime into a net incapacitation effect and a marginal deterrent effect. Table 13.3 displays the effects of

TABLE 13.1 Individual Crime Rates as a Function of Elasticity Value[a]

	Offender Category		
Elasticity	Low Rate	Medium Rate	High Rate
0	2.0	10.0	30.0
−0.3	2.38	9.57	25.09
−1.0	3.56	8.63	16.54

[a]Crime rates are calculated for the case when low-, medium-, and high-rate offenders are sentenced (when caught) to prison for 12 months, 29.2 months, and 60 months, respectively.

TABLE 13.2 Effects of Selective Sentencing for Three Elasticity Values

Type of Sentencing	Percent of Offenders Free	Number of Offenders in Prison (000)	Crimes Prevented by Incapacitation Per Year (000)	Crimes Committed Per Year (000)	Percent Change in Crimes Per Year
		Low-Rate Group: $N = 50,000$			
Uniform sentencing	90.6	4.68	9.4	90.6	
Selective, $E = 0$	95.1	2.45	4.9	95.1	5.0
Selective, $E = -0.3$	94.2	2.89	6.9	112.0	23.6
Selective, $E = -1.0$	91.6	4.20	15.0	162.9	79.8
		Medium-Rate Group: $N = 12,000$			
Uniform sentencing	66.0	4.08	40.8	79.2	
Selective, $E = 0$	61.4	4.63	46.3	73.7	-6.9
Selective, $E = -0.3$	62.5	4.50	43.1	71.7	-9.5
Selective, $E = -1.0$	64.8	4.22	36.4	67.2	-15.2
		High-Rate Group: $N = 9,000$			
Uniform sentencing	39.2	5.47	164.0	106.0	
Selective, $E = 0$	20.5	7.15	214.6	55.4	-47.7
Selective, $E = -0.3$	23.6	6.88	172.5	53.3	-49.7
Selective, $E = -1.0$	31.9	5.13	101.4	47.5	-55.2
		All Groups Combined: $N = 71,000$			
Uniform sentencing	80.0	14.23	214.2	275.8	
Selective, $E = 0$	80.0	14.23	265.7	224.3	-18.7
Selective, $E = -0.3$	79.9	14.27	222.5	237.0	-14.1
Selective, $E = -1.0$	79.5	14.55	152.8	277.6	0.7

TABLE 13.3 Effects of Changing From Uniform to Selective Sentencing Policy

E	Net Incapacitation Effect (000)	Marginal Deterrence Effect (000)	Net Crime Reduction (000)
0	51.5	0	51.5
−0.3	8.3	30.5	38.8
−1.0	−61.4	59.6	−1.8

changing from uniform sentencing to selective sentencing. If $E = 0$, there is no deterrent effect, and the reduction in the overall crime rate results entirely from an increased incapacitation effect. However, the increase in incapacitation is much smaller if offenders exhibit even a small degree of responsiveness to threat ($E = -0.3$), and for $E = -1.0$ the total incapacitation effect is actually greater for uniform sentencing than for selective sentencing. This last result is perhaps counterintuitive. How could a selective incapacitation strategy result in a reduction in the number of crimes prevented by incapacitation? The answer is simply that those who are locked up under a selective sentencing policy have a lower offense rate on the average. Even though a higher percentage of prisoners are from the high-rate group, this group's offense rate has been reduced by the increased threat level. Selective sentencing does *not* necessarily produce a more efficient use of prison capacity than uniform sentencing.

The point of this extended example is to show that the claims made for selective incapacitation depend critically on the assumption that offenders' crime rates are insensitive to the severity of punishment. To the extent that active criminals are well informed about sentencing policies and tend to adapt their behavior to the severity of punishment, selective incapacitation will accomplish less reduction in crime than implied by the usual incapacitation models.

Although the incapacitation theorists may be overstating the potential efficacy of a selective incapacitation policy, they are surely underestimating the overall effect of imprisonment on crime rates. Cohen (1983) reported that the aggregate incapacitation effect achieved by imprisonment circa 1980 was to reduce crime rates by at most 20%. Furthermore, she reported estimates indicating that imposing longer prison sentences on convicts is generally not a promising strategy for reducing crime, because achieving even small gains against crime requires large increases in an already unprecedentedly large prison population. Her analysis is consistent in ignoring deterrent effects of prison sentences, and for that reason it is misleading. Surely the rate of serious crime would increase by far more than 20% if all prisoners were released and imprisonment were no longer a sentencing option available to judges. Other currently available sentencing options—fines and restitution requirements—are intrinsically less punitive than imprison-ment, particularly for indigents, and hence have less of a deterrent effect. As long as the only available modes for imposing severe punishment also incapacitate the convict, deterrence and incapacitation effects are inextricably linked. A change in sentencing policy will influence the crime rate via both mechanisms, and both should be considered in evaluating the change to avoid invalid results.

Expanding the Conceptual Framework

Conclusions about the effect of imprisonment on crime are determined by one's choice of conceptual framework for understanding the linkages between sentencing policy and criminal behavior. The framework adopted in recent writings on incapacitation effects is very simple: imprisonment and the threat thereof are assumed to have no effect on individual criminal behavior except to physically prevent criminal activity by those criminals who are incarcerated. Thus portions of predetermined criminal careers are not acted out due to incapacitation. My alternative framework, which allows for a deterrent effect, generates quite different predictions about the consequences of alternative sen-tencing policies, as shown in the preceding section.

Even this alternative framework is simplistic. The interaction between criminal behavior and the actions of the CJS is properly viewed in a larger context that takes account of the positive incentives to participate in criminal activity. Each predatory criminal act can be viewed as an instance in which the criminal perceived an opportunity, decided that it was worthwhile, and acted on this decision (see, generally, Clarke, 1983, and Clarke and Cornish, 1985). The criminal may evaluate opportunities along a number of dimensions, including likelihood of successful completion of the crime, payoff if successful, probability of arrest and conviction, and severity of punishment if convicted (Carroll, 1978; Smith and Thompson, 1983). The availability of attractive opportunities may influence the structure and distribution of criminal activity and also the overall volume of crime. Opportunities are provided by the public as a generally inadvertent byproduct of the routine activities of everyday life. Potential victims will exercise more or less care in protecting themselves and their property depending on their circumstances, but also on their perception of the likelihood of victimization. Thus the threat of crime engenders private self-protection activities, and these activities may in turn prevent or discourage some criminal activity.

In this conceptual framework, observed crime rates are the net result of a dynamic interaction between criminals, the CJS, and the public at large (Ehrlich, 1981, 1982; Cook, 1977, 1985). If CJS resources and effectiveness are increased, then the initial reduction in crime (caused by enhanced deterrence and/or incapacitation) may provoke compensatory behavior by potential victims. If, for example, potential victims reduce self-protection efforts, then the initial success of the CJS in reducing crime may be lost, at least in part. Thus the notion of danger compensation applies to potential victims as well as to criminals and has potentially important implications for assessing the ultimate consequences of CJS policy.

Mechanical models of crime determination generate clear results, but these results are not reliable if criminals and victims do not behave in a mechanical fashion. The additional complexity introduced by allowing for adaptive behavior is justified if nothing else by the need to judge the appropriate degree of confidence to place on the implications of the mechanical model. I conclude that the results of the recent incapacitation research program, resting as they do on mechanical, simplistic assumptions about criminal behavior, should be viewed as subject to great uncertainty.

References

Blomquist, G.C. and S. Peltzman
  1981   "Passive restraints: an economist's view." Pp. 37–52 in R.W. Crandall and L.B. Lave (eds.), The Scientific Basis of Health and Safety Regulation. Washington, DC: Brookings Institution.
Blumstein, A., J. Cohen and D. Nagin
  1978   Deterrence and Incapacitation: Estimating the Effects of Criminal Sanctions on Crime Rates. Washington, DC: National Academy of Sciences.
Carroll, J.S.
  1978   "A psychological approach to deterrence: the evaluation of crime opportunities." Journal of Personality and Social Psychology 36:1512–20.
Clarke, R.V.
  1983   "Situational crime prevention: its theoretical basis and practical scope." Pp. 225–56 in M. Tonry and N. Morris (eds.), Crime and Justice: An Annual Review of Research, Volume 4. Chicago: University of Chicago Press.
Clarke, R.V. and D.B. Cornish
  1985   "Modelling offenders' decisions: a framework for research and policy." Pp. 147–85 in M. Tonry and N. Morris (eds.), Crime and Justice: An Annual Review of Research, Volume 6. Chicago: University of Chicago Press.
Cohen, J.
  1983   "Incapacitation as a strategy for crime control: possibilities and pitfalls." Pp. 1–84 in M. Tonry and N. Morris (eds.), Crime and Justice: An Annual Review of Research, Volume 5. Chicago: University of Chicago Press.

Cook, P.J.
  1977   "Punishment and crime: a critique of current findings concerning the preventive effects of punishment." Law and Contemporary Problems 41: 164–204.
Cook, P.J.
  1980   "Research in criminal deterrence: laying the groundwork for the second decade." Pp. 211–68 in N. Morris and M. Tonry (eds.), Crime and Justice: An Annual Review of Research, Volume 2. Chicago: University of Chicago Press.
Cook, P.J.
  1986   "The demand and supply of criminal opportunities." In M. Tonry and N. Morris (eds.), Crime and Justice: An Annual Review of Research, Volume 7. Chicago: University of Chicago Press.
Ehrlich, I.
  1981   "On the usefulness of controlling individuals: an economic analysis for rehabilitation, incapacitation, and deterrence." American Economic Review 71(3): 307–22.
Ehrlich, I.
  1982   "The market for offences and the public enforcement of laws: an equilibrium analysis." British Journal of Social Psychology 21:107–20.
Erickson, M.L. and J.P. Gibbs
  1979   "On the perceived severity of legal penalties." Journal of Criminal Law and Criminology 70:102–16.
Farrington, D.
  1979   "Longitudinal research on crime and delinquency." Pp. 289–348 in N. Morris and M. Tonry (eds.), Crime and Justice: An Annual Review of Research, Volume 1. Chicago: University of Chicago Press.
Graham, J.D. and S. Garber
  1984   "Evaluating the effects of automobile safety regulation." Journal of Policy Analysis and Management 3:206–24.
Greenwood, P.W.
  1982   Selective Incapacitation. Santa Monica, CA: Rand.
Greenwood, P.W. and F.E. Zimring
  1984   Last Clear Chance: The Role of Rehabilitation in Reducing the Criminality of Chronic Serious Juvenile Offenders. Santa Monica, CA: Rand.
Huelke, D.F. and J. O'Day
  1981   "Passive restraints: a scientist's view." Pp. 21–35 in R.W. Crandall and L.B. Lave (eds.), The Scientific Basis of Health and Safety Regulation. Washington, DC: Brookings Institution.
Martinson, R.
  1974   "What works?—questions and answers about prison reform." The Public Interest 35:22–54.
McKenna, F.P.
  1985   "Do safety measures really work? an examination of risk homeostasis theory." Ergonomics 28:489–98.
Moore, M.H., S.R. Estrich, D. McGillis and W. Spelman
  1984   Dangerous Offenders: The Elusive Target of Justice. Cambridge, MA: Harvard University Press.

Orr, L.D.
1982 "Incentives and efficiency in automobile safety regulation." Quarterly Review of Economics and Business 22:43–65.

Peltzman, S.
1975 "The effects of automobile safety regulation." Journal of Political Economy 83:677–726.

Petersilia, J.
1980 "Criminal career research: a review of recent evidence." Pp. 321–79 in N. Morris and M. Tonry (eds.), Crime and Justice: An Annual Review of Research, Volume 2. Chicago: University of Chicago Press.

Sechrest, L., S.O. White and E.D. Brown (eds.)
1979 The Rehabilitation of Criminal Offenders: Problems and Prospects. Washington, DC: National Academy of Sciences.

Shinnar, R. and S. Shinnar
1975 "The effect of the criminal justice system on the control of crime: a quantitative approach." Law and Society Review 9:581–611.

Slovic, P. and B. Fischhoff
1982 "Targeting risks." Risk Analysis 2:227–34.

Smith, M.E. and J.W. Thompson
1983 "Employment, youth, and violent crime." Pp. 96–113 in K.R. Feinberg (ed.), Violent Crime in America. Washington, DC: National Policy Exchange.

Von Hirsch, A.
1976 Doing Justice: The Choice of Punishments. New York: Hill and Wang.

Wilde, G.J.S.
1982 "The theory of risk homeostasis: implications for safety and health." Risk Analysis 2:209–25.

Zimring, F.E.
1978 "Policy experiments in general deterrence: 1970–1975." Pp. 140–86 in A. Blumstein, J. Cohen and D. Nagin (eds.), Deterrence and Incapacitation: Estimating the Effects of Criminal Sanctions on Crime Rates. Washington, DC: National Academy of Sciences.

Zimring, F.E. and G.J. Hawkins
1973 Deterrence: The Legal Threat in Crime Control. Chicago: University of Chicago Press.

14
Practical Reasoning and Criminal Responsibility: A Jurisprudential Approach

ALAN NORRIE

Editors' Note

Whatever their own beliefs about the wider implications of a rational choice approach, criminologists need to become aware of how their work may be perceived and used by others. Alan Norrie's chapter raises in a very clear way two important issues: the likely impact of a rational choice perspective on traditional images of the criminal, and its possible effect on the criminal justice response to offenders. As he comments, criminological theories that focus upon the offender as a rational decision maker appear at first glance very close to classical juridical conceptions of the criminal as rational and hence responsible and punishable. Norrie goes on to argue that such similarities are no accident: The former encourages, and the latter incorporates, a similar view of human rationality, one that recognizes the ability of human beings to be practical reasoners, but fails to locate (or "situate") this process in the reasoner's social and personal context. Deracinating or abstracting the reasoning offender in this way, Norrie argues, makes it possible to treat the offender as an isolated, responsible agent. And because rational choice approaches may similarly appear to decontextualize criminal reasoning they give further credence to justice model approaches. More importantly, by neglecting the broader social context in this way, rational choice approaches may encourage simplistic situational solutions to crime which, instead of reducing, merely displace it. The issues are complex and not resolvable within this short space. Our own view would be, first, that a concept of human reasoning as "situated" is not only compatible with but given explicit recognition in a rational choice approach. It is true that event models, considered alone and out of context, might seem to encourage that image of the offender to which Norrie objects. The reason, however, is that the variables with which they deal relate primarily to the restricted and immediate strategic issues of crime commission itself (cf. Carroll and Weaver). Each event, however, is linked to a previous (new, standing, or revised) involvement decision sequence, and it is there, where wider social forces and personal histories have most impact on decision making, that the situated nature of practical reasoning is most clearly to be appreciated and structural explanations of offending to be sought. Second, the rational choice approach was designed to be policy relevant. It therefore introduced an analytical distinction between events and involvement in order to provide the framework within which a wide variety of short-term and long-term policies—social preventive, rehabilitative, situational, and deterrent—in relation to criminal behavior could be explored. That some of these policies pay less attention than others to the implications of a situated view of practical reasoning is true, but it is a counsel of despair that implies that only changes to distal factors will reduce rather than simply (and perhaps more dangerously) displace it. Third, the rational choice approach was developed, in part, to provide an alternative framework within which to investigate displacement behavior—a framework that would explicitly replace assumptions about its inevitability by estimating its likelihood in terms of the costs and benefits involved.

In this essay, I compare legal ideas of rationality and responsibility with recently developed ideas within criminology that are in many ways similar. I focus upon the rational choice or decision-making approach to criminal behavior expounded by Clarke and Cornish (1983, 1985). In so doing, I recognize that a number of different disciplinary approaches (economic, psychological, sociological) have converged in this perspective, but I make no attempt to distinguish their differential implications. To do so would not be possible within the limited scope of this essay, but the focus on Clarke and Cornish's work is valid given its practical policy implications. My aim is to argue, as an outsider to the field, that certain fundamental problems with legal conceptions of agency and responsibility are replicated, albeit in a slightly different fashion, within the criminological decision-making perspective. I suggest that these problems might limit the approach's practical value as a source for crime-control policy.

Historically, the relationship between law and criminology has been one of complexity and change. Classical criminology had its roots in legal reform and adopted an essentially juridical world view (Ferri, 1901; Foucault, 1977). At the same time, the work of penal reformers such as Beccaria and Bentham exhibits a confluence of ideas of legal reform, criminal behavior, and economic rationality (Halevy, 1972; Norrie, 1982). At their heart, all these ideas manifest a rational individualism whose different aspects are now juridical, now economic, now criminological.

However, the nineteenth-century focus on discipline and control (Foucault, 1977) disrupted this cozy unity of approach by leading to the development of forms of criminological positivism antithetical to the penal reformers' rational individualism. These new ideas emphasized, philosophically, behavioral determinism and the irrelevance of the individual reasoning process, and practically, state intervention to "cure" individual or social ailments. These new ideas, as Pashukanis (1978:130) put it, "directed their fire at legal individualism" and established the decisive rift between criminological and legal viewpoints that has been evident for the greater part of this century.

Recently, however, that division has itself come under attack as the orthodoxy of criminological positivism has been questioned from a number of perspectives. Two in particular draw upon ideas that either directly or indirectly can be traced back to classical juridical positions. First, the "justice model" (Von Hirsch, 1976; Bottoms and Preston, 1980) has made a return to the legal fold an explicit aim, adopting the juridical ideas of philosophical retributivism as its theoretical basis, and second, the decision-making approach of Clarke and Cornish can be seen to follow, implicitly if not explicitly, a similar route. Although they themselves present their perspective as being limited in its scope and implications, as having heuristic and pragmatic value alone (1985:178), and decline to affirm any more general positions as regards questions of criminal responsibility and justice, there is surely no denying that the idea of the criminal as a rational decision maker lies foursquare with the traditional conceptions of criminal law and that doctrine's analysis of whether or not punishment is appropriate. Judges, at least, who frequently extol the virtues of pragmatism in dealing with questions of criminal responsibility themselves, are unlikely to be put off recognizing a kindred intellectual spirit by perfectly proper expressions of academic caution.

But in what ways are the legal and the rational choice perspectives similar? I would argue that the similarity lies in their sharing a conception of the individual criminal as a rational, decision-making agent. Clearly such a conception is contained within the rational choice approach; in what way is it contained within the law? One of the major concerns of criminal lawyers is to delimit the ways in which individuals may be held responsible or irresponsible for their criminal acts. Hart (1968:181) suggested that the principle of criminal responsibility could rest on the idea that "unless a man has the capacity and a fair opportunity or chance to adjust his behaviour to the law its penalties ought not to be applied to him." These two criteria of capacity and fair opportunity have recently been elaborately developed by Moore (1984), who argued that the law of criminal responsibility rests upon the two philosophical concepts of autonomy and practical rationality. It is only when agents are practical reasoners (I use the terms *practical reasoning* and *practical rationality* synonymously) and autonomous that they should be held responsible for their actions by law.

In practice these two concepts are exceedingly difficult to separate because they often appear as simply different facets of the same phenomenon: human agency. However, an analytical separation will be made here, for the question of autonomy, concerning philosophical issues of free will and determinism, is not directly relevant to our discussion of practical reasoning and its implications, upon which alone

I propose to concentrate. Moore (1984:ch. 1) explained the ability of human beings to be practical reasoners as entailing an ability to adopt "practical syllogisms" which have as their major premise a factual belief, and as their outcome an action. For example:

1. Let it be the case that the wine is chilled.
2. If I open the window, then the wine is chilled.
   Therefore
3. I open the window. (Moore, 1984:13)

The enjoining of beliefs and desires leads to practical conclusions as to what ought to be done; the establishment of "belief/desire sets" gives rise to reasons for action, and actions carried out are both exhibited as rational and explained as a consequence of a process of individual practical reasoning. It is this philosophical idea of agents as practical reasoners that unites the legal conceptions concerning criminal responsibility with the criminological conception of crime as the product of rational decision making and as a response to situational factors in the experienced environment.

The questions I want to ask are: How adequate are these conceptions of practical reasoning to their different tasks within law and criminology? How well do they describe the reality of human agency in the commission of crime? In the legal context, how successfully does the practical reasoning conception legitimate the punishment of criminals who break the law? In the criminological context, how successful is the same perspective likely to be in limiting the amount of crime? In turning first to the legal context, I hope to establish certain arguments which can then be transferred to the criminological context.

Juridical Individualism and Practical Rationality

Before discussing the recent work of Michael Moore, I shall outline a position I myself developed prior to its publication, and which forms the basis for the analysis presented here. In a short article (Norrie, 1983), I argued that one could identify two antithetical conceptions of practical reasoning within criminal law discourse. The first of these I called *situated reasoning*. Its distinguishing feature is its insistence that human reasons and actions are to be understood in the context of the social and personal biography of the individual. The social context provides the material conditions within which the individual acts, and the individual's reasoning power serves to mediate between individual, subjective agency and the social, objective context of individual life. To be human is to act according to one's ability to reason, not in the abstract, but in the already-given context of a social situation. Put slightly differently, situated reasoning is reasoning from premises derived from the observation and understanding of the world in which the individual is both located and locates himself or herself.

The value of this approach is that it both recognizes individual autonomy (grounded in the ability to be a practical reasoner and an agent) and situates individual agency within a social context. This two-sided approach is necessary to avoid the twin errors of voluntarism and reductionism which are so prevalent in both legal and criminological thought. However, it is precisely this approach's strength in refusing to isolate individual reason and agency from the context in which it occurs that makes it peripheral and unpopular within the discourse of the criminal law, for the central feature of that discourse is the idea of the individual subject as an isolated, responsible agent. Such an idea is not easily sustained within a conception that, while recognizing individual powers (to reason, to act), insists that they are only and always utilized within contexts already given to the individual. How can one see individuals as responsible for their actions if they are only responding rationally to situations within which they find themselves?

The discourse of the criminal law is therefore centered around a second conception of practical reasoning, which is marked by its abstract quality. *Abstract reasoning* is a view of practical reasoning that stresses its asocial and purely individual character. At most, it is tied to moral notions of individual wickedness and the like, but it is rigorously separated from the social context that provides the premises of reasoning and action. For example, criminal law discourse in general (there are exceptions, such as the defense of duress discussed below, and in Norrie, 1983) focuses solely upon the existence of rationally formed intentions and excludes from its gaze questions of how individuals come to form them—their motives, their motives' contexts, and so on. Criminal law discourse decontextualizes actions and intentions, abstracts them from their social context, and does so in order to attribute criminal responsibility to individuals. (At the end of the day, of course, once the legal tests and procedures have been complied with, the law puts on its human face and hears any pleas of mitigating circumstances that counsel may be able to supply, but by then the legal texts have already been packed away.)

This distinction between situated and abstract rationality was later confirmed by the publication of the work of Michael Moore. In an extended analysis of the doctrines of criminal responsibility, Moore sought to defend the abstract legal conception of the individual while claiming to present a realist account of human action, and thereby to justify the legal process of conviction and punishment. In so doing, however, he was forced to confront the limits imposed upon that conception by its abstract nature, and in the process, the consistency of his account is broken, as I shall now argue.

For Moore, practical reasoning entails the formation of practical syllogisms from belief/desire sets which establish reasons for acting.

Actions stem from the process of practical reasoning, and those who cannot be practical reasoners cannot be legally responsible because they cannot be persons "in moral theory or legal doctrine" (Moore, 1984:49). This position is coupled with a strong commitment to realism, to describing "the way human beings really are." The legal and moral concepts employed in discussing issues of responsibility:

are not empty labels for a moral or legal conclusion reached on other grounds, or on no grounds at all; they are concepts having a descriptive and explanatory function, no matter what other expressive, prescriptive, or ascriptive functions they may serve in contexts such as those of responsibility assessment. It accordingly makes sense to seek the meaning of persons and its related terms (action, intention, and the like) in terms of the facts that must be true if such concepts are to be correctly employed. (Moore, 1984:47).

However, later this claim is modified by virtue of a limit imposed on Moore's realism stemming from his focus only on the *form* of practical reasoning and not its *content*. That is, he concentrates upon the universal features of practical reasoning rather than the concrete and specific nature of what an individual might syllogize, or how individuals might come to formulate and act upon one syllogism rather than another in any given situation. Moore acknowledges as much at the end of a long discussion of legal doctrine and practical reasoning when he concludes that:

the very abstract view of persons in terms of autonomy and rationality is of course radically incomplete as a picture of any person we know. In particular, left out is the life of the emotions where, if anywhere, the "affection of other men" is gained. Yet the radical incompleteness of the law's view of a person is no argument that it is wrong. As far as it goes, the law's view of persons could be quite correct even if radically incomplete." (Moore, 1984:112, emphasis added)

A more striking omission than the "life of emotions" within Moore's discussion is the "life of society," or social life, and its effects upon individual behavior. These are not touched upon in his analysis, and this can be shown to have problematic consequences for his defense of abstract legal rationality. I shall now pick out two particular problems within his analysis, which I shall argue are generated by its formalistic and abstractive character.

Moore's Discussion of Compulsion (Duress)

In analyzing compulsion as a legal defense, Moore argues that the operation of duress (compulsion by threats of violence) involves "a restriction on the freedom of [the individual's] decisions imposed by something other than his own character" (Moore, 1984:88). The person acting under duress "obviously has a constraint upon his alternatives" (1984:88), and so should not be held responsible for his actions. In the language of practical rationality, duress is an "impediment to practical reasoning" (1984:87); practical reasoning is "interfered with" (1984:363).

Now in what sense is practical reasoning "interfered with" in the duress situation? It is not that the individual concerned cannot form practical syllogisms: Belief in the reality of the threat coupled with the desire to stay alive lead the individual to act as he or she does, and so the individual remains a practical reasoner. If the ability to be a practical reasoner lies at the heart of the legal conception of responsibility, why then does the law excuse the person acting under duress? Moore argues that duress stems from "*a feature of the actor's situation* that significantly limits the alternative courses of action that he may choose" (1984:88, emphasis added). Although the actor remains in form a practical reasoner, the content of his or her actions is derived from the immediate social context. Duress is therefore admitted as a legal excuse on the basis that the individual acting under it remains a practical reasoner, but is excused because of the particular context of his or her action. The ability to reason practically is only relevant in that it is the process whereby the external coercion is mediated and translated into individual action. Duress cannot be understood as resting upon the presence or absence of any individual human capacity abstracted from the social context within which it operates.

It is this fact, I have argued elsewhere (Norrie, 1983), that sets the duress defense apart from most other criminal defenses. More than this, however, it represents a chink in the law's iron curtain of abstract rationality. Logically, once the significance of the context of reasoning is acknowledged in one situation, how is the law to distinguish between a context of threats and a context of, say, bad social conditions, inadequate housing and education, unemployment, police harrassment, and so on? Such conditions form the context for the bulk of crime, and the individual acting and reasoning within it is as irresponsible for the social environment as is the compelled individual for the threats imposed upon him or her.

In a slightly different but related context, Moore meets this criticism and seeks to evade its consequences for his defence of abstract rationality. We have already seen that he defines compulsion as "a restriction on the freedom of [the individual's] decision imposed by something other than his own character." Why should he wish to distinguish between restrictions on individual freedom derived from an external source and those derived internally (from the character)? The answer is that if he did not do so, then one might "think that an actor's characteristic evaluations constrain his choices in the way in which a gun at his head would" (Moore, 1984:88). Clearly, however, if one did that, the scope for any doctrine of individual responsibility would be radically diminished, even annihilated: Is anyone responsible for his or her own character?

Thus, the practical requirement to defend the abstract legal conception of individual rationality yet explain the defense of duress leads Moore ultimately into inconsistency, for he is now forced to back off from his earlier claim to realism. He evades the objection raised by the analysis of character by arguing, "*stipulatively*," that, "One's character does not constrain one in this way; rather, characters are themselves constructs created by generalising about what one does when one's choices are unconstrained" (Moore, 1984:88, emphasis added). This kind of stipulative, functionalist account of character, however, is precisely the kind of approach to the legal view of persons that Moore had earlier foresworn in his claim that legal philosophical concepts must remain true to the entities they describe.

Moore's Discussion of the Work of R.D. Laing

Laing has argued that "without exception the experience and behavior that gets labelled schizophrenic is a special strategy that a person invents in order to live in an unlivable situation" (quoted in Moore, 1984:162). In effect, this means that behavior that the law would regard as insane and excusable is seen as the product of a process of practical reasoning. So Laing's analysis of schizophrenia threatens Moore's analysis in a similar way to the existence of the duress defense, and for the same reason. In Laing's work, the form of practical reasoning remains preserved through the schizophrenia, whereas the content of the reasoning process (the schizophrenic behavior) is generated by the contradictory nature of the lived environment and the need to survive it.

In this, however, the schizophrenic is no different from anyone else. All that marks him or her out from the rest of humanity is a particularly problematic lived situation. Laing's work, in other words, focuses attention upon the context of behavior as determining its content in a manner similar to that encountered in Moore's analysis of the duress defense. The actual process of reasoning is again real, but only mediatory in its effect. Accordingly, one conclusion from Laing would be that the ability to be a practical reasoner is no different between the sane and the insane, and therefore cannot provide a basis for distinguishing between the responsible and the irresponsible. As a corollary, the ability to be a practical reasoner cannot ground any notion of individual responsibility, because the determining factor in action is not individual reasoning but the social environment, which practical reasoning only mediates to produce individual action. To put that more briefly: The sane are as irresponsible for the world they are born into as the insane (the schizophrenic), so why punish the former if we excuse the latter?

Again Moore seeks to evade the significance of the context of actions by buttressing his (and the law's) distinction between sanity (responsibility) and insanity (irresponsibility). Although, he concedes, the schizophrenic may be minimally rational and therefore may form practical syllogisms, the substance of the reasoning process is irrational. In their practical reasoning, schizophrenics employ qualitatively irrational beliefs and desires. Now one may accept Moore's argument here (1984:162–164), yet note that in order to make it he is forced to shift his ground from consideration of the form of practical reasoning (the element of minimal rationality) to its content. From the subjective form of mental activity (the formulation of belief/desire sets), Moore shifts once more to the content of those belief/desire sets in order to ground and justify a legal conception. Whereas in duress the content of the relevant set is provided by the context of threats, in schizophrenia/insanity the content derives from the context of an unlivable situation.

This discussion has perhaps been rather abstract, but its aim is important. I have been concerned to show the inadequacy of the legal approach to practical reasoning through analysis of a most sophisticated formulation and defense of it. Practical reasoning must be understood as a *unity* of form and content, of individual capacity and social context. To do otherwise, to focus solely on the former, may be necessary to produce an alienated form of individualism (Pashukanis, 1978; Balbus, 1978), which can serve as a more or less coherent defense of a particular social practice (the law), but it cannot replicate the reality of the individual's life in society. The claim made by Moore that the legal view may remain true yet radically incomplete turns out to be hollow, for the radical incompleteness of the law is precisely a means of evading the truth of how individuals reason practically in social contexts. The *de*scription of human action and the *as*cription of legal responsibility are not coherent but contradictory tasks, for the one stems from a model of abstract, the other from a model of situated, rationality.

Situated Reasoning and the Rational Choice Model of Crime

What does the above discussion of law have to do with the rational choice model of crime? I shall argue that the rational choice model involves a narrow focus on the process of rational decision making that has more in common with the law's abstract rationality than the conception of situated rationality I have discussed. It is not the same as the abstract model, but it is nearer to it in its effects and implications than it is to the situated model. However, I shall suggest that this latter model is better suited to the business of understanding and ultimately combating the problem of crime.

I will begin by developing slightly further the conception of situated reasoning, in so doing following closely the work of Bhaskar (1979), then show how it fits into the question of how people come to commit crimes, and then compare this view with that of the rational choice theorists,

Clarke and Cornish. As should by now be clear, the idea of situated reasoning has two aspects: On the one side, there is the view that mind is real both as an entity and in its effects. It is, in the words of Bhaskar (1979:103), a *"sui generis* real emergent power of matter." On the other side, individuals only reason within societies that preexist them, so that individuals can only produce or transform societies, and never create them in a first, original act. Individuals act rationally and intentionally but must act upon a preexisting reality; they must take their society as a material cause, to be worked on by their practice. Agency must be located within given social structures, and it is necessary to designate points of contact between individual agency on the one hand and social structures, institutions, and so on, on the other.

To develop this idea, Bhaskar argues for the conceptualization of a "position-practice system" consisting of *"positions* (places, functions, rules, tasks, duties, rights, etc.) occupied (filled, assumed, enacted, etc.) by individuals, and of the *practices* (activities, etc.) in which, in virtue of this occupancy of these positions (and vice versa), they engage" (1979:51). Human agency and reason play their part in relation to the individual's self-orientation to this system. The formulation of practical syllogisms occurs in attempts to make sense and best use of the available options in a given situation. Against Moore, who concentrates purely and simply upon the ability to be a practical reasoner, practical reasoning must always be seen as "the situated doings of agents at places in time" so that desires and beliefs "both express, and arise in response to, the practical business of living" (Bhaskar, 1979:104, 123).

Now, in relation to depicting the reality of crime, this philosophical standpoint is expressed in the best social ethnography, which identifies both the objective structures that delimit individual options and the subjective orientation of the individual to the social structure. Criminal behavior is seen as the product both of social structure and individual reason. Thus in Parker's work (1976) on the "cats-eye kings," a group of delinquent boys in an English inner-city area, it is argued that "through their brief adolescence the Boys were continuously reacting to constraining influences which limited their range of choice and freedom" (1976:45). The boys mediate the effects of social structure by way of a rational appraisal of means and ends, beliefs and desires:

The Boys' delinquency was intimately tied up in the local job situation, for given their desire for the good times the balance between legitimate and illegitimate pathways to cash was fundamental to decisions both about getting involved in and getting out of the cats-eye business .... [This was] an available and in context a rational strategy, almost 'praxis', allowing an immediate termination of the bad times and the celebration of the good times.... [It] was a choice made from limited alternatives and...was a product of their immediate situation... (Parker, 1976:46)

Throughout, Parker emphasizes the need for "structural analyses which emphasise the accommodative and rational nature of decision making by actors faced with the constraints of a particular social context" (1976:29). This idea embodies most clearly the philosophical ideas of situated rationality and contextualized action developed above.

Turning now to the rational choice approach of Clarke and Cornish, we find first of all that there is a conscious limit imposed upon the degree of understanding of crime that the approach can generate, and this limit derives from their orientation to questions of social and political practice:

the models have been developed primarily for the limited purposes of improving crime-control policies and developing policy-relevant research. Such models have only to be "good enough"; they may not necessarily be the most appropriate or satisfactory for more comprehensive explanations of criminal behaviour— though it seems likely that a decision approach might provide a useful starting point even for academic purposes. (Clarke and Cornish, 1985:178)

The limits imposed upon the approach concern a distinction, first, between criminal involvement and criminal events, and second, between background factors and situational influences. The distinctions are connected, and the rational choice approach is regarded as relevant to the latter elements in each pair. As regards the distinction between involvement and events, the rational choice approach does not deny the relevance of questions of involvement, but consigns their investigation to traditional positivistic views in which "people may be propelled by predisposing factors to the point where crime becomes a realistic course of action . . . " (Clarke and Cornish, 1985:164). It is concerned with the actual criminal acts and the factors taken into consideration in deciding whether to commit them or not.

As regards the second distinction, this is tied up with the first, separating the question of how people come to the point of committing crimes from that of the actual decision to commit a particular crime. Again, the former is understood in traditional positivist fashion, whereas the latter involves the rational choice model:

It is with the influence of [psychological, familial, and sociodemographic] factors that traditional criminology has been preoccupied; they have been seen to determine the values, attitudes and personality traits that dispose the individual to crime. In a decision-making context, however, these background influences are less directly criminogenic; instead they have an orienting function—exposing people to particular problems and particular opportunities and leading them to perceive and evaluate these in particular (criminal) ways. Moreover, the contribution of background factors to the final decision to commit crime would be much moderated by situational and transitory influences . . . (Clarke and Cornish, 1985:167)

My concern about these distinctions is, first, that they are false. An analysis such as Parker's and the philosophical position advanced here both argue that behavior should be seen as a rational response not only to a particular, immediate situation (giving rise to an opportunity to commit a crime) but also to the broad structural processes that operate in any society and to which individuals respond in either a criminal or a noncriminal way. The structural situation is as important, if not more important, to the decision to commit crime as the particular opportunities available in a given situation. It is true that Clarke and Cornish make reference to the role of social structure (for example, in their flow diagrams), but the focus of the situational model excludes them from *its* concerns through the distinctions noted above.

I can illustrate this point. Clarke and Cornish note (1985:151) that one of the reasons why Parker's delinquent boys gave up stealing from cars was the increased police activity that their behavior generated. Now it is true that that was one factor, but reading Parker's analysis makes it clear that it was only one among many, and had to be seen within the context of the boys' overall "brief adolescence"—their development into manhood and the associated responsibilities. If these more fundamental factors had not existed, would increased police activity have encouraged desistance, or would it have encouraged diversification and displacement? In other words, if the fundamental structural features are not considered (and the situational approach consciously separates them off), will not crime-control strategies directed at restricting criminal opportunities be like holding a lid on a boiling pan when the heat should be turned off?

Clarke and Cornish mention the problem of displacement, although not in detail. The implication of the analysis presented here is that it may be an issue of no little consequence for the rational choice approach. I recognize the force of their claim that attention needs to be focused on individual forms of crime rather than crime in general. Consequently it is not possible to mention here the possible forms of displacement that could occur across the spectrum of crimes. Displacement could involve developing different techniques of committing the same crime, or doing it in different areas. It could also involve diversification into different crimes. One example can be briefly cited that entails aspects of both: bank theft and robbery. Banks have over the years developed a whole situational technology to discourage thieves and robbers. In the process they have only succeeded in encouraging more professional and more violent forms of the art. From being a crime based upon techniques of stealth it has developed into an activity of highly organized armed gangs. Could one not suggest analogues in relation to other crimes to which a rational choice approach might be applied?

Conclusion

In this essay, I have sought to explore some of the philosophical issues associated with legal and criminological approaches to practical reasoning. What the legal approach and the rational choice approach have in common is a tendency to bracket off important aspects of the reasoning process. Practical reasoning involves a unity of form (the ability to be a practical reasoner) and content (a concrete set of socially specific practical syllogisms generated within a particular context). The legal approach brackets off the questions of content and context, grounding individual legal responsibility in the ability to be a practical reasoner. However, because it adopts this abstract approach, it cannot be adequate to the reality of social life nor even adequately rationalize a legal defense such as duress, which entails a recognition of form and content, without throwing into question the validity of the whole idea of individual responsibility.

The rational choice approach within criminology faces a parallel danger. While for it the immediate context of decision making is recognized, an artificial division is made between that and the wider social context, so that its approach is abstractive too. Thus what the approaches have in common is a tendency to focus on the decision to commit a particular criminal act and to abstract that decision from the wider context. Further, both do so on policy grounds: the law in order to attribute responsibility to individuals, the rational choice approach in order to develop practical schemes for crime prevention. Both must fail, however, in their respective tasks because they inadequately characterize the phenomena they seek to represent. Whereas in the law the result is anomaly and injustice (see Norrie, 1983), in the criminological decision-making approach the result is a potential narrowness of focus that fails to see the forest for the trees.

References

Balbus, I.
    1978   "Commodity form and legal form." Pp. 73–90 in C. Reasons and R. Rich (eds.), The Sociology of Law: A Conflict Perspective. Toronto: Butterworths.
Bhaskar, R.
    1979   The Possibility of Naturalism. Brighton, England: Harvester.
Bottoms, A. and R. Preston
    1980   The Coming Penal Crisis. Edinburgh: Scottish Academic Press.
Clarke, R. and D. Cornish.
    1983   Crime Control in Britain: A Review of Policy Research. Albany: State University of New York Press.
Clarke, R. and D. Cornish
    1985   "Modelling offenders' decisions: a framework for research and policy." Pp. 147–85 in M. Tonry and N. Morris (eds.), Crime and Justice: An Annual Review of Research, Volume 6. Chicago: University of Chicago Press.
Ferri, E.
    1901   The Positive School of Criminology. Chicago: Kerr.

Foucault, M.
  1977 Discipline and Punish. Harmondsworth, England: Allen Lane.
Halevy, E.
  1972 The Growth of Philosophic Radicalism. London: Faber.
Hart, H.
  1968 Punishment and Responsibility. Oxford: Clarendon.
Moore, M.
  1984 Law and Psychiatry. Cambridge, England: Cambridge University
        Press.
Norrie, A.
  1982 "Pashukanis and the 'commodity form theory': a reply to Warrington."
        International Journal of the Sociology of Law 10:419-37.
Norrie, A.
  1983 "Freewill, determinism and criminal justice." Legal Studies 3:60-73.
Parker, H.
  1976 "Boys will be men: brief adolescence in a downtown neighbourhood."
        Pp. 27-47 in G. Mungham and G. Pearson (eds.), Working Class Youth
        Culture. London: Routledge & Kegan Paul.
Pashukanis, E.
  1978 General Theory of Law and Marxism. London: Ink Links.
Von Hirsch, A.
  1976 Doing Justice: The Choice of Punishment. New York: Hill and Wang.

Author Index

Ageton, S.S. 111, 118, 168
Ajzen, I. 160, 161, 163, 166, 167, 168
Akers, R.L. 159, 168
Ali, M.M. 136, 151
Allport, F. 46, 51
Andriessen, J.H. 136, 142, 151
Arrow, K.J. 133, 150–51
Assembly Committee on Criminal Procedure
    (California) 21, 35
Athens, L. 14, 15

Baker, A.J. 101
Balbus, I. 225, 229
Ball, J.C. 100
Bandura, A. 20, 35
Bar-Hillel, M. 136, 151
Barmash, I. 25, 35
Baumer, T. 35, 37
Beach, L.R. 131, 151
Beccaria, C.B. 218
Becker, G.S. 20, 35, 129, 130, 151, 171, 183
Becker, H.S. 87, 88, 99
Bell, D.E. 138, 151
Bennett, T. 5, 7, 9, 12, 15, 41–42, 48, 50,
    51, 67, 70, 83, 162, 163, 168
Bentham, J. 218
Berk, R.A. 169
Beyleveld, D. 157, 168
Bhaskar, R. 225–26, 229
Bickman, L. 31, 34, 35, 37
Bishop, D.M. 158–59, 164, 168
Blackwell, J.S. 91, 100
Blazicek, D.L. 8, 15
Blomquist, G.C. 207, 214
Blumstein, A. 24, 35, 72, 73, 81, 131, 151,
    206, 214
Bordua, D. 123

Bottoms, A. 229
Bowden, C.L. 93, 100
Boyer, R. 82
Braiker, H. 201
Braly, M. 74–75, 76–77, 78, 81
Brantingham, P.J. 45, 48, 51, 126, 128
Brantingham, P.L. 45, 48, 51, 126, 128
Braunstein, M.L. 16, 37, 175, 185
Brier, S.S. 131, 151
Bronner, A. 187, 200
Brown, B.S. 90, 93, 100
Brown, E.D. 216
Bruner, J.S. 46
Burroughs, W. 100
Bursik, R. 188, 189, 199

Cacioppo, J.T. 20, 37
Canter, R.J. 111, 118, 168
Carey, S.H. 178, 184
Carr, J. 78, 81
Carroll, J.S. 5, 8, 9, 12, 16, 20, 21–22, 24,
    35, 37, 39, 131, 151, 162, 168, 170,
    171, 173, 181, 182–83, 185, 213, 214,
    217
Cauthen, N. 36
Chaiken, J. 67, 70, 188, 189, 199
Chaiken, M. 67, 70, 188, 189, 199
Chambers, C.D. 89, 100
Chien, I. 87, 91, 100
Chiricos, T.G. 33, 37, 38, 169
Christenholz, C. 35
Chung, J. 168
Cicourel, A. 84, 100
Cimler, E. 131, 151
Clarke, R.V. 1, 2, 12, 15, 16, 20, 33, 35,
    36, 66, 67, 70, 81, 84, 86, 98, 100,
    113, 118, 126, 128, 159, 167, 168,

171, 175, 181, 182, 183, 187, 198,
200, 213, 214, 218, 219, 226, 227–28,
229
Clarkson, G. 25, 36
Claster, D.S. 33, 36, 131, 151
Clinard, M.B. 41, 51, 187, 200
Cloward, R.A. 87, 100, 110, 118, 187, 200
Coghlan, A.J. 85–86, 101
Cohen, A.K. 110, 118
Cohen, J. 35, 72, 73, 81, 100, 151, 204,
205, 206, 208, 212, 214
Cohen, J.L. 138, 153
Cohen, L.E. 121, 123, 125, 128, 159, 168
Coleman, S.B. 87, 100
Colvin, M. 110–11, 118
Commission of Inquiry into the Non-Medical
Use of Drugs, 89, 92–93, 100
Conklin, J. 187, 200
Connell, P.H. 90, 100
Cook, P.J. 12, 16, 20, 23, 33, 36, 131, 152,
202, 203, 206, 213, 215
Coombs, F.S. 160, 168
Corbin, R.M. 134, 152
Cormier, B.M. 77, 78, 79, 82
Cornish, D.B. 1, 2, 12, 15, 16, 20, 33, 35,
36, 66, 70, 81, 84, 98, 100, 113, 118,
167, 171, 175, 176, 181, 182, 183,
187, 198, 200, 213, 214, 218, 219,
226, 227–28, 229
Corrigan, B. 182, 184
Craig, S.R. 90, 100
Crelinsten, D.R. 72
Crum, R. 185
Cusson, M. 5, 8, 9, 72, 83, 126, 128

Davis, D.I. 87, 100
Dawes, R.M. 182, 184
de Finetti, B. 133, 152
DeFleur, L.B. 91, 100
Dill, F. 70
Dobash, R.E. 14, 16
Dobash, R.P. 14, 16
Dole, V. 85, 100
Dosher, B.A. 180, 185
Dudraine, N.S. 101
Dunham, J.D. 169
Dunn, C.S. 184
Duran, A.S. 36
Durkheim, É. 107, 108, 159

Edwards, W. 133, 137, 152
Ehrlich, I. 24, 36, 131, 144, 152, 213, 215

Einhorn, H.J. 21, 36, 136, 152, 182, 184
Einstadter, W.J. 41, 51
Elliott, D.S. 109, 111, 118, 159, 168
Erickson, M.L. 158, 168, 169, 189, 201,
206, 215
Ericsson, K.A. 24, 25, 35, 36
Estrich, S.R. 215

Faria, A.J. 25, 36
Farrington, D.P. 67, 70, 157, 168, 204, 215
Feeney, F. 5, 8, 12, 14, 19, 40, 53, 69, 70
Feldman, M.P. 21, 36
Felson, M. 10, 119, 121, 123, 125, 128, 159,
168
Ferri, E. 218, 229
Fienberg, S.E. 131, 151
Figlio, R. 16, 71, 191, 200, 201
Fischhoff, B. 38, 179, 184, 185, 208, 216
Fishbein, M. 156, 160, 161, 163, 166, 167,
168
Fishburn, P.C. 137, 152
Forster, B. 169
Foucault, M. 218, 230
Friedman, M. 132, 136–37, 138, 149, 152

Gandossy, R.P. 93, 100
Garafolo, J. 126, 128
Garber, S. 208, 215
Gardner, R. 90, 100
Gauvey, A.B. 100
Gay, G.R. 90–91, 102
Gendreau, L.P. 86, 101
Gendreau, P. 86, 101
Gerard, D.L. 100
Gibbons, D.C. 41, 52, 187–88, 200
Gibbs, J.P. 158, 168, 169, 206, 215
Glaser, B. 98, 101
Glueck, E. 72, 79, 82, 92, 101, 115, 118
Glueck, S. 72, 79, 82, 92, 101, 115, 118
Gold, S.R. 85–86, 101
Goldstein, P.J. 101
Gottfredson, M. 79, 82, 113–14, 118, 123,
125, 126, 128, 160, 169, 184
Graham, J.D. 208, 215
Grasmick, H.G. 158–59, 169
Greaves, G. 86, 101
Green, D.E. 158–59, 169
Greenwood, P.W. 48, 52, 67, 70, 118, 200,
204, 206–7, 208, 209, 215
Grether, D.M. 134–35, 152
Gristwood, J. 50, 52
Guillo, F. 75, 82

Gunn, J. 50, 52
Guttmacher, M. 187, 200

Haertzen, C.A. 101
Halevy, E. 218, 230
Handa, J. 137, 152
Hannum, T.E. 21, 38
Hart, H. 219, 230
Harwood, H.J. 100
Haslem, P. 93, 101
Hassebrock, F. 36
Hawkins, G.J. 157, 169, 206, 216
Healy, W. 187, 200
Henshel, R.L. 178, 184
Hershey, J.C. 133, 135, 136, 137, 152
Hewett, B.B. 101
Hey, J.D. 132, 133, 149, 152
Hindelang, M. 126, 128, 177, 184
Hirschi, T. 10, 15, 79, 82, 105–6, 108–9,
        112, 113–14, 118, 119, 121, 125, 128,
        159, 160, 166, 169
Hogarth, R.M. 21, 36, 136, 152
Home Office 99, 101
Hope, T. 2, 16
Hough, M. 126, 128
Huelke, D.F. 207, 215

Inciardi, J.A. 22, 36
Interdepartmental Committee on Drug Addic-
        tion 98–99, 101
Irwin, J. 78, 82

Jackson, H. 15, 16
Janzen, W. 36
Jensen, G.F. 158, 169
Johnson, B.D. 91, 101
Johnson, E.J. 11, 14, 23, 36, 140, 144, 170,
        176, 180, 181, 182, 184
Johnson, P.E. 25, 36
Jonas, A.D. 85, 101
Jonas, D.F. 85, 101
Jones, J.P. 100

Kahneman, D. 21, 36, 129, 131, 134, 135–
        36, 137, 138–43, 153, 154, 155, 165,
        166, 169, 173–79 *passim*, 184, 185
Kaplan, H.B. 87, 101
Karmarkar, U. 137, 153
Kemeny, J. 191, 200
Kempf, K. 12, 186

Kennedy, M. 82
Khantzian, E.J. 86, 101
Klein, M.W. 125, 128, 188, 198, 200
Kleinmuntz, B. 184
Kleinmuntz, D.N. 184
Klockars, C. 9, 16
Knight, F.H. 134, 153
Knight, S. 35
Kochenberger, G.A. 137, 152
Kornhauser, R. 108, 109, 118
Krauss, H.H. 21, 36
Kraut, R.E. 31, 33, 36
Krohn, M.D. 168
Kudel, M. 35, 37

LaFave, W. 67, 70
Laing, R.D. 224
Langenauer, B.J. 93, 100
Langer, E.J. 136, 142, 153
Lanza-Kaduce, L. 168
Larkin, J. 23, 37
Lattimore, P. 11, 129
Laughlann, D.J. 185
Laver, M. 41, 52
Lavin, M. 48, 52, 118, 200
Lee, R.S. 100
Lejeune, R. 8, 14, 16
Letkemann, P. 22–23, 37, 41, 52, 76, 82
Lichtenstein, S. 22, 38, 134–35, 153, 154,
        175, 185
Lingley, L.P.A. 102
Long, S.K. 131, 155
Luce, R.D. 149, 153
Lynch, J. 138, 153

McBride, D.C. 89, 102
McCaghy, C. 187, 200
McDermott, J. 37
McDonald, W. 69, 70, 71
McElroy, J. 160, 169
McFarland, D. 191, 200
McGillis, D. 215
McKenna, F.P. 208, 215
Maguire, M. 41, 52, 67, 70, 76, 77, 81, 82,
        162, 169
Markowitz, H.M. 137, 153
Martin, W.R. 85, 101
Martinson, R. 206, 215
Matza, D. 109
Mayhew, P. 126, 128, 159, 168
Merton, R.K. 87, 101, 107, 108, 110, 118
Meyer, R.J. 182, 184

Meyers, M.B. 100
Middlestadt, S.E. 168
Misner, G. 70, 71
Misra, R.K. 87, 101
Moffett, A.D. 100
Moller, J.H. 36
Moore, M. 219, 220, 221–25, 226, 230
Moore, M.H. 204, 215
Morgenstern, O. 131–32, 133, 138, 149, 155
Morton, R. 31, 37
Mosteller, F. 134, 153
Murphy, B.C. 88, 101

Nagin, D. 35, 151, 214
Neustatter, W. 187, 200
Newell, A. 21, 25, 27, 37
Nisbett, R.E. 24, 37, 176, 184
Nogee, P. 134, 153
Norrie, A. 13, 217, 218, 220, 221, 223, 229,
    230
Nye, F. 109
Nyswander, M.E. 85, 100

Obert, A. 82
O'Day, J. 207, 215
Ohlin, L.E. 87, 100, 110, 118, 187, 200
Oppenheimer, E. 91, 102
Orne, M.T. 24, 37
Orr, L.D. 207, 216

Parisi, N. 184
Parker, H. 226–27, 228, 230
Pashukanis, E. 218–19, 225, 230
Paternoster, R. 21, 25, 37, 158, 169
Pauly, J. 110–11, 118
Payne, J.W. 10, 11, 14, 16, 23, 25, 27, 37,
    140, 144, 165, 169, 170, 175, 180,
    184, 185
Peltzman, S. 207, 208, 214, 216
Perkowitz, W. 35, 37
Petersilia, J. 48, 52, 116, 118, 188, 189, 200,
    201, 204, 216
Peterson, M. 189, 201
Petty, R.E. 20, 37
Pinsonneault, P. 5, 8, 9, 72, 73, 82, 83
Plant, M.A. 89, 90, 102
Plott, C.R. 134–35, 152
Polich, S. 189, 201
Postman, L. 46
Pratt, J.W. 133, 150–51, 153
Preston, R. 219, 229

Puto, C. 179, 185

Quinney, E.T. 41, 51
Quinney, R. 84, 102, 187, 200

Radosevich, R. 168
Ragsdale, E.K.E. 25, 37
Raiffa, H. 149, 153
Ramsey, F.P. 133, 154
Rawson, H.E. 21, 37
Ray, M.B. 93, 102
Reckless, W.C. 109
Reiss, A.J., Jr. 109
Rengert, G. 126, 128
Reppetto, T.A. 12, 16, 115, 118
Rettig, S. 21, 37
Richard, S.F. 146, 154
Richards, P. 160, 169
Riley, D. 11, 156
Robins, L.M. 87, 91, 92, 102
Robinson, F. 36
Roebuck, J. 187, 201
Rojek, D. 189, 201
Rosenbaum, D. 25–26, 35, 37
Rosenfeld, E. 100
Ross, L. 176, 184
Ross, M. 136, 154
Roth, J.A. 130, 154
Russo, J.E. 180, 184, 185

Sadava, S.W. 89, 102
Saltzman, L.E. 37, 169
Samenow, S.E. 14, 16, 165, 169
Sangovicz, J. 82
Savage, L.J. 132, 133, 136–37, 138, 149,
    152, 154
Schlaiffer, R. 153
Schmidt, P. 130, 144, 146, 154
Schoemaker, P.J.H. 132, 133, 134, 135, 137,
    152, 154, 172, 185
Schrag, C. 187, 201
Scott, A. 67, 70
Sechrest, L. 206, 216
Sellin, T. 16, 71, 188, 201
Shave, P.L. 25, 38
Shinnar, R. 205, 216
Shinnar, S. 205, 216
Shinyei, M.J. 88, 101
Shover, N. 75, 77, 78, 82
Sicoly, F. 136, 154
Silberman, M. 158, 169

Simon, D.P. 37
Simon, H.A. 1, 13, 16, 20, 21, 24, 25, 27,
    35, 36, 37, 38, 78, 82, 134, 154, 165–
    66, 169, 172, 181, 185
Sinn, H. 132, 154
Slovic, P. 21, 22, 36, 38, 84, 102, 134–35,
    153, 154, 175, 178, 184, 185, 208,
    216
Smith, D.E. 90–91, 102
Smith, M.E. 213, 216
Snarr, R.W. 100
Snell, J. 191, 200
Spelman, W. 215
Stanfield, H. 102
Stark, S.D. 100
Stefanowicz, J.P. 21, 38
Stephens, R.C. 89, 102
Stevenson, G.H. 86, 87, 102
Stimson, G.V. 91, 102
Strauss, A. 98, 101
Sturman, R. 126, 128
Sutherland, E.H. 41, 52, 73, 82
Sviridoff, M. 160, 169
Sykes, G. 187, 201

Taub, R.P. 160, 169
Taylor, D.G. 169
Taylor, S.E. 136, 154
Thiffault, A.L. 82
Thompson, J.W. 213, 216
Thorley, A. 92, 102
Toby, J. 109
Tracy, P. 190, 201
Trasov, G.E. 102
Trottier, M. 82
Tuck, M. 11, 156, 160, 169
Tversky, A. 36, 129, 131, 134, 135–36, 137,
    138–43, 153, 154, 155, 165, 166, 169,
    173–79 *passim*, 184, 185
Tyler, T.R. 33, 38

Von Hirsch, A. 204, 216, 219, 230
von Neumann, J. 131–32, 133, 138, 149, 155

Waldo, G.P. 33, 37, 38, 169
Waldorf, D. 91, 93, 102
Walsh, D.P. 5, 8, 9, 10, 14, 39–40, 43, 52,
    67, 71, 162, 170
Wasilchik, J. 126, 128
Weaver, F. 5, 8, 9, 12, 14, 39, 170, 181,
    182–83, 185, 217
Weir, A. 54, 70, 71
Weppner, R.S. 9, 16
West, D. 79, 82
West, W.G. 77, 82
White, S.O. 216
Wilde, G.J.S. 208, 216
Williams, J.R. 100
Williamson, H. 84, 102
Wilson, T.D. 24, 37
Winchester, S.W.C. 15, 16
Winick, C. 90, 92, 93, 102
Witte, A.D. 11, 84, 102, 129, 130, 131, 144,
    146, 154, 155
Wolfgang, M.E. 12, 16, 67, 71, 188, 201
Wright, P. 180, 185
Wright, R. 9, 12, 15, 41–42, 48, 50, 51, 67,
    70, 162, 163, 168

Yochelson, S. 14, 16, 165, 169

Zimring, F.E. 157, 169, 204, 206, 215, 216

Subject Index

Abstract reasoning (*see* Practical reasoning, abstract reasoning as)

Adaptive choice framework (*see also* Displacement; Risks of offending, changing the)
  cognitive aspects of 203
  danger compensation thesis in 202, 203, 207–8
  on incapacitation 12, 202–14
  justification for 205–8
  policy relevance of 202, 203, 213–14 (*see also* Rational choice perspective)
  in robbery 209–12
  victimization and 203

Age
  and crime 72–73, 79, 80, 105, 159, 228 (*see also* Criminal careers)
  influence of, on desistance 75–77, 80, 92 (*see also* Desistance; Maturing out)
  as a situational variable 105, 117

Alcohol, use of, in crime 40, 47, 50, 67

Anomie 87

Aspiration level (*see* Prospect theory, reference levels of wealth in)

Attachment (*see* Social control theory)

Autotheft 41, 177, 181

Availability heuristic (*see* Judgmental heuristics)

Awareness space 45

Backsliding, resistance to 79–80 (*see also* Desistance)

Behavioral decision theory 21, 84, 170, 171, 173 (*see also* Decision processes)

Belief in norms (*see* Social control theory)

Bentham-style rationality 50, 66 (*see also* Expected utility model)

Body build, as a situational variable 105, 117

Bounded rationality (*see* Decision processes, bounded rationality of)

Burglary 9, 65, 68, 109, 114–16, 161
  commercial 2, 5
    assessment and planning in 39, 40, 45–46, 47–48 (*see also* Criminal decision making; Robbery)
    influence of drink or drugs in 40, 47, 50
    rationality of 47–48 (*see also* Rational choice perspective, rationality of offending and)
    research on 43–51
    role of determination in 48
    role of intuition and experience in 39, 46–47 (*see also* Experience; Expertise)
    role of luck and fatalism in 47
    target-selection in 39, 43–49
    use of knowledge-market in 43–45
  crime-specific focus on 2–5, 6, 7, 8, 39 (*see also* Crime-specific focus; Rational choice perspective)
  economic model of 132–33, 138, 139, 143
  increasing perceived risks of 177–78 (*see also* Risks of offending)
  noncompensatory strategies in 170, 180 (*see also* Decision processes)
  offense specialization in 190, 193–98 (*see also* Offense specialization)
  process-tracing research on 9 (*see also* Research on criminal decision making)
  prospect theory and continued involvement in 175–76
  rational choice perspective on 2–5, 39–51, 83
  residential
    continuing involvement in 2, 5, 6 (*see also* Continuing involvement)

Burglary(*cont.*)
  desistance from 2, 5, 6, 7, 81 (*see also*
      Desistance)
  event model of 2, 4, 5 (*see also* Event)
  initial involvement in 2, 3, 4, 5 (*see also*
      Initial involvement)
  target-selection in 4–5, 42–43
  role of skill in 113–16
  target-selection in 162, 163, 173, 181 (*see
      also* Decision processes)

California *F* Scale 164
Capable guardian (*see* Informal social control)
Career-criminal prosecution units 188, 205
Certainty effect 177
Certainty equivalent model 137
Cessation (*see* Desistance; Opioid addiction)
Choice (*see* Criminal decision-making; Ra-
      tional choice perspective)
Commitment (*see* Social control theory)
Compensatory choice strategies 180 (*see also*
      Decision processes)
Compulsion (*see* Criminal responsibility)
Conflict theory 110–11
Contingent processing (*see* Decision processes)
Continuance (*see* Continuing involvement)
Continuing involvement
  application of theory of reasoned action to
      156, 163
  in burglary (*see* Burglary, residential)
  in burglary, prospect theory and, 175–76
  decision model of 2, 5, 6, 8, 9, 182, 187
      (*see also* Desistance; Event; Initial in-
      volvement; Rational choice perspective)
  methods of studying 14–15
  offense specialization and 187
  in opioid addiction (*see* Opioid addiction)
  in robbery (*see* Robbery)
Control theory (*see* Social control theory)
Corporate crime 11, 14
Cramer's rule 146
Crime-specific focus 2, 5, 113 (*see also* Ra-
      tional choice perspective)
  on burglary 2–5, 6, 7, 8, 39
  need for 67–68, 114–15, 170, 182, 186,
      198, 228
  on opiod use 5, 84
  on robbery 2, 8, 39, 53
  on shoplifting 2, 19
Criminal behavior, rationality of (*see* Rational
      choice perspective, rationality of of-
      fending and)
Criminal careers 5, 54 (*see also* Continuing

involvement; Desistance; Initial in-
      volvement; Opioid addiction)
  age and 72–73 (*see also* Age)
  criticism of concept of 114, 115–16
  research on 12, 81, 186–99
  specialization during 12, 186–99 (*see also*
      Offense specialization)
Criminal choice 119, 126–27 (*see also* Crimi-
      nal decision making; Rational choice
      perspective; Routine activities theory)
Criminal decision making (*see also* Decision
      processes; Rational choice perspective)
  adaptive choice and 203
  assessment and planning in 9, 10, 13, 23,
      39, 45–46, 53, 59–61, 115–16 (*see
      also* Burglary; Robbery)
  decision models of (*see* Continued involve-
      ment; Desistance; Event; Initial in-
      volvement; Rational choice perspective)
  deterrence research and 158–59, 160
  empirical studies of 5–10 (*see also* Bur-
      glary; Opioid addiction; Robbery;
      Shoplifting)
  expected utility model of (*see* Decision pro-
      cesses; Expected utility model)
  information-processing analysis of (*see* De-
      cision processes)
  intellectual sophistication of offender and
      50, 105, 115–16 (*see also* Rational
      choice perspective, rationality of of-
      fending and)
  nature of processes in 1, 2, 8, 11, 14, 19,
      156 (*see also* Decision processes)
  policy-relevance of research on 11, 54, 67–
      70, 130, 136, 157, 160, 170, 171,
      173, 174–79, 182 (*see also* Rational
      choice perspective, policy-relevance of)
  practical reasoning and 217–29
  prerequisites for models of 159–60
  prospect theory and (*see* Prospect theory)
  role of experience in (*see* Experience)
  role of expertise in (*see* Expertise)
  roles of luck and fatalism in (*see* Luck)
  role of offenders' perceptions in (*see* Of-
      fenders' perceptions)
  role of opportunities in (*see* Opportunities
      for crime)
  situational crime prevention and (*see* situa-
      tional crime prevention)
Criminality
  measuring 115
  in social control theory 105, 106, 113–14,
      117

Criminal law
  conception of the offender in 217, 219 (*see also* Criminal responsibility)
  relationship between criminology and the 218–19
Criminal responsibility
  compulsion (duress) and 222–25
  criminal law conceptions of 221–25, 229
  criteria for imputing 218–19
  of opioid addicts 83
  and practical reasoning 217–29
  and the rational choice perspective 13, 84, 99, 217, 218–19, 220, 229
Criminal thinking patterns 14, 164–65
Criminology
  classical 218–19
  explanations of offending in 105–17
Cultural deviance theory 109, 111

Danger compensation thesis 202, 203, 207–8, 213–14 (*see also* Adaptive choice framework; Highway safety)
Decision-making approach (*see* Criminal decision making; Decision processes; Rational choice perspective)
Decision making in the criminal justice system 160, 171
Decision making under uncertainty (*see* Expected utility model; Prospect theory)
Decision problem
  constructing representations of the 135, 170, 173–79, 180–82 (*see also* Prospect theory)
  treatment of, in the theory of reasoned action 162–63
Decision processes
  bounded rationality of 19, 20–22, 39, 41–42, 50–51, 53, 66–67, 170, 172–73 (*see also* Rational choice perspective, rationality of offenders and)
  contingent-processing models of 23, 39, 165, 166, 182
  criminal thinking patterns and 14, 164–65
  and deterrence 21–22 (*see also* Deterrence; Risks of offending)
  for evaluating alternatives 170, 179–83
  expected utility model of 8, 132–33, 144–46 (*see also* Expected utility model)
  hierarchical thinking in 28–29
  information-processing strategies used in 1, 2, 8, 11, 14, 19, 20–23, 129, 134, 172–83
  investigating, through process tracing (*see* Research on decision making; Shoplifting)
  involved in handling fear, guilt and shame 11–12, 14 (*see also* Expertise; Fear; Moral scruples)
  judgmental heuristics and (*see* Judgmental heuristics)
  multistage characteristics of 2, 165, 166, 217
  nature of, in event decisions 11–12, 19–39, 156, 165–67 (*see also* Rational choice perspective)
  nature of, in involvement decisions 11–12, 156, 165–67 (*see also* Rational choice perspective)
  need for separate decision models in relation to (*see* Rational choice perspective)
  negative thinking and flaw-hunting in 39, 45–46, 51
  problem representation in relation to (*see* Decision problem)
  prospect theory and 39, 129, 146–48, 173–79
  role of expertise in 8, 11–12, 14, 19, 22–23, 27–34, 170, 181 (*see also* Experience; Expertise)
  satisficing 39, 170, 181–82
  sequential aspects of 22–33, 33
  simplifying 129, 170, 179, 180–182 (*see also* Prospect theory)
  time constraints on 1, 5, 23, 32, 129, 170, 179
  use of compensatory choice strategies in 180
  use of noncompensatory choice strategies in 11, 14, 170, 180–82
Deinstitutionalization 188
Delayed deterrence (*see also* Desistance)
  concept of, as a factor in desistance 8, 72, 73, 75–77, 80
  cumulative risks of offending and 76–77
  increased difficulty of "doing time" and 76–77
  severity of punishment and 77
Desistance
  age at 72–73
  application of theory of reasoned action to 156, 163
  backsliding and 8, 72, 79–80
  from burglary (*see* Burglary, residential)
  decision model of 2, 5, 6, 7, 8, 9, 72, 74, 187 (*see also* Continuing involvement; Event; Initial involvement; Rational choice perspective)

Desistance(*cont.*)
  delayed deterrence as a factor in (*see* De-
      layed deterrence)
  effects of employment on 80, 93
  effects of marriage and family on 5, 79–80,
      93
  effects of maturation on (*see* Age; Maturing
      out)
  fear and 74–75
  methods of studying 14–15
  offense specialization and 187
  from opioid addiction (*see* Opioid addiction)
  policy-relevance of research on 67, 80–81
  probability of 192–93, 196, 198
  process of, from robbery 74
  reasons for 72–81, 92–93, 96–97
  reevaluation of goals and 5, 77–78, 83, 93
  from robbery (*see* Robbery)
  role of situational factors in 83, 92–93, 98
  shock as a factor in 8, 72, 73–75, 77
Deterrence 12, 13, 20, 68, 99, 106, 116, 130,
    202, 203, 218 (*see also* Risks of
    offending)
  effects of, on incapacitation 209–13
  expected utility analysis of 20–21, 177, 178
  legal sanctions and 157–59
  moral commitment and 158–59
  policy-relevance of decision-making research
      to 20, 21–22, 24, 35, 171, 173
  prospect theory analysis of 177–79
  research on effectiveness of 24, 157–59,
      160, 206–7
  of robbers 53, 69–70
  of shoplifters 29–30, 31, 34
  social disapproval and 158–59
Differential association 80
Differentially weighted product-averaging
    model 137–38
Directive state theory 46
Displacement 12, 114, 228
  rational choice perspective on 12, 217, 218,
      228
  situational crime prevention and 181, 217
Dispositional theories
  of crime 84, 111, 113, 162
  limitations of 98–99
  of opioid addiction (*see* Opioid addiction)
Diversion 188
Drugs, use of, in crime 40, 47, 50, 67
Drug-taking (*see* Opioid addiction)
Duress (*see* Criminal responsibility)

Economic criminals (*see* Burglary; Robbery)

Economic models of criminal decision-making
    (*see* Expected utility model)
Escalation
  to robbery 65
  theory of drug abuse 88–89
EU model (*see* Expected utility model)
Event (criminal)
  application of theory of reasoned action to
      the 156, 161, 162–63, 167
  of burglary (*see* Burglary, residential)
  correlates of the 116–17
  decision model of the 2, 4, 5, 8, 11, 12,
      19, 187 (*see also* Continuing involve-
      ment; Desistance; Initial involvement;
      Rational choice perspective)
  methods of studying the 15
  nature of decision-making processes in the
      (*see* Decision processes)
  rational choice perspective as a theory of the
      105, 106, 113–16 (*see also* Social con-
      trol theory)
  risks of offending in relation to the (*see*
      Risks of offending)
  routine activities and the 120, 127
  situated reasoning and the 217–18
Expectancy-value theories 156, 160–61, 167
    (*see also* Theory of reasoned action)
Expected utility (EU) model 8, 32, 33, 40–42,
    50, 55, 66, 84, 130, 133, 140–41, 218
    (*see also* Decision processes)
  assumptions underlying 132–37, 138, 149–
      50, 171
  attitudes to risk in 133–34, 136–37, 140,
      144, 150–51
  bounded rationality versus 19–22, 172–73
  calculation of EU in 130–33
  concept of probability in 130, 132–33, 135,
      136, 140, 141–43, 171
  contrasted with prospect theory 129–30,
      131, 140–43, 144, 146–49, 174–75,
      179
  criticisms of 11, 20–22, 50–51, 129, 131,
      134–37, 148, 156, 160, 165–66, 170,
      172–73, 178–79, 182–83
  development of 131–32, 137–38, 144–46
  empirical research on 129, 131
  nature of utility function in 147–48, 171,
      174
  normative rationality of 19, 20, 39, 50–51
  policy-relevance of 146–49, 171
  preference reversal in 134–35
  and social control theory 109
  use of compensatory choice strategies by
      180 (*see also* Decision processes)

use of, in event decisions (*see* Decision processes, nature of)

use of, in involvement decisions (*see* Decision processes, nature of)

Experience (*see also* Expertise)
role of, in criminal decision making 9, 34, 39, 46–47, 60
role of, in developing criminal thinking patterns 165

Expertise (*see also* Experience)
noncompensatory strategies and 170, 181 (*see also* Decision processes)
role of, in criminal decision making 5, 8, 11, 12, 14, 19, 22–23, 181
role of, in fear and guilt management 11–12, 14
role of, in involvement decisions 11
role of, in shoplifting (*see* Shoplifting, expert strategies in)

Fatalism (*see* Luck)

Fear (*see also* Risks of Offending)
and desistance 74–77
experienced by novice robbers 61, 65
experienced by novice shoplifters 33, 34
management of, by offenders 11–12, 19, 39, 48, 61, 65–66

Fines 212

Flaw-hunting (*see* Decision processes, negative thinking and flaw-hunting in)

Force (*see* Robbery, use of weapons and force in)

Fuzzy logic (*see* Decision processes, negative thinking and flaw-hunting in)

Gambling behavior 2, 135, 136, 143, 148, 176

Gang membership, as a situational variable 105, 117

Generalists, offenders as (*see* Offense specialization)

"Good enough" theories 98, 227 (*see also* Rational choice perspective)

Grounded theory 98

Guilt (*see* Moral scruples)

Handled offender (*see* Informal social control)

Highway safety
danger compensation thesis and 202, 203, 207–8 (*see also* Adaptive choice)

improving, through prospect theory applications 176, 178
role of subjective norms in 163

Home Office 1

Homicide 8, 14

Illusion of control 136, 142

Images of man
in opioid addiction theory 98–99
in the rational choice perspective 105, 106, 113, 117, 217
in social control theory 105, 106, 113, 117
in sociological explanations of crime 105–10 *passim*, 113, 117

Impulsive crimes, rationality of (*see* Rational choice perspective, rationality of offending and)

Incapacitation
assumptions underlying policy of 203, 205, 210, 212–214
criticisms of selective 204–5, 212, 213, 214
effects of adaptive choices on 12, 202–14
neglect of deterrent effects of 206–7, 209–13
prediction of high-rate offenders for 204–5
previous research on 203, 204–5
of robbers 70, 208–13
simulated effects of selective versus uniform 202, 203, 208–13

Informal crime control, web of 122–23, 128 (*see also* Informal social control)

Informal social control 119 (*see also* Routine activities theory)
obstacles to 124–25, 126
role of capable guardian in 121, 122–28
role of handled offender in 121–28
role of informant in 123, 124
role of intimate handler in 122–28
social control theory and 121–22, 125
variations in strength of 123–28

Information
nature of, used by offenders 14, 21, 39, 43–45, 68

Information processing (*see* Decision processes)

Initial involvement
application of theory of reasoned action to decisions about 156, 161, 167
in burglary (*see* Burglary, residential)
decision model of 2, 3, 4, 5, 8 (*see also* Continuing involvement; Desistance; Event; Rational choice perspective)
methods of studying 14–15

Initial involvement(*cont.*)
  nature of decision processes in (*see* Decision
    processes, nature of)
  in opioid addiction (*see* Opioid addiction)
  risks of offending in relation to (*see* Risks
    of offending)
  in robbery (*see* Robbery)
  roles of fears and moral scruple in (*see* Fear;
    Moral scruples)
  situated reasoning and model of 217–18,
    227–28
Institute of Criminology, Cambridge 85, 93
Insurance purchasing 135, 136, 143, 148
Integrated theory in sociology 109–11, 117
Internalized normative constraint 158–59, 164
Interviewing offenders (*see* Research in crimi-
    nal decision making)
Intimate handler (*see* Informal social control)
Intuition (*see* Experience)
Involvement in crime, social control theory of
    (*see* Social control theory)

Judgmental heuristics 134, 135–36, 165–66,
    172, 176 (*see also* Prospect theory)
Juridical individualism 13, 220–22
Justice model 13, 217, 219

Knowledge brokers (*see* Knowledge market)
Knowledge market 39, 43–45, 51

Labeling theory 110
Leakmen 39, 44
Limited rationality (*see* Decision processes,
    bounded rationality of)
Luck, role of, in crime 39, 42, 47

Markov chain analysis 191
Markowitz utility function 137
Maturing out (*see also* Age; Desistance)
  of crime 79, 80, 228
  of opioid addiction 92, 93
Moral commitment 158–59, 164–65
Moral scruples
  implication of, in desistance 78–79
  influence of, of decision to shoplift 29, 33,
    34
  management of, by experienced offenders
    11–12, 14, 19, 29, 65–66
  treatment of, in theory of reasoned action
    164–65

about use of weapons 64
Mugging 2, 8, 14, 54, 109 (*see also* Robbery)

Negative thinking (*see* Decision processes,
    negative thinking and flaw-hunting in)
Noncompensatory choice strategies (*see* Deci-
    sion processes)
Normative rationality (*see* Expected utility
    model)

Offenders' perceptions 5, 19–35, 159, 162–
    63, 176, 202, 205, 206 (*see also* Op-
    portunities for crime; Risks of offend-
    ing; Target selection)
Offense specialization
  early research on 187–89
  evidence of 186–99
  and the generalism–specialism issue 12,
    105, 114
  juvenile 188–91 *passim*, 192–98
  methodological problems of research on
    186, 187–89, 198
  policy-relevance of research on 186, 188,
    198
  probabilities of, for adult offenders 192,
    198
  race of offender and 191–99
  rational choice perspective and 12, 186–87,
    198
  in residential burglary 41
  in robbery 66
  serial specialization as 186
  sex of offender and 191–99
  type of crime in 190, 193–98
  use of offender typologies to study 187–88
Opioid addiction
  the addiction-prone personality in 86
  automedication in 86, 91, 96
  continuing involvement in 90–92, 95–96
    (*see also* Continuing involvement)
  control of, by user 83, 90–91, 96, 97
  desistance from 83, 91, 92–93, 96–98 (*see
    also* Desistance)
  developing a habit in 83, 90–92, 94–95
  as a deviant career 87, 88–98
  dispositional theories of 83, 84, 85–88, 91,
    92, 98–99
  escalation in 88–89
  image of user in (*see* Images of man)
  initial involvement in 7, 83, 88–90, 92, 94–
    95, 97 (*see also* Initial involvement)
  as a medical problem 98–99

as a motive for robbery 55–56, 61–62 (*see also* Drugs, use of in crime)
patterns of use in 90–92, 95–96, 97
policy-relevance of rational choice perspective on 83, 85, 99
rationality of 87, 88, 89, 90 (*see also* Rational choice perspective, rationality of offending and)
reasons for 7, 90, 91, 95, 96, 97
research on 5, 83–99
role of individual factors in 85–86
role of professional pushers in 83, 89, 94
role of social factors in 86–88
role of social group in 83, 90, 94–95
treatment of 98–99
Opportunities for crime
changes in 120–21, 125–26, 157
perception of (*see* Offenders' perceptions)
routine activities and 119–23 *passim*, 126–27, 213

Pathological motivation (*see also* Dispositional theories; Rational choice perspective, rationality of offending and)
role of, in crime 2, 5, 14, 15, 84, 172
role of, in opioid addiction 85–89 *passim*, 98
Philadelphia Birth Cohort
(1945) 188, 189
(1958) 186, 189, 192, 198, 199
Planning (*see* Criminal decision making, assessment and planning in)
Police, interviews with 15
Policy making, need for decision-making perspective in (*see* Criminal decision making; Rational choice perspective)
Positivism 84, 107, 108, 111, 112, 113, 115, 117, 218–19, 227
Practical reasoning
abstract reasoning as 13, 217, 221, 223, 225, 229
belief/desire sets and 220, 221–22, 225
and criminal responsibility 217–29
Moore's treatment of 221–25
practical syllogisms in 220–25
and the rational choice perspective 217–18, 220, 225–27, 229
in schizophrenia 224–25
as situated reasoning 13, 217, 218, 220–29
Prediction of criminal behavior 158–59
Preference reversal (*see* Expected utility model)
Professionalism (*see* Expertise)

Property offences, offense specialization in 190, 193–98
Prospect theory (*see also* Decision processes)
attitude to risk in 129, 143–44
coding of prospects in 138, 143, 147
contrasted with expected utility model 129–30, 131, 140–43, 144, 146–49, 174–75, 179
current limitations of 179
editing of prospects in 39, 129, 138–39, 147
evaluation phase in 139–40, 147
framing and reframing in 170, 173, 178, 179
model 131, 137–44
model of criminal choice, developed 146–48
nature of decision weights in 129, 139–40, 141–42, 143, 147, 176–77
nature of value function in 129, 139–41, 143–44, 147–48, 174, 177
policy-relevance of 144–46, 148–49, 170, 174–79
reducing tax evasion through 140, 175, 177
reference levels of wealth in 140, 143–44, 148, 174, 175–76
representing the decision problem by means of (*see* Decision problem)
Pseudocertainty effect 178

Race of offender, offense specialization and 191–99
Rand Corporation 188, 189
Rape 14, 114
Rational actor model (*see* Rational choice perspective)
Rational choice perspective 1–5
adaptive choice and 202
assumptions of 105, 106, 109, 112–13
on burglary (*see* Burglary, residential)
commonplace nature of offending asserted by 5, 15, 84
concept of cause in 112, 116
correlates of crime in 116–17
crime-specific focus of 2, 7, 8, 106, 113, 186 (*see also* Crime-specific focus)
and criminal responsibility (*see* Criminal responsibility)
criticisms of 105–110, 115–16, 217, 218, 227–29
decision models in 2–5, 6, 7 (*see also* Continuing involvement; Desistance; Event; Initial involvement)

Rational choice perspective(*cont.*)
  determinism and 112–13
  and displacement 12, 218, 228
  generalism–specialism issue and 12, 114–
    15, 186, 187, 198 (*see also* Offense
    specialization)
  as a "good enough" theory 98, 227
  history of, in sociology 105–17
  image of man in (*see* Images of man)
  implications of routine activities theory for
    10, 11, 119, 126–28
  need for separate decision models in 2, 7,
    8, 13, 19, 33, 35, 67, 167, 170, 182,
    187, 218, 227–28
  on opioid addiction (*see* Opioid addiction)
  policy-relevance of 1, 2, 11, 12, 13, 15,
    20, 67–70, 98, 99, 105–6, 182, 202,
    217, 218–19, 227 (*see also* Criminal
    decision making, policy-relevance of)
  and practical reasoning (*see* Practical
    reasoning)
  rationality of offending and 1, 2, 5, 7, 8,
    10, 13, 14, 15, 19, 20–23, 40–42, 47–
    49, 50, 66–67, 83, 84, 156, 171–72
  relationship to social control theory of 10,
    11, 105–6, 113–17
  on robbery (*see* Robbery)
  on shoplifting (*see* Shoplifting)
  situated reasoning critique of 13, 217, 218,
    225–29 (*see also* Criminal responsibil-
    ity; Practical reasoning)
Rational choice theory (*see* Rational choice
    perspective)
Rational crime theory 121 (*see also* Rational
    choice perspective)
Rationality
  bounded (*see* Decision processes, bounded
    rationality of)
  limited (*see* Decision processes, bounded ra-
    tionality of)
  normative (*see* Expected utility model, nor-
    mative rationality and)
  of offending (*see* Rational choice perspec-
    tive, rationality of offending and)
  of outcomes 32
  precedural 19, 31, 32, 129
Reasoning criminal (*see* Rational choice
    perspective)
Regret theory model 138
Rehabilitation 2, 12, 99, 130, 157, 202, 206,
    218
Research on criminal decision-making
  difficulties encountered in 8–10, 14–15, 192

empirical studies (*see* individual forms of
    crimes)
  interview 9–10, 14, 15, 39, 43, 57, 67, 72,
    73, 83, 92–94
    methodological problems of 9, 22, 24–
      25, 35, 43, 49, 72, 73, 116
  life history 14, 15, 72, 73, 74–75
  participant observation 9, 14
  process-tracing 9–10, 14–15, 19, 25, 26–
    28, 34–35, 162–63, 179–80, 182
    methodological problems of 31–32, 182–
      83
  triangulation of methods in 15, 35, 67
  use of ex-offenders in 9, 73
  use of offenders at liberty in 9, 25–26
  use of prisoners in 9, 43, 49, 54
  in vitro methods 9–10, 22, 25, 43, 47–48
  in vivo methods 9, 19, 20, 22, 25, 183
Restitution 213
Retributivism 219
Risk
  attitude to (*see* Expected utility model; Pros-
    pect theory)
  dimensions 20–21
Risks of offending 116, 174
  changing the 68–70, 130, 146, 148, 149,
    176, 177–79, 205, 206–7
  control of, by offender 39, 42, 47 (*see also*
    Expertise; Fear)
  cumulative 76, 77
  distal 13, 19, 32–33
  novice offenders' estimates of 33, 61, 69–
    70
  perceived 21, 23, 55, 60–61, 68–70, 158,
    213
  proximal 5, 13, 19, 32
  salient beliefs about 163 (*see also* Theory
    of reasoned action)
Robbery 9, 109, 112, 114
  "accidental" 55, 57–58
  armed 41, 73
  assessment and planning in 5, 8, 14, 39,
    40, 45–46, 48–49, 53, 55, 59–61 (*see
    also* Burglary; Criminal decision
    making)
  commercial 8, 54, 59, 64, 228
  continuing involvement in 54, 65–66, 67
    (*see also* Continuing involvement)
  desistance from 8, 66, 72–73, 74, 75–81,
    83 (*see also* Desistance)
  harm to victims in 64–65
  individual 8, 54, 59, 64 (*see also* Mugging)
  initial involvement in 54, 61, 65, 67 (*see
    also* Initial involvement)

life history research on 74–75, 76–77
motives for 55–59, 62
need for crime-specific focus on (*see* Crime-
    specific focus)
noncompensatory strategies in 170 (*see also*
    Decision processes)
offender-mobility and 62–63
offense-specialization in 190, 193–98 (*see
    also* Offense specialization)
opportunistic 48, 53, 59–61, 70
pattern planning in 14, 59, 60
perceived risks of capture in relation to 60–
    61 (*see also* Risks of offending)
rational choice perspective on 39–51, 83
rationality of 48–49, 53, 66–67 (*see also*
    Rational choice perspective, rationality
    of offending and)
reasons for choosing, as a means 61–63
research on 39–51, 53–70, 72–81
robbers' views on preventing 68–69
role of determination in 48
role of drink or drugs in 40, 47, 50, 67
role of experience in 39, 46–47, 66 (*see
    also* Experience; Expertise)
role of luck in 39, 42, 47
simulated effects of selective incapacitation
    on rates of 208–12 (*see also* Adaptive
    choice; Incapacitation)
situational crime prevention strategies and
    53, 68, 70
statistics on 53, 54, 177, 208–9
target selection in 8, 39, 43–49, 62–63 (*see
    also* Decision processes)
use of knowledge-market in 43–45
use of weapons and force in 14, 47, 63–65
Routine activities theory 10, 105, 119–28,
    159 (*see also* Informal social control)
activity patterns in 120–21, 123, 125, 126
and criminal opportunities 121, 126–27,
    159–60, 213
policy implications of 127–28
rational choice perspective and 10, 119
role of criminal motivation in 120, 125
social control theory and 10, 114, 117,
    119, 121–22, 125
and victimization 120–21, 126–27

Safebreakers 41
Salient beliefs (*see* Theory of reasoned action)
Satisficing 39, 170, 181–82 (*see also* Decision
    processes)
SEU model (*see* Subjective expected utility
    model)

Sex of offender
offense-specialization and 191–99 (*see also*
    Offense-specialization)
as a situational variable 105, 117
Shock, as a factor in desistance (*see*
    Desistance)
Shoplifting 2, 5, 41, 42–43, 61, 62, 65, 68,
    162
empirical study of contemplated, 19–35
expert strategies in 18, 19, 20, 26, 27–34,
    181 (*see also* Experience; Expertise)
facilitators of 29–30, 39
noncompensatory strategies in 170, 181 (*see
    also* Decision processes)
novice strategies in 19, 20, 26, 27–34
process tracing as a method of studying 19,
    25–28 (*see also* Research on criminal
    decision making)
rational choice perspective on 19–35, 42–
    43, 83
rationality of 41, 172 (*see also* Rational
    choice perspective, rationality of of-
    fending and)
situational deterrents to 29–30, 31, 34, 39
target selection in 42–43 (*see also* Decision
    processes)
Situated reasoning (*see* Practical reasoning)
Situational crime prevention
and displacement 12, 217 (*see also*
    Displacement)
rational choice perspective and 217, 228,
    229
in robbery 53, 68, 70
theory 13, 84, 157, 159, 202, 218
theory, and theory of reasoned action 162–
    63
Situational variables 4–5, 30–31
individual-level properties as 105, 106, 117
role of, in desistance 83, 92–93
Social bond (*see* Social control theory, concept
    of attachment in)
Social control theory
assumptions of 105, 108–9, 111, 113
concept of attachment in 108–9, 121, 122
concept of belief in norms in 108–9, 121,
    122, 159, 166
concept of commitment in 108–9, 121, 122
concept of involvement in 108–9, 121, 122,
    125
and criminality 105–6, 113–15, 116–17
criticisms of 109, 110–11, 117
and economic rationality 109
image of man in (*see* Images of man)
and informal social control 121–22, 125

Social control theory(*cont.*)
 of involvement in crime 105–6, 113–15, 116–17
 rational choice perspective and 10, 105–6, 109, 113–17
 and routine activities theory 10, 117, 119, 121–22, 125
Social crime prevention 13, 157, 218
Social disorganization theory 108
Social learning theory 87, 110, 117
Social structure, role of, in offending 226–29
Sociological explanations of crime 105–117, 159
 criticisms of 106–7
 image of man in (*see* Image of man)
Specialization (*see* Offense specialization)
Spouse abuse 14
Status offenses, offense specialization and 190, 193–98 (*see also* Offense specialization)
Strain theories 110
Strategic analysis 126 (*see also* Rational choice perspective)
Structural-Marxist perspectives on crime 110–11
Subjective expected utility (SEU) model 137, 156
 and deterrence research 158–59, 160
 and theory of reasoned action 161, 163
Subjectively weighted utility model 137
Subjective norms (*see* Theory of reasoned action)
Suitable target (*see* Informal social control)
Syllogisms
 elided 45–46
 practical (*see* Practical reasoning)

Target-selection
 role of salient beliefs in 162–63
 routine activities and 126–27
 strategies of 50, 179–83 (*see also* Burglary; Decision processes; Robbery; Shoplifting)
Tax evasion, prospect theory and 140, 170, 175, 177

Terrorists 41
Theft 41, 73
Theory of reasoned action (TORA) 11, 156–67
 "attitude to an act" in 161–62, 163, 166
 behavioral intentions in 156, 161–62, 166, 167
 place of judgmental heuristics in 165–66
 policy-relevance of 11, 156, 162–67
 in relation to the rational choice perspective 156, 167
 salient beliefs in the 156, 162–63, 166–67
 and situational crime prevention theory 162–63
 subjective norms in 156, 161–62, 163–64, 166, 167
 treatment of moral commitment in 164–65
Tipsters 44
TORA (*see* Theory of reasoned action)
Treatment (*see* Rehabilitation)
Typologies of offenders 187–88

Utility maximization 106 (*see also* Expected utility model)

Vandalism 41, 162
Verbal protocols (*see* Research on criminal decision making, process tracing)
Victimization
 adaptive choice and 208, 213–14, 303
 resistance and harm in relation to 64–65
 routine activity patterns and 120–21, 126–27, 160
 studies of, needed 15
Violent crime, offense-specialization in 190, 193–8 (*see also* Offense-specialization)
von Neumann–Morgenstern expected utility paradigm (*see* Expected Utility model)

Weapons, use of, in robbery 63–65
White-collar crime 109
Window of vulnerability 45